RACE AT THE TOP

Race at the Top

ASIAN AMERICANS AND WHITES IN PURSUIT OF THE AMERICAN DREAM IN SUBURBAN SCHOOLS

Natasha Warikoo

THE UNIVERSITY OF CHICAGO PRESS | Chicago and London

The University of Chicago Press, Chicago 60637
The University of Chicago Press, Ltd., London
© 2022 by The University of Chicago

Published 2022
Printed in the United States of America

31 30 29 28 27 26 25 24 23 22   1 2 3 4 5

ISBN-13: 978-0-226-63681-8 (cloth)
ISBN-13: 978-0-226-81933-4 (e-book)
DOI: https://doi.org/10.7208/chicago/9780226819334.001.0001

Library of Congress Cataloging-in-Publication Data

Names: Warikoo, Natasha Kumar, 1973– author.
Title: Race at the top : Asian Americans and Whites in pursuit of the
    American dream in suburban schools / Natasha Warikoo.
Other titles: Asian Americans and Whites in pursuit of the American dream
    in suburban schools
Description: Chicago ; London : The University of Chicago Press, 2022. |
    Includes bibliographical references and index.
Identifiers: LCCN 2021054530 | ISBN 9780226636818 (cloth) | ISBN
    9780226819334 (ebook)
Subjects: LCSH: Home and school—United States. | Academic
    achievement—Social aspects. | Suburban high schools—Public opinion. |
    Education, Secondary—Public opinion. | High school students—United
    States—Attitudes. | Asian American high school students—Attitudes. |
    Elite (Social sciences)—United States—Attitudes. | Parents—United
    States—Attitudes. | Asian American parents—United States—Attitudes. |
    United States—Race relations.
Classification: LCC LC225.3 .W366 2022 | DDC 373.09173/3—dc23
    /eng/20211109
LC record available at https://lccn.loc.gov/2021054530

♾ This paper meets the requirements of ANSI/NISO Z39.48-1992 (Permanence of Paper).

Contents

Preface

SABRINA IS FORTY-FIVE AND WHITE, a mother of three.[1]

Her house looks like picture-perfect suburban wealth—a broad, shimmering lawn, tall trees, big windows—close, but not too close, to the quaint main street of her town. Street parking is not allowed.

Sabrina brewed coffee for us while I sat on a barstool at the island in her kitchen. She wore stylish boots, fitted pants, a dress shirt. It was quiet: her kids were at school, her husband at work. She told me that she and her family moved to the town when her oldest was about to start kindergarten so that the children could attend the town's highly regarded schools. From the moment Sabrina started speaking, it was clear that her days were filled with supporting her kids and their schools. Achievement and happiness were a full-time job; the skills required were numerous.

When Sabrina's son Michael was not placed in the math level she felt he deserved in eighth grade, she and her husband met with Michael's teacher. "Can you help us understand why this is the recommendation?"[2] She recounted their conversation with the teacher. "My son is devastated that this is his level." The school relented, and moved him up. I found myself stiffening as she told me this story—I knew that this was the kind of behavior that perpetuates educational inequality, even if Sabrina didn't realize it and was simply thinking of the best for her son, like all parents do.[3]

Beyond academics, Sabrina supported Michael's aspirations in sports, too, especially soccer and lacrosse. Sabrina's cultivation of Michael's athletic skills when he was young seemed to be paying off. He had previously played with an elite town soccer team—more elite than the usual town and travel teams—but quit that team to join an even more elite private "club" lacrosse team "in anticipation of going to high school and trying to make the team." Club teams in her area typically cost thousands of dollars every year, and provide, among other things, a paid professional coach and game locations well beyond the usual maximum hour-long drive for travel teams. Weekend tournaments and costly hotel stays are common. Again, I found myself feeling uneasy, partly for the implications for inequality and partly, I have to admit, because the conversation was beginning to make me worry about my own parenting, which was feeling more lax by the minute. The phrase "intensive parenting" kept coming to mind as she shared her kids' accomplishments and problem-solved their difficulties.[4]

Sabrina also was adamant about the importance of racial diversity. She particularly appreciated her town's busing program that brought a small number of students—mostly Black and Latinx—from the urban school district near her children's schools.[5] In fact, Sabrina's family volunteered to be the local contact for a child in the program for a number of years, frequently having that child over to their house. Beyond the busing program, the number of Asian immigrants was growing in her town—in fact, Michael was one of only three white students in his class. She gave me her take on those changes:

> When I look at his kindergarten picture, it looks like the UN, which we love. Diversity is important to us, something we embrace. And it was about 15 percent [students of color] when we moved in. And now I think we have, at least within the school-age population, close to 40 percent. So that is a huge change in ten years. . . . I'm delighted we're preparing our kids for a flat world.[6]

But as she gushed about diversity, a sense of dismay crept into our conversation. She hesitated, uneasy, before describing the growing diversity as also having "some very meaningful implications on life in this town." Sabrina was frustrated at how other families' decisions sometimes negatively affected her own children. She got most visibly upset when she described how her children sometimes lose out to kids whose parents do things differently.

Sabrina particularly resented Michael's Asian American peers who improved their math skills by taking supplementary classes outside of school.[7] In fact, she blamed Michael's initial eighth-grade math placement on those classes. Michael told his mom that eighteen of the twenty-one students in his class had a supplementary math class outside of school—he was one of the three who did not. Given the matching numbers, I guessed that the other two white kids in class were the other two who did not do supplementary math. Sabrina's liberal identity may have prevented her from naming their ethnicities explicitly, but the association was implicit.

I felt myself getting defensive at Sabrina's disapproval. Those other parents could have been my own Indian immigrant parents a generation ago. If there had been supplementary math classes in my western Pennsylvania town, I am certain my parents would have signed me up. Instead, they assigned me pages of a math workbook every day during summer vacation before they went off to work—and I did them. While I hated those assignments—mostly, I think, because my red-headed best friend across the street never had any summer work, and so it added another reason for me to feel different in my predominantly white town—as an adult I have more empathy for my parents' choices. Still, after talking with parents like Sabrina I was happy that I did not live in a town like hers. I even felt a newfound appreciation for the gentle pace of my own children's schools—fewer demanding parents, less pressure. I wondered if I too would come to resent the parents Sabrina described if I lived in her town and felt my kids would need to sign up for a supplemental course if I wanted them to take honors math.

Sabrina lamented the impact of this intensive parenting on Michael's self-esteem and self-confidence: "So my son is being compared to kids who are doing the supplemental math and he's suffering in his estimation of himself because of it." Sabrina labeled the impact of supplemental math on kids who do not participate "comparative distress," claiming that it had led her child to think he wasn't good at math. These kids, she shook her head, "think they're stupid." She made her view clear: "I think it's a problem. And I think it's creating some of the stress and the tension and the anxiety." The message—like so many things in her town—was implicit but clear. Asian parenting choices make white children like her own feel less competent and miss out on advantages to which they feel they are entitled. She loved racial diversity and the prospect of a "flat world," but when these things threatened her son's academic position, that love seemed to sour.

Sabrina did not simply complain about the problems she perceived, she set out to do something about them. She ran for elected office in her town. She also organized community-wide discussions aimed at reducing student stress related to academic achievement and joined the board of a local nonprofit providing free mental health services to teens.

Her efforts were noticed. Asian parents sometimes sensed the resentments of parents like Sabrina. Mei-Ling, an immigrant Chinese mother of two, was blunt: "There are people who are blaming the influx of immigrants for the heightened stress." I chatted with Mei-Ling as we sat on couches at the local public library first thing on a Monday morning. She was dressed in clothes suitable for the office, though when she told me she recently quit her corporate job to found a start-up, I wondered if she had gotten dressed up to meet me. After all, she saw herself as a community leader and was part of the leadership for a Chinese American organization in town.

Mei-Ling too lamented student stress—she told me that "stress is definitely a concern." But she felt placing the blame for it on her community was unwarranted. She went on to draw an analogy between sports and academics:

> In sports, when somebody does better, people winning Olympics, we celebrate them, right? We celebrate their success because these people, they have talents. They work very hard. So we say if you lose at least you lose gracefully, right? If you win, of course you show grace as well. So in success, academics and other activities, I feel people should embrace the same attitude. . . . I think sometimes when the status quo is challenged, people feel threatened. They say "Oh, well, my child used to be the best." Now you have the new influx of competition. "Now my child has become less than the best. . . ." It can be hard. But the world is changing, as always. . . . It used to be a high school diploma meant something. Now it doesn't mean something. It used to be a child performing at such level is great. Now it's *not* great.

Mei-Ling moved to town at the request of her older child, who had admired the high school's robotics team as a middle schooler. Eventually, her son found the robotics team too competitive—perhaps he didn't make the cut, though she didn't say—and he joined the school's Science Bowl team instead, which "played to his strength a little more." Mei-Ling's son took all honors classes, which led him to spend most of his evenings on schoolwork. Still, she disagreed with a proposed new homework policy to reduce homework in the district, which administrators had recently designed as part of an overall plan to reduce academic stress among students. The plan included ending homework in elementary school and banning homework on all school vacations and religious holidays. Mei-Ling explained why she disagreed with the new policy:

> If you don't build a foundation, both in terms of knowledge
> and in terms of skill, and in terms of habits—so I think this is
> just nonsense. For the first graders, second graders . . . maybe
> you give some option of homework. If they're busy or if they
> have other stuff, they don't do it. But for higher elementary and
> middle school, you have to build a foundation.

Despite the concerns of parents like Mei-Ling, the new homework policy eventually passed. Given that her daughter's middle school homework was "not much," Mei-Ling sent her to supplementary math for which she had to do additional homework. Soon after I began this research, I learned that Sabrina was right at least about one thing: classes at the local Russian School of Math (RSM), despite its name, were dominated by Asian American students. Still, Mei-Ling felt her daughter had too much time on her hands because of the lack of significant schoolwork: "She spends so much time making slime and playing with slime. And then watching TV. . . . It's a lot of free time."

Mei-Ling made me anxious too, but because of academics, not sports. When I got home I looked up RSM classes near me, determined to help my children keep up. But when I learned that the classes are two hours long with homework assigned every week, I didn't bother to ask my children to go. I knew it would be a fight. And like Sabrina, I wasn't sure it was what I really wanted for my kids.

Mei-Ling's own biography is, in many ways, a classic American dream story. For college she "went to the MIT equivalent in China," then came to the United States with a graduate school scholarship and "two thousand dollars of borrowed money." She described to me "the insecurity of having a visa, getting a green card, getting citizenship, without the support of extended family." Her story was so much like my own parents' story. On the surface, their experiences appear to bolster the idea that hard work can propel anyone to success in the United States. But they accumulated college degrees, cultural know-how, and high incomes both in Asia and the United States, which enabled them to provide substantial opportunities to their children. Mei-Ling also benefited from the inequality baked into American life that renders communities like the one she shared with Sabrina inaccessible to Americans without fancy degrees and jobs. There they could pour resources into the public schools together and prevent the schools from using those resources to support more than a handful of children from economically disadvantaged families, because those families simply could not afford to live in the town. The American dream narrative blinds many to the vastly unequal opportunities in American society.

Sabrina and Mei-Ling, and the other families in this story, all live a few miles from each other, in the same suburban town. Let's call this town "Woodcrest."[8] The town is on the East Coast, packed with highly educated parents who make good money and seek excellent educations for their kids. Many parents are alumni of well-known selective colleges in both the United States and Asia. For many years professional, well-paid parents and parents-to-be have moved to Woodcrest because of its public schools. Over thirty percent of residents in Woodcrest are Asian American, with most others identifying as white.[9] Four out of every five adults in town have a bachelor's degree (compared to one-third of American adults overall); a majority also have a master's degree.[10]

The town is both idyllic and intense. Residents know what they want and are willing to work hard to get it. Parents in Woodcrest, like parents everywhere, mobilize their resources to bolster their children's excellence in academic achievement and in their extracurricular endeavors. In many ways, this is what we parents instinctually *do*, one way or another, with whatever we have. Yet that access to resources—to money, networks, time, and cultural practices to help our kids succeed—varies enormously from one family, and one town, to the next. Parents in towns like Woodcrest, no surprise, have exceptionally rich resources of many kinds to propel their children ahead.

I spent three years visiting Woodcrest, to try to understand the impact of the growing and academically successful Asian community in town. I interviewed 121 people—parents, kids, and other community members. I also spent time shadowing students at the public high school, and at high school games, performances, and more.

The origins of this story, like all good stories, was born of curiosity. I was curious about the assumption, embedded in both research on immigration and the popular imagination, that suburbs are places where immigrants blend seamlessly into the American mainstream. The story goes that someone like Mei-Ling would fit in easily in Woodcrest—her academic degrees, fluency in English, and high income would lead to a blurred boundary between families like hers and the white American families in town.[11] This assimilation would be bolstered by the liberal sensibilities of most whites in town. In other words, so the story goes, a recent immigrant will do everything they can to move to a place like this, knowing that their kids will get a good education, learn how to fit in, and become a successful American. And suburban liberal whites will welcome the diversity that immigration brings with open arms. After all, in towns like Woodcrest, Black Lives Matter signs are common, growing in number after the murder of George Floyd by a police officer while three others looked on. And when Asian women were killed by a gunman outside Atlanta, "Stop Asian Hate" signs were placed next to the BLM ones.

And yet decades of research on the incorporation of immigrants has produced surprisingly little knowledge about professional immigrants living in suburban communities, implicitly promoting the assumption that when well-educated, well-paid immigrants and their children move into suburbs, their integration is smooth.[12] This may be because we are comparatively more worried about children of immigrants whose families are not able to get this far, so to speak. Also, early theories of assimilation were based on the experiences of white eastern and southern European immigrants of previous generations, a model that may not apply to immigrants of color, even if they are well-educated and earn high incomes.[13]

I also knew that historically, the majority group has always found ways to protect its interests, often by redefining "merit" in ways that suit themselves and maintain their position in the status hierarchy.[14] To take a century-old example, when administrators at Ivy League universities disliked the increasing proportion of Jewish students getting in based on standardized testing, they shifted their criteria of admission. Suddenly, Ivy League colleges required demonstrations of "character," photographs, and more in thinly veiled attempts to limit the number of Jewish students admitted.[15] The list of such examples is long. Protecting privilege has motivated the advantaged for centuries.

My hunch was that the growing presence of Asian Americans might make life in town more complicated than a simple story of assimilation, especially since Asian American kids are outperforming white kids academically in a variety of places around the country: in SAT scores, in admissions to the most desirable public schools with competitive entrance exams, and more. I wondered if an influx of Asian families in town might disrupt supposedly sacred American ideas about meritocracy, achievement, and excellence. How might whites respond when they notice that Asian American kids are surpassing the academic achievement of their own kids?

White Americans, of course, have a long history of finding ways to separate their children in school from children of color, even after the Supreme Court, in *Brown v. Board of Education*, outlawed segregated schools.[16] The "best" schools across much of the country are heavily white, via legal machinations that separate these kids from Black and Latinx kids whose parents are economically disadvantaged.[17] Would these white communities try to exclude Asian Americans in the same way, even if those kids were high achievers and had well-educated parents? On the other hand, I also wondered if some white parents might even start copying their Asian neighbors when they saw Asian American kids catapulting ahead of their own academically. As for Asian families, I had a hunch that they might be experiencing academic success not by assimilating into the white "mainstream," but rather by resisting assimilation.

I came to this research as a parent myself, the daughter of Indian immigrants, and a scholar who recently wrote a book about college students' views on, among other things, meritocracy, diversity, and college admissions. In *The Diversity Bargain* I described how white Ivy League undergraduates expressed great appreciation for diversity, but only to the extent that such diversity benefited themselves. They liked how Black and Latinx peers on campus broadened their perspectives—so they supported affirmative action. But the second they experienced a setback, many pulled out the "reverse discrimination" script that lay in their back pockets. After that research, I started to wonder how whites make sense of Asian American academic success. And I began to wonder how Asian families too make sense of meritocracy and diversity as they put down roots and become a part of American suburbs. This time, though, I thought I would catch families before the frenzy of college admissions had begun.

These questions about who belongs and who is deserving are practically as old as our country is. But this research is also shaped by another social anxiety: how to be a good parent. Of course, mothers and fathers have always tried to do right by their kids, but the question of how to parent has perhaps never been asked with quite the same level of intensity—and worry—as it is today.[18] Before I began the research, I had heard a growing chorus of concerns about intensive parenting. Some worried that the determination of parents to promote their children's success was worsening mental health, particularly among upper-middle-class kids.[19] Others sounded the alarm about kids becoming "excellent sheep"—good at excelling in tests and competitions, but not so good at thinking for themselves about who they want to be and the role they want to play in the world.[20] The whole conversation seemed to tilt toward exaggeration. Even well-meaning parents—and after all, aren't we *all* well-meaning parents?—became stereotypes. White wealthy parents were lambasted for being "helicopter parents"—overly involved in their children's lives—and Asian parents for being "tiger parents"— overly demanding of excellence.[21] I wondered how parents caricatured by both of these stereotypes really thought about parenting and how those views might be different for white and Asian parents of the same social class. How did they make sense of the drive to achievement? What did they think about concerns over the emotional well-being of kids like theirs? At the heart of all these questions was the simplest, and most complicated, one of all: how do you define what makes a good parent?

There is so much we don't know about what parents in towns like Woodcrest think. How do they make sense of achievement and the best ways to attain it? How do they try to balance their children's emotional well-being with achievement? What do they see as fair ways of helping children succeed, and perhaps more importantly to parents, the unfair ways? What interracial tensions emerge as a result of parents' different perspectives and actions? These questions, and the ways they get messy and entangled as we try to answer them, are the focus of this book.

White parents move to Woodcrest to take advantage of its "excellent" schools, assuming their children will be virtually guaranteed success by doing so. But over the last decade, their multicultural sensibilities have been tested like never before; the Asian population has continued to grow and Asian American children have continued to outshine their white peers. Unlike with the Black and Latinx kids who are bussed in, Asians are arriving on their own accord—no one can stop them. And they threaten the status of their white peers in ways that Black and Latinx students do not, because they are not stuck in the low-track classes that many bussed students are. In response, white parents attempt to maintain their position at the top of the racial hierarchy by, among other things, pushing their schools to reduce academic work and shaming Asian parents for a parenting style they deem unworthy for its supposedly excessive focus on academics. In other words, while parents like Sabrina express excitement about a supposedly flat world, that appreciation seems to rest on the assumption that she and her children will sit comfortably at the top of that world. Their pushback is rarely described in racial terms—that would be anathema to the town's liberal sensibilities. Still, the alignment with race is unmistakable to anyone paying attention.

Asian parents also seem to appreciate the affluence and socioeconomic segregation in Woodcrest that enable them to reap the benefits of a town designed to keep Black, economically disadvantaged families out, even if most are unaware of that history. They and their children also excel in a system of meritocracy that has historically rewarded whites and justified Black exclusion from top tracks in high school and from top colleges.[22] In other words, in a situation of great irony, Asian Americans in Woodcrest benefit from a system designed to maintain white advantage.

In reading this book you will come to understand that while white and Asian parents alike simply do their best to provide for their children, they do so in an education system that concentrates privilege by allowing well-off parents to separate their children from lower-income children with fewer resources. So much of the handwringing in Wood-crest, it seemed to me, happened with little awareness of how privileged they all were and how their lives were built around a system designed to perpetuate inequality and myths of meritocracy. Instead, they seemed to be fighting for gold versus silver or bronze, forgetting that practically everyone in town was already assured of a medal.

Good Parenting in an Age of Migration

THE COMMON STORY ABOUT RACE in the United States goes something like this: whites pretty much always manage to retain their status at the top of society; racial minorities struggle to succeed in systems that seem designed to privilege whites. That story is the one that gets told the most, and has been told the longest, for good reason. Such inequality is baked into our country, found almost anywhere we look hard enough.[1]

It's certainly true in education. Standardized tests were designed to demonstrate the superiority of whites over other races.[2] They often include cultural biases that render them unfair to Black test takers and seem to be almost as good at predicting a taker's household income as their eventual grades in college.[3] In school Black kids are more likely than white kids to be referred for special education testing, and less likely to be referred to honors or AP classes.[4] They are also more likely to be punished for "defiant" behaviors.[5] And they learn in classrooms run by teachers who often hold anti-Black bias.[6] When they get to college, Black and Latinx Americans are more likely to attend community colleges than are whites and less likely to attend selective four-year colleges, which partially explains why they are less likely to graduate college.[7] Beyond education, whites are much less likely to be arrested and incarcerated than Blacks.[8] Real estate agents continue to discriminate against racial minorities, shaping where we live and where our kids go to school.[9] Racial bias shapes hiring decisions.[10] The list is endless.

When racial minorities do succeed, they are often forced to leave their cultures behind. For centuries, to get ahead some African Americans have been forced to engage in "respectability politics"—emulating "white" behaviors, speech patterns, and styles to demonstrate moral worthiness of social mobility—and in general, convincing established whites that they are in fact much like them.[11] Scholars of immigration have traced the Europeans who arrived in the US over a century ago and found that over generations their communities did a version of the same thing for social mobility: assimilate.[12] Early immigrants from non-Western countries even tried to convince established whites that they were indeed "white" (and not Black), and hence deserving of US citizenship.[13] At that time they were usually turned down, but today, in a society defined by the Civil Rights Movement and multiculturalism, the exclusion is rarely so overt. Sometimes assimilated racial minorities are even welcomed by whites eager to demonstrate their belief in racial equality.[14] As long, of course, as Black women go to great lengths to make their hair adhere to white norms of beauty; racial minorities work hard and ignore the racism they experience; and, overall, in ways large and small, minorities leave their cultures behind.[15]

Alongside this widespread story of assimilation and cultural shedding is a quieter but no less pervasive reality: racial minorities have always drawn on their own resources to facilitate their flourishing. Long before the end of slavery, African Americans drew on a unique "African American philosophy of education" to learn to read and claim their humanity.[16] Working-class immigrants draw on their social connections in ethnic enclaves to earn a living despite their lack of proficiency in English.[17] Professional minority organizations such as the National Medical Association, an association of Black doctors, facilitate the sharing of ideas and skills to deal with experiences like racism in professional settings.[18] Further, a bicultural identity can also facilitate success.[19] Biculturalism enables racial minorities to draw strength from their ethnic or racial groups while also finding "success" via white-identified dominant culture. This leads many immigrant youth to educational outcomes on a par with their US-born peers.[20] But all of these examples assume that racial minorities succeed by adopting at least some aspects of the dominant, privileged white culture in the US.

All of these explanations fail to help us make sense of situations in which racial minorities catapult *ahead* of established whites. Today, Asian Americans are outperforming whites in many of the areas deemed most important to educational success. From standardized test scores to admission to elite high schools and colleges, Asian Americans have jumped ahead of white Americans.[21] Income is another area. Asian American adults have higher average incomes than whites, even when compared to whites who grow up in households of the same income.[22] In high-income towns with a large and growing Asian American population, most Asian Americans who grew up in those towns also go on to earn higher incomes than their white peers from the same town.[23] In this book I focus not on why Asian Americans are experiencing this success, but rather on what happens next. We assume that no one minds or even much notices professional minorities because they seamlessly blend into the top of society and cannot be portrayed as draining our social welfare programs. But when Asians start to loosen the racial hierarchy, whites can start to feel less comfortable and can grow to resent Asians for seeming to encroach on their status.

Woodcrest is a town that captures this pattern. While both Asian American and white children do well in Woodcrest—most go on to attend four-year colleges, and selective ones at that—Asian American kids are outperforming their white peers academically. And the growth of the Asian American population in the town means that the academic success of Asian Americans is impossible to ignore. When growing diversity related to Asian immigration starts to threaten white parents' comfortable status as the highest-achieving group in a town they chose so they could give their children every advantage, they begin to push back. They offer arguments about the right way to parent and advocate for changes at school that would preserve their status. In other words, they attempt to guarantee their children a spot at the top of a supposedly flat world, but when that move is emulated by Asian families that go on to best them at their own game, they attempt to change the rules.

Asian parents, in turn, push back on these judgments. At the same time, they too benefit from a community that was originally designed to keep out the vast majority of African Americans in the area, as well as middle- and lower-income families. The exclusivity of Woodcrest means that Asian American children reap the benefits of resource hoarding that segregation drives—they get a top-notch education supported by high property taxes, and a parent community with high educational levels. As a result, they maintain full faith in American meritocracy, a system that sometimes seems designed to maintain social standing across generations rather than to promote equal opportunity.

ASIAN IMMIGRANTS IN THE UNITED STATES

While Asian immigrants have been coming to the United States for well over a hundred years, both the pace of new arrivals and their profile dramatically shifted after the passage of the 1965 Hart-Celler Act. The act launched both the temporary skilled-worker program and employment-based permanent residency, paving the way for significant Asian immigration. Today, more than fifty years later, hundreds of thousands of Asian immigrants come to the United States every year. Asian Americans are the fastest-growing racial group in the United States, and the countries sending the most immigrants annually are China and India.[24] Around four million Americans identify as Chinese American, and a similar number identify as Indian American.[25]

Because visas for highly skilled workers have been a key avenue through which Indian and Chinese immigrants arrive in the United States, immigrants from India and China tend to be the elites of those countries. They are much more likely to have a bachelor's degree than the average adult in India and China, as well as compared to adults in the United States.[26] More than half of Chinese American adults hold a bachelor's degree, and one in four also hold an advanced degree.[27] Among Indian Americans, three in four hold bachelor's degrees, and 40 percent also hold advanced degrees.[28] These high levels of education are associated with high incomes. The median household incomes of Indian and Chinese Americans ($127,000 and $86,000, respectively) are higher than any other ethnic or racial group in the United States, including white Americans (median household income for whites is $70,000, and the national median income is $66,000).[29]

Like other well-off Americans, high-achieving Chinese and Indian immigrants tend to have high-achieving children.[30] The average SAT score for Asian Americans is 100 points higher than the average for white Americans, and that gap continues to grow.[31] Over the past two decades, all but four winners of the national spelling bee have been

Indian Americans.[32] Asian Americans are overrepresented in selective universities: 35 percent of Asian Americans who go to college attend a very selective college, compared to 25 percent of whites who go to college.[33] At Harvard, Asian Americans are overrepresented by more than a factor of five—while over 25 percent of domestic Harvard undergraduates are Asian American, Asian Americans make up just 5 percent of all adolescents in the United States today; every other group, including whites, is underrepresented.[34]

Education and high incomes are cardinal features of today's idealized American suburbs (even while the reality of suburbs is, and always has been, much more complex). No surprise, then, that more and more Asian Americans are moving to upper-middle-class suburban communities and enrolling their kids in the local schools, a move aided by considerably less housing discrimination toward Asian Americans now than a century ago, as well as compared to African Americans and Latinx Americans today.[35] Today, six in ten Asian Americans live in a suburb.[36] Many upper-middle-class suburban communities across the country, especially in California, Texas, and the northeast, are seeing increasing numbers of Asian American families, in part due to the development of technology hubs and the presence of highly ranked schools.[37] In these seemingly idyllic communities, it is easy to assume that immigrant families rapidly assimilate into the mainstream. In America's cities, such fitting in is more challenging, as immigrants are often undereducated, with limited knowledge of English, and gripped by economic hardship. But we all assume that life is different in the suburbs.

Again and again across the last century, Jews, Catholics, Irish, and numerous other formerly marginalized groups have moved to the suburbs and into the American mainstream.[38] Why wouldn't Asian immigrants do the same? After all, moving to the suburbs combined with high incomes, college degrees, and intermarriage with whites all weaken the boundary between "white" and "Asian," right?—especially in an increasingly inclusive American society that values diversity.[39] The optimistic scholars of "neo-assimilation theory" suggest that any remaining anti-Asian racism and discrimination in the labor market will likely dissipate in the coming years, leading to full assimilation for Asian Americans.[40]

But the extent to which Asian Americans are incorporating into some kind of dominant, and increasingly expanding, "white" group remains to be seen. More than twenty years ago, sociologist Mia Tuan asked whether Asian Americans are "forever foreigners or honorary whites."[41] The question lingers. In the past, white immigrants always held privilege over African Americans and immigrants of color, leading many to conclude that the particular shade of your skin—let alone the amount of education you have or your country of birth—doesn't matter as long as you are not white.[42] Indeed, studies of the increasing numbers of Asian Americans in Los Angeles suburbs during the 1990s found significant racial discrimination and efforts to minimize the visibility of Asian cultures, such as local politicians pushing English-only laws, and the exclusion of Asian food at neighborhood block parties.[43] Today, Asian Americans still report experiencing racial discrimination, especially at work; such reports have increased, rather than decreased over the past decade.[44] After the 2001 attacks on the World Trade Center, hate crimes toward South Asians increased, and more recently attacks on East Asians have increased in response to associations between the COVID-19 virus and China.[45] In school, Asian Americans are more likely than peers of all other races to report experiencing racial discrimination from their peers.[46] At work, many Asian Americans report of so-called bamboo ceilings.[47] And despite the high overall incomes and educational achievements of Asian Americans, white men still earn more than Asian American men with the same level of education, type of job, and location; Asian American women too experience disadvantages at work that white women don't face.[48] Indeed, perceptions of this discrimination are one reason Asian Americans sometimes give for their emphasis on achievement, and particularly on STEM fields, which they view as holding less room for the bias that can feel inevitable in more subjective fields.[49] While different from stereotypes that Black and Latinx Americans have long endured, stereotypes of Asian Americans can nonetheless prevent their full assimilation into the mainstream.[50]

Despite racial exclusion, many Asian Americans are socioeconomically successful. Neo-assimilation theory predicts that their high levels of education and good jobs will go hand in hand with the blurring of the boundary between Asian Americans and whites, especially within the upper-middle class. But professional Asian Americans may succeed through *different* avenues rather than by following the pathways of upper-middle-class whites.[51] Overall, the research on Asian Americans shows the complexity of the process of becoming American, even for a highly educated group of immigrants.

HOW DOES IMMIGRATION SHAPE NONIMMIGRANTS?

How do US-born whites react when an immigrant community seems to outshine them, playing the game of meritocracy even better than the white society that wrote the rules to their own advantage?[52] Most studies of immigration have focused exclusively on immigrants and their children, as if they had no impact on the people they encountered when they arrived. But in a recent study of Cupertino, California, an upper-middle-class suburb that is now over two-thirds Asian, Tomás Jiménez found white residents concerned about their shifting school culture. While the arrival of Asian immigrants brought about many positive interactions between immigrants and their US-born white neighbors, some whites in Cupertino responded by moving to towns with fewer Asians.[53] And many perceived a shift in which white students went from being at the top to being perceived as "slackers."[54] In other words, Jiménez describes a changed racial hierarchy in Cupertino in which Asians have achieved higher status than whites. Still, we do not hear from immigrants in Cupertino in Jiménez's study—I suspect they may have a different take on the town's racial hierarchy. And it is hard to get a sense of how whites in Cupertino may hold on to their status by speaking only to them. We are usually quite unaware of the ways we hold on to our privileges—disadvantage is much more legible to those who experience it.

A different response to Asian American academic success by some whites is to change the criteria for success. In recent years, more and more whites seem to concede that our typical criteria for evaluating students—especially standardized tests—are seriously flawed. Tests like the SAT have been critiqued for decades for their systematic exclusion of African Americans and for their biases, whether conscious or not, in favor of those with resources. Why are we only taking these critiques seriously now? There may be some whites who have genuinely gotten "woke" and are reckoning with this small but ubiquitous example of systemic racism. But more likely? Whites started paying attention to the very real flaws in standardized testing precisely because Asian Americans started to outperform them.

Whites questioning the worth of the SAT when Asian Americans excel on the test dates back to the 1980s. Back then, administrators at the University of California shifted their practice of affirmative action because of perceptions of "racial imbalance" due to the over-representation of Asian Americans on campus (but not, it needs to be said, because of the underrepresentation of Black and Hispanic students).[55] More recently, Frank Samson has demonstrated that when white undergraduates at UCLA are reminded of Asian Americans' high GPAs, they downplay the importance of GPA in selective college admissions; on the other hand, when they are reminded of Black Americans' low GPAs, they express strong belief in the use of GPA to judge applicants.[56] On the east coast, as the percentage of Asian Americans attending New York City's coveted Stuyvesant High School has crept up to 73 percent of the student body (in a city whose public schools are just 16 percent Asian), a growing chorus of liberal white New Yorkers is now criticizing the school's exam-based system of selection, even though activists for equity for Black and Latinx students have been advocating for alternative admissions for decades.[57] Until whites were no longer dominating the exam, whites fought to maintain it.[58] What we see over and over again is white people adjusting their beliefs about merit not to be racially equitable, but rather to maintain their own status as the top-performing group, especially in the face of Asian American achievement. It is only Asian American academic success that causes some whites to question the systems of evaluation they have long benefited from. In other words, questions of meritocracy move front and center when Asian American academic achievement takes off.

So, does moving to upper-middle-class, predominantly white suburbs lead to Asian American "assimilation" into the white, upper-middle-class culture of parenting and ideas about achievement and merit? Or does Asian American achievement lead white parents to adopt Asian American styles of parenting and ideas about achievement and merit? Or do whites attempt to redefine merit when Asians beat them at their game? Do some simply exit for whiter communities?

Towns like Woodcrest are filled with suburban liberals—white professionals who support policies like busing to create school integration in urban areas, but who turn a blind eye to policies that create the need for that busing in the first place, such as minimum housing lot size policies instituted many decades ago to exclude working-class African Americans.[59] In my research I discovered new forms of jockeying for status among whites and Asian Americans alike. That is, rather than whites and Asians assimilating, parents seem more often than not to be at odds with each other. I found a persistent and underlying conflict about the most basic issues of parenting.

GOOD PARENTING

Across all ethnicities and incomes, parents have a lot in common. After all, we are all participating in the same thankless, exhausting, thrilling task. We all do what we can to help our kids. That is the simple premise from which I began researching this book. But what parents do to help their kids, and what they think is best, can vary a lot from one parent to another, and from one neighborhood to another. And when differences emerge, judgments are right behind. Too often parents who are working class, or immigrants, or just not white are blamed for their parenting decisions, while the behaviors of white middle-class parents are considered "normal" and therefore go unexamined. As researchers try (with only the best intentions) to explain why Black and Latinx kids do worse in school than their white peers, and why Asian kids do better, the implicit assumption is that what white kids and parents do is the norm; any deviation from them is what requires explanation.

What we do know so far is that the differences start with money. It's clear that how much money we have, whether earned or inherited, affects what we can provide for our children. In fact, recent research shows that as economic inequality has grown, so too has inequality in how much parents are able to spend on their children, which plays a big role in the college admissions process.[60] This includes spending on extracurricular activities, which cultivate soft skills transferrable to the classroom and beyond.[61] Beyond economic resources, college-educated parents tend to have more cultural know-how to help their kids. They know how to cultivate behaviors in their children that are rewarded in school (like being proactive in getting teachers' attention through verbal reasoning and negotiation skills), and they know how to communicate with school staff in ways that more often than not gets their wishes granted.[62] Annette Lareau describes this parenting as "concerted cultivation."[63] Most middle-class parents genuinely believe

9

that their style is the "right" way to parent, one that aligns with their philosophy and goals for parenting. Still, their style also strategically helps their children get ahead. We can also find many college-educated mothers spending significantly more time and energy on parenting than previous generations of parents, a practice called "intensive parenting."[64] These supports extend well beyond the childhood years, and they pay off again and again: in college admissions, college success, job opportunities, and more.[65]

Upper-middle-class white parents are particularly adept at deploying their resources and, as some describe it, "opportunity hoarding" for their school-aged children, often to the detriment of Black kids, even within the same school.[66] Upper-middle-class Black parents also think about issues that whites rarely notice, often trying to ensure diversity in their children's school and extracurricular environments; seeking positive images of African Americans in the books their children read; and teaching their children specific skills to avoid the harmful, even deadly, consequences of racial stereotypes.[67] All of this is in service of building a strong racial identity, known to support success among African American youth.[68] Middle-class immigrant parents also try to foster strong ethnic identities, sometimes through cultural heritage and language classes.[69] Many immigrant parents instill a sense of duty or obligation in their children to succeed, given the sacrifices they made to come to the United States to provide them with a better life—some call this an "immigrant bargain."[70] Middle-class immigrants are particularly skilled at leveraging community resources, their social networks, and ethnic identities to support their children's success.[71] Nonimmigrant white parents don't have to spend their time, money, or energies on any of this.

What about Asian parents? It has become commonplace, both in academic writing and popular culture, to attribute the academic achievements of Asian Americans to some kind of innate set of cultural values in their parents. It is true that parents in India and China are more likely to place stronger demands and harsher punishments on their children, with less emphasis on autonomy, than parents in the West.[72] And the ideals of Confucius may in fact influence some East Asian parents to some extent.[73] And yes, there are some self-proclaimed tiger moms out there. But these controversial, and quotable, cultural simplifications ignore a more banal but much more meaningful explanation: selective migration from Asia, and the education systems Asian immigrant parents left behind. Entrée into the most elite universities of India and China is through standardized exams; the higher a college is ranked, the more intense the competition for spots. The most elite colleges in India and China have lower admission rates than top colleges in the United States.[74] For academically ambitious and well-resourced students in both countries, hours of grueling study is common; tutors are ubiquitous.[75] These Asian parents' previous contexts carry abiding influence over the achievements of the next generation.[76]

Of course, most people in India and China do not go to college, let alone an *elite* college. However, immigration policies in the United States have meant that most immigrants from those countries are, by necessity, highly educated. In well-off American suburbs, almost all adults, across ethnic lines, have a bachelor's degree, and many of those degrees are from top universities in the United States, China, and India. In other words, what gets you into an elite college in India and China is not the same as what gets you into an elite college in the United States, and most professionals in suburban America from India and China got to the suburbs because of their elite education back home. In turn, in both India and China, landing a spot at an elite college sets an individual on a pathway to lucrative jobs beyond college.[77] While a degree from an elite college helps in getting selected for jobs in elite management consulting, law, and finance firms in the United States as well, pathways to success in the United States are more diverse.[78] In the US, top business executives and government leaders are more likely to *not* hold degrees from elite colleges.[79] This means that elite degrees are more critical in Asia than in the US, heightening the importance there of academic excellence as the primary pathway to a comfortable life (and the main pathway to highly skilled migration to the United States). Suburban Asian immigrants bring these experiences with them as they parent in the United States.

Immigrant parents in well-off American suburbs bring strategies for success to the United States from their own experiences of success in Asia, so it should come as no surprise that they emphasize academic achievement even more than other American parents.[80] In their study of US-born children of Chinese and Vietnamese immigrants in the Los Angeles area, Jennifer Lee and Min Zhou found that many Asian parents define success with unusually high standards: "earning straight

A's, graduating as the high school valedictorian, earning a degree from an elite university, attaining an advanced degree. . . ."[81] Not surprisingly, their children seem to take on at least some of those high expectations and strategies for academic achievement, at least in part due to a stronger sense of family obligation than other American kids hold.[82] It was these success frames that seemed to propel many in Lee and Zhou's study to high levels of achievement.[83]

And what about sports? How do Asian and white parents cultivate their children's athletic skills? American high schools spend more money on sports and extracurriculars per pupil than on academics.[84] And the growing high school sports industry enables parents to spend their own money as well—sometimes shockingly large amounts of it—cultivating athletic prowess.[85] While there have been attempts over the years to end sports teams at both the high school and college levels in order to redeploy funds toward academic success and other priorities, those attempts have been met with fierce resistance.[86] Upper-middle-class parents in the US are spending more than ever on developing their children's sports skills, a primary reason that the gap between wealthy and poor parents' spending on their children has grown.[87] During the COVID-19 pandemic, many sports teams played interscholastic games even while their schools were shuttered for academic learning. In contrast, the sports industry in Asia struggles to gain a foothold.[88] There, childhood sports are not the norm and most high schools do not have sports teams—which is presumably at least in part because Asian colleges pay little heed to athletic skills in their admissions process. Playing sports outside of school is associated with lower achievement in Asia (but higher achievement in the US).[89] Parents also bring their perspectives on the importance of athletic excellence to their children's development, as we'll see.

Beyond the pursuit of advancement for their children, both academic and athletic, parents in Woodcrest and around the country are increasingly concerned about their children's emotional well-being.[90] America today is influenced by therapeutic culture, which means we think about emotion more than ever.[91] Recent studies have hinted at potential downsides of intensive parenting, including psychological strain in children, conflicts between teachers and parents, family conflict, and excessive competition between students.[92] Some are questioning whether today's adolescents are, as in the titles of two recent books, "overloaded and underprepared," insisting that we acknowledge the "price of privilege."[93] A popular book among upper-middle-class moms, *How to Raise an Adult*, provides guidance on how to "break free of the overparenting trap."[94] A growing nonprofit based at Stanford University, Challenge Success, states its vision that

> Extrinsic metrics such as grades, test scores, and selective college admissions have become the primary markers of success in too many communities. We know that this narrow definition of success can interfere with healthy child development and effective education, leaving many kids feeling stressed, marginalized, or misunderstood. . . . A largely singular focus on academic achievement has resulted in a lack of attention to other attributes of a successful life.[95]

An increasing number of voices in the US—from bestselling books to magazine and journal articles to podcasts—describe a full-blown mental health "crisis" among American adolescents. Upper-middle-class children are pegged as particularly vulnerable to bouts of depression and anxiety related to the dogged pursuit of excellence.[96] Diagnoses of psychological distress among adolescents have grown dramatically in recent years, and the increases are largest in high-income families.[97] This maladjustment is tied to *community*-level affluence, rather than a family's individual level of income or the expectations of individual parents.[98] While these studies tend to spotlight concerns about white upper-middle-class youth, there is worrying data about Asian American youth as well. They tend to have lower self-esteem and higher rates of suicidal thoughts than white youth.[99] High parental expectations and a sense of obligation to succeed can damage emotional well-being among Asian Americans, especially those who are not able to meet their parents' expectations or who lack strong relationships with their parents.[100]

Concerns about emotional health are growing in Asia too.[101] As early as the 1990s, protesters in Taiwan—a test-heavy country—chanted "We want happy childhood!"[102] Urban upper-middle-class parents in Asia are often influenced by ideas they hear from friends and relatives living in the United States, and in the global news and social media they read.[103] As a result, they emphasize emotional well-being, autonomy, and individual identity more than in the past.[104] Affluent Asian parents are particularly able to emphasize nonacademic concerns, because they can fall back on sending their children abroad for college if they do not attain high scores on the standardized tests necessary for college enrollment at home; they can also afford more engaging and empathetic tutors than working-class parents can.[105] This means that many upper-middle-class Asian immigrant parents are likely to share with upper-middle-class US-born parents concerns about emotional well-being and a desire for their children to have room for autonomy rather than strict parental direction.[106]

How do parents manage all these concerns? Given the stakes of parenting—to be a good parent, after all, feels for many of us like the most important job in our lives—making the "right" decisions and providing the "right" guidance can feel like a moral imperative, so we do our best to signal that we are good, moral parents.[107] It also leads us to make moral judgments of those whom we see as "bad" parents—whether that's because they coddle their children emotionally, or don't instill a value for hard work, or push their kids too hard.[108] Parents who diligently assist their children, as we have already seen, can be pathologized for being *too* focused on achievement—this is especially true when white parents observe Asian American youth outperforming their own.[109] Parenting choices, ever fraught ground, can easily spill into moral judgments and ethnic generalizations.

And yet there *are* differences between certain ethnic groups. All parents do what they can to support their children's development, yet even when we have the same economic resources, our choices can be quite different. Everything from our level of involvement as parents, to the messages we give to our children, to the ways we interact with teachers, to the places we choose to live—all of these can be different for white and Asian parents. What is crucial to acknowledge here is that many of our decisions are shaped by what sociologist Ann Swidler refers to as "cultural repertoires," or "habits, skills, and styles from which people construct 'strategies of action'" that guide what we do in any given moment.[110] Our cultural repertoires stem from a variety of sources—mostly what we have encountered in our lives through our families, our neighbors wherever we have lived, and our social networks. These influences can lead to ethnic patterns, and those patterns can lead to racial tensions. On the other hand, our cultural repertoires are diverse.

Moving to a different neighborhood or country can often lead to an expanded cultural repertoire, so the cultural repertoires of Asian parents are not all the same (nor are the cultural repertoires of white parents all the same). One of the aims of this book is to reckon with the vicious influence of stereotypes, while acknowledging the reality of cultural differences.

So while we can assume that all parents care deeply about their children and their flourishing, how we attempt to facilitate that flourishing, and the resources we bring to bear on those attempts, vary considerably, based on our levels of education, our race, our own experiences of schooling and migration, and much more. And when those differences sit side by side in suburban communities, the tensions are probably inevitable.

WOODCREST, USA

Most contemporary studies of how immigrants become part of American life are based in cities, but for over two decades a majority of immigrants have been living in suburbs.[111] In fact, suburbs are increasingly the first destination for immigrants, rather than a place to aspire to once you have some money in the bank.[112] In this research I was particularly interested in suburbs in which upper-middle-class white and Asian families brought their styles of parenting and achievement together in one community. When I looked at the data I found a growing number of suburbs that are home to families with high incomes and significant and growing Asian American populations—I counted thirty-four such suburbs using 2010 U.S. Census data, but the number has likely grown since then.[113] Many of these towns have already experienced "white flight," with whites leaving as the percentage of minorities (in these cases, mostly Asians) increases.[114] Settings like Woodcrest, then, are increasingly common in the United States (see appendix A for more details on Woodcrest and the research basis for this book).

Woodcrest has historically been filled with what Lily Geismer describes as "suburban liberals"—liberals who, since the 1960s, have supported liberal policies on a national level, like environmentalism and racial integration, while simultaneously instituting restrictive laws in their own towns.[115] Indeed, over three times as many Woodcrest residents are registered Democrats over Republicans, and for decades most white residents have enthusiastically supported a busing program that brings students from a nearby urban district to Woodcrest schools, an early effort at school integration. In the past, some Woodcrest residents organized to advocate for fair housing laws to prevent racial discrimination as well. Still, in the 1950s the town passed a minimum housing lot size policy, requiring all new construction to be single-family homes, and severely limiting commercial land usage. All were thinly veiled efforts to ward off the racial integration and development appearing in other nearby towns. And they were successful—by 1970 the town was over 95 percent white.[116] In the 1960s, white residents of Woodcrest also fought proposals to integrate the town's public schools with those of the urban center in which it is embedded. In fact, some advocates for the urban-suburban busing program cited the danger that without busing, the district could be pushed to integrate more fully.[117] Programs like busing allowed Woodcrest residents to express support for "diversity" while maintaining Woodcrest as a separate, economically advantaged school district. While the city those kids are bused from is less than ten miles away from Woodcrest, the percentage of students who are economically disadvantaged in that urban district overall is more than ten times the percentage of economically disadvantaged students in Woodcrest schools (most of whom in fact reside in the urban district and are bused to Woodcrest).[118]

Since the 1990s large numbers of immigrants from Asia have arrived in the area to take up highly paid jobs in the tech industry. While social policies of a half century ago were designed to shut out one minority group—African Americans—today another minority group—Asian Americans—is able to benefit from that racial exclusion.[119] In other words, in towns like Woodcrest, highly skilled immigrants with high levels of education are able to reap the benefits that whites initially established for themselves. Further, the diversity Asians bring to towns like Woodcrest bolsters white residents' identities as racially progressive liberals, despite their town's foundations in Black exclusion. The town, to its credit, has acknowledged its shifting demographics, and created commissions to address, among other things, how to increase Asian Americans' civic participation. Today, just under one-third of Woodcrest residents is Asian. Median household income is over $150,000, and less than 5 percent of residents live in poverty (see appendix A for more details on Woodcrest).[120]

One high school serves the town of Woodcrest, with over two thousand students. Over one-third of students at Woodcrest High School are Asian, just over half are white, and the rest identify as mixed, Black, or Latinx.[121] While the number of Asian American students in each cohort grows as the group moves from grade to grade, white cohort sizes are shrinking slightly, suggesting that Asian families with school-aged children continue to move into Woodcrest as their children grow older while more white families either leave the town or move their children from public to private schools.

It will come as no surprise that most students excel academically at Woodcrest High School. On state exams, 96 to 100 percent of students achieved proficiency or higher, depending on the subject.[122] The school's average SAT score is close to 1300, well above the state average (and even noticeably higher than the 1180 national average for Asian Americans).[123] Three of every four students take at least one Advanced Placement exam during high school.[124]

Just as we've seen for the country as a whole, Asian American students at Woodcrest High School outperform their white peers academically. They are overrepresented in the top 10 and top 20 percent of student GPAs, and substantially underrepresented in the bottom 10 and bottom 20 percent.[125] Further, Asian American students are overrepresented in AP courses in both STEM and the humanities.[126] Asian students at Woodcrest High School outperform their white peers on the state exams as well; for example, 99 percent of Asian students were rated advanced in mathematics, while 92 percent of white students were. In English language arts, 90 percent of Asian students were rated advanced, compared to 83 percent of white students.[127] And this academic performance translates into college admissions: while almost all graduates of Woodcrest High School go on to attend four-year colleges (and mostly highly selective ones at that), Asian American graduates are more likely to attend four-year colleges and less likely to go on to two-year colleges.[128]

On the other hand, white students at Woodcrest are outperforming their Asian American peers when it comes to sports. Asian Americans are underrepresented on twenty-one of the twenty-seven varsity sports teams, appearing in proportion to their schoolwide population (or overrepresented) only in ultimate frisbee (co-ed), boys and girls volleyball, boys and girls tennis, and boys swimming.[129] And just one of every ten athletes from Woodcrest recruited by coaches at selective colleges to play for their teams were Asian American.[130]

For all these reasons, Woodcrest is a rather unusual piece of America, and also a place that is becoming more and more common. Both because it is exceptional and at the same time increasingly common, the tensions in town are more and more relevant for understanding achievement, immigrant assimilation, and parenting in the United States today.

WHAT'S NEXT

What I report in this book is based on my three years of ethnographic work in Woodcrest. I spent time shadowing students at Woodcrest High School; attending sports games, music performances, and a science fair; and speaking with students during focus group discussions, informal conversations in the cafeteria, and one-on-one in-depth interviews. I also spent time listening to parents in Woodcrest at discussions about mental health, community events, and in in-depth interviews. I spoke with community leaders as well, and even to a real estate agent to help me understand the shifting population of Woodcrest. In addition to the many hours of observation at Woodcrest High School and beyond, I conducted 121 in-depth interviews altogether, mostly with white, Chinese, and Indian parents and the children of white, Chinese, and Indian residents (see appendix A for details on the research methodology, and appendix B for in-depth interview questions).

So often studies of immigrants and their children attempt to explain why immigrant families are different from middle-class white families. But rather than frame Asian Americans as the ones in need of explanation, we should compare their ways of doing things to their non-Asian neighbors.[131] In the pages that follow I take you on a tour of Woodcrest to reveal how white parents make sense of and react to the ways Asian Americans are competing in the meritocracy game that white families have been taking advantage of for decades, and how their Asian neighbors respond. Along the way, I'll show how all parents work hard to maintain their social position—for whites, viewing themselves as better parents than Asian parents, even ones whose children might now be surpassing their children academically, and for Asian parents, unwittingly reaping advantages from the class and racial segregation that historically benefited whites at the expense of African Americans. By highlighting tensions over both academic and extracurricular excellence, we see how these two groups of parents are often doing the same thing: they both give more weight to the areas in which their children excel, and they both frame their own choices as the morally correct pathway to success for their children.

Overall, the voices in this book demonstrate that well-off suburbs are not simply landing places for ethnic assimilation, even for those highly skilled newcomers whom many Americans find desirable. Rather, these suburbs are the places where new forms of ethnic tensions and integration play out. Early theories of immigrant assimilation did not account for what it would look like when people arrive who are *more* highly educated and *more* likely to be professionals, but who are also visibly distinct from the white mainstream. Indeed, most of our understanding of the immigrant trajectory focuses on people who arrive with much lower levels of education and "skills." The stories we know are about how fast and through what processes these newcomers and their descendants "catch up" with US-born whites—not surpass them entirely. So as the pages that follow will show, what we take for granted about assimilation can't fully explain the Asian American experience today.

What I found in Woodcrest suggests that cultural influence when it comes to immigration is no longer a one-way street. It is not only the natives who are shaping the lives of the new arrivals. Immigrants' success in a meritocracy that historically worked to privilege the white upper-middle class may lead to contestations between white natives and immigrant Asians over the very terms of that meritocracy, shaping whites' views on merit. Our current age of economic anxiety across class lines makes those struggles feel even more urgent among parents. Parents are desperate to ensure their children will enjoy the same status as they do, and even well-off parents today feel a sense of anxiety about their children's futures.[132] And these tensions play out even in a system of education that allows well-off parents (of all ethnicities) to surround their children at school with other well-off, well-educated famlies with abundant resources and connections to ensure their future success.

After the various threads of our story are woven together here, in chapter 1 I describe similarities between white and Asian families in Woodcrest—how they ended up there, as well as their shared high standards for excellence in academics and extracurriculars. Most parents moved to town in order to enroll their children in its highly regarded public schools, and most of their children did not disappoint. Across ethnic lines, most students worked hard and achieved at high levels, both in academics and in their extracurricular pursuits. But all of this achievement was built on an unacknowledged truth. While explicit racism no longer prevails, the socioeconomic segregation created by expensive housing costs and various local laws in Woodcrest and towns like it means that the upper-middle-class families in Woodcrest, immigrant and US-born alike, benefit from a remarkable concentration of resources. Asian Americans and white residents alike benefit from the legacy of racism that built towns like Woodcrest.

Despite somewhat similar paths to and aims in Woodcrest, the ways that Asian and white parents support their children's achievement differs; the ethnic breakdown of those differences is impossible to miss. In chapter 2 I describe those differences with respect to academic achievement. Immigrant Chinese and Indian parents came of age in educational systems in which only academic excellence brought success and opportunity, and they tended to impart this focus onto their children. White parents, on the other hand, sometimes limited their children's academic ambitions, fearing that taking too many advanced classes would damage their children's emotional well-being and feeling more confident that their children could have a good life without achieving the highest academic levels in school. These differences sometimes led to ethnic tension over what constitutes fair ways of supporting children's academic success and the effect of Asian students' academic success on their white peers' sense of self-worth, as some white parents described it. Overall, rather than any blurring of the boundary between white and Asian parenting—whether Asian families emulating their white neighbors' ways of pursuing success, or white families emulating their Asian neighbors' strategies for academic advancement—I witnessed divergence. As Asian Americans continued to do better on tests, ethnic tensions grew, and the boundaries that everyone created about the "right" way to parent become more and more contentious.

In chapter 3 I turn to parents' perspectives on extracurricular participation. As with academics, the ethnic patterns are clear. Parents' preferences shaped students' choices. Ethnic differences in parents' beliefs about the importance of children's autonomy also influenced extracurricular participation, with Asian parents playing a stronger role in determining how their kids spent time outside of school and white parents wanting to feel that their children chose their own activities. White families also tended to place a higher priority on excellence in sports, whereas Asian American families tended to see sports as a means for exercise, not excellence.

In chapter 4 I turn to emotional well-being. Aside from excellence in academics and extracurriculars, the thing that parents in Woodcrest worried most about was their children's emotional health. Community leaders, local elected officials, and school administrators alike all fretted along with parents about the health of the next generation. Still, parents differed in their views on what should be done about these concerns, and these differences were patterned by ethnicity. White parents tended to advocate for reducing academic work; a few transferred their children to elite private schools where they felt their children would face less academic pressure—but notably, not to lower-resourced public schools in nearby towns. Both solutions protected white children's ability to gain admission to an elite college, the former by dampening the increasing academic competition from Asian American students, and the latter by shifting to schools that were arguably even more well-regarded and known to enable entrée into the most selective colleges. In contrast, most immigrant Asian parents did not want the school to limit how much academic work a student could take on. They wanted to protect the high academic standards in which their children tended to excel.

Which approach was better? Chapter 5 describes the moral boundaries that parents drew in their quest to defend themselves as good parents. Given the high stakes of parenting, and the seemingly endless concerns expressed in Woodcrest over the burdens of academic and extracurricular expectations, parents worked hard to justify their own parenting. And they spent considerable energy judging the worthiness of *others'* parenting, especially (but not exclusively) along racial lines. Many white parents told stories, in varying degrees of hushed tones, of unreasonable immigrant Asian parents who were supposedly obsessed with academic achievement. Immigrant Asians were aware of these critiques, often defending themselves against them—either by acknowledging that some of their fellow parents of the same ethnicity were unreasonable while they themselves were not, or by comparing their ethnic group's emphasis on academics with some white parents' emphasis on sports, highlighting a hypocrisy they perceived in white parents' disapproval of their children's intensive academic work.

In the conclusion I describe the consequences of the tensions over parenting in Woodcrest and what they mean for our understandings of intensive parenting and for immigrant assimilation. I argue that scholars and other social observers should reframe discussions of "intensive parenting" and supposed Asian "tiger parenting" to help make sense of parents' different cultural repertoires. That is, I found similar values and concerns across nearly all parents in Woodcrest, but their cultural repertoires—and thus the way they responded to those concerns—differed widely. The patterns were clearly shaped by ethnicity, in part due to different experiences and observations in their own lives about getting ahead, as well as ideas about what would help their children get ahead. Ultimately, Asian immigrants seem to be forging new pathways to achievement, and those pathways seem to serve them and their children well. And white parents find new ways to protect their position in the face of Asian success.

Ultimately, as I argue in the conclusion, there is one clear group that loses out in these struggles: urban Black and Latinx youth who go to school in cities adjacent to suburban enclaves like Woodcrest, close by and yet a world of resources apart. Those among them who are lucky enough to be bused to Woodcrest acquire a solid education, but they are limited by the raft of structural burdens they face in the rest of their lives, not to mention racism in Woodcrest and beyond and being forced to leave their neighborhoods physically and culturally to attend Woodcrest's schools. These are the kids who were originally kept out of white American suburbs, or only allowed in in small numbers and under certain conditions. They are the ones for whom America's myth of meritocracy is exposed as the lie that it is. They live in a world of blocked and mediocre opportunities, they are the ones for whom the expectations of standardized testing are not calibrated, and they are the ones who are shockingly unlikely to attend an elite college. As upper-class Asian and white families engage in a race at the very, very top of the achievement hierarchy, both are standing on the backs of other students of color, supported by a long-standing system of economic and racial exclusion.

Chasing Excellence
in the Suburbs

MY FIRST VISIT TO WOODCREST was to see a friend who had recently moved there. She and her family were renting an apartment until they could find a house to buy. What I encountered when I got there came as a surprise. I did not expect to find an apartment complex full of families in this suburban community known for large single-family homes. And I did not expect to see so many people who were not white. The complex, built in the 1990s, was centered around a courtyard, and we ventured out to explore after brunch. As soon as I turned the corner, I felt as if I were in New York City's Little India, or maybe Chinatown, albeit with different architecture. At first glance, it seemed everyone was South Asian or East Asian. Much later, I learned that the complex attracts many Asian professionals who can afford the $3,000+ monthly rent but not yet a down payment on a house in Woodcrest. Some, like my friend, moved there temporarily until they could find a house to buy. These parents were eager to send their children to Woodcrest's schools, which was usually their motivation to live there. The complex, at the edge of town, is visited by multiple school buses every morning.

Other housing feels very different in Woodcrest. Most families live in single-family homes. Huge mansions sit alongside older houses closer to 1,000 square feet, but those smaller homes are disappearing. Many buyers these days tear down the small houses and replace them with properties two or three times the original size. Most family homes I visited were the larger, more modern style; I guessed that parents with smaller homes were more likely to suggest we meet at the public library or a café. The town is, like most suburbs, mostly a car-oriented place, with one car for each adult in a family. A few lucky families I met live within walking distance of the quaint town center, and some live within walking distance of the high school. Almost everyone I met drives to work, even if they work in the nearby city. Even during the prepandemic rush hour, it was quicker to drive than to take the bus and then subway to get to the city.

Long after that brunch with friends, my research visits to Woodcrest frequently took me to the town center. Some parts have an old-town feel, like a century-old shoe store known for patience with fitting children in shoes just their size. Other storefronts are newer—I spent countless hours writing up fieldnotes and passing time between events and interviews in town at the requisite Starbucks and Peets Coffee. Downtown was quiet during weekdays while school was in session, but on weekends the neighborhood was bustling, the town's diversity clearly visible and audible as bits of Mandarin or Hindi caught my ear. Up the road the newly renovated public library acts as a community hub. There, I tried to snag time in the private meeting rooms to conduct interviews with parents whenever I could. Frequently we'd end up in a nook elsewhere in the library—private tutors came early in the day to sign up for the rooms so they could hold their sessions with students after school. The library boasts an impressive Mandarin collection, and a growing collection in a variety of Indian languages as well.

A fifteen-minute walk from the town center, Woodcrest High School's busy and sprawling campus feels like a small college. For many months I frequently needed directions. Some of the outdoor space is filled with temporary classrooms; the district has plans to rebuild the school to increase capacity. Students move from one building to another for their classes, getting fresh air as they do so—each building serves a different discipline. On nice days I sometimes saw small groups of students during their free period playing hacky sack or sitting on the ledge and chatting. Mostly, though, everyone usually seemed rushed to get to class, to the school bus, or to the next activity after school. They walked with purpose, even while chatting with friends. It was surprisingly hard to catch their attention. They did not want to be late to class, or they were distracted by whatever new Instagram post was occupying them on their phones or the latest song playing on their headphones.

Inside, the school could feel claustrophobic, especially between classes. I frequently got stuck in the hallway between classes, and learned to wait patiently to the side of the hallway as students passed; I would not need a late pass to get into class like they would if I delayed them. Students were warm and sometimes greeted each other in the hallways. Teachers also seemed genuinely affectionate toward them. One day as I walked with a student in search of a space to sit down for an interview, the principal asked him for a high five, and then replied with a twinkle in his eye, "That's so weak! Try again!" And he obliged.

But still, despite the friendliness, I sensed that these were kids with somewhere to be, something to accomplish. They did not linger until the school bell rang, let alone after it rang as I was used to in other schools. The place felt busy and focused from the moment I stepped on campus. And the determination to achieve was evident from the complex experiments on display at the school science fair, to the perfectly delivered lines at school performances, to the swarm of eager students hoping for extra help from their chemistry teacher during study hall.

The hallway displays give you a sense of the school's priorities. One showcase features trophies from activities ranging from sports championships to debate tournaments. Another strikes a different tone: "If you really knew me, you'd know . . ." with stars filled out by students ending with handwritten lines such as "I am insecure" and "I love to run." A different bulletin board holds rejection letters from a range of colleges, from Ivy League colleges to others less selective. Peers added handwritten notes to the applicant, such as "You rock, Ellie!" and "This does not take away from your amazing generosity, kindness, and wit!" and "You didn't want to go here, anyway!" These dual messages—of excellence, and of self-care, were signs of what I would come to understand much more deeply during my time in Woodcrest.

The school library is expansive. Still, I often could not find a quiet space to sit and write up my notes, let alone interview a student. Eventually I became friendly with the librarians, and they gave me access to a media room to conduct interviews there. Some students really did sit alone and get to work, while others took out their books and laptops and ended up chatting quietly with their friends at the same table.

Many students were around long after the end of the school day. One day an hour after the last bell of the day rang, I wrote in my fieldnotes, "It's over an hour after school ended. There are many kids in the hall. I can hear balls in the gym—perhaps basketball practice." And I later wrote, "As I left the school, I heard the sound of multiple instruments playing warm-up scales through the windows—it sounded like they were just getting started." Even the scales sounded so precise and even, as if they had been practiced for years already.

I found excellence almost everywhere I turned in Woodcrest, whether in the classroom or on the playing field. Privilege and achievement abound in towns like Woodcrest. In what follows I explain how families ended up in Woodcrest, how parents support their children's achievement, both academic and extracurricular, and what kids do with all the resources they have. White and Asian families in Woodcrest have much in common, as we'll see.

GETTING TO WOODCREST

Woodcrest's property taxes are as high as the high school's standardized test scores. To most families, the trade-off is well worth it. This was true for both Asian and white parents I met. Three-fourths of parents specifically named the schools when I asked how they ended up in Woodcrest, and the percentage was similar across ethnic groups. Radha, an immigrant Indian mother, told me that she and her husband moved to Woodcrest before they had children, because "we thought that it would be a good town to raise a family." She explained that she had a friend who lived in Woodcrest who was happy with the town, which led her there. Yan, an immigrant Chinese mother, said of her family's move when her children were young, "We moved here so my kids could go to Woodcrest High School." Xin, another immigrant Chinese mother, told me that her family moved to Woodcrest after watching multiple immigrant families move from her previous suburb to Woodcrest:

> The neighbors near me, most of them were Chinese families or Russian families. Once their kids were almost middle school aged, they kept moving out to Woodcrest. So we had in mind that when our child was about to graduate from elementary school, probably we needed to look at houses in Woodcrest. And we did that.

White parents too more often than not named the school system as a reason for living in Woodcrest. Robin, a white mother of two, said, "My husband and I, we were living in [nearby town], and we were thinking of starting to have a family. And I think it's not unusual. A lot of people move to Woodcrest for the schools." When I asked Robin about her favorite aspects of Woodcrest High School as a parent, she said, "I value the community. I value that they value education."

Some white parents were less direct about their desire for strong schools. Jennifer explained her and her husband's move from the urban center where they previously lived: "I think rent control changed. And at that point it felt like it would make sense for the same money to go toward investing towards a home we could own. So we looked in neighboring towns. We were definitely motivated by schools. But also community quality of life."

Bill, a white dad, told me that heard about Woodcrest through friends. He and his wife previously lived in the nearby urban center, but when school enrollment loomed for their two young children they considered either moving or applying to private schools:

> At the time, we were just looking at private school. We were going to stay in [the city] and look at private schools. . . . I never imagined I was going to live in a suburb. But there's this little neighborhood in Woodcrest that we, through a friend of a friend, found out about. . . . And moved here when the kids were one and three.

A few white parents, especially those who worked as programmers or engineers, were drawn to the focus on STEM fields among many families in Woodcrest, especially Asian families. Fred was one such parent. He and his wife trained as computer programmers. Before moving to Woodcrest when their older son was in fifth grade, Fred and his family lived in a nearby suburb with a median household income that is more than 50 percent above the US median, and where median property values are close to half a million dollars. He told me about the previous town:

> To me, [that town] was just not as energized, an intellectually energized community. The schools weren't as good. . . . It just

didn't have the same culture of achievement and energy in the school system. I thought [Woodcrest] was a really pretty place, friendly place, interesting place.

Fred's son attended a Jewish school when they lived in that town. Fred told me he was "very enthusiastic about the Asian presence" in Woodcrest, adding, "In fact, we encouraged our [younger] son to study Mandarin Chinese. He's been learning that for a while. And actually, most of his friends are from the Chinese community." Fred told me about a "computer school" in Woodcrest where his son took classes and then worked as a teaching assistant, which he said was started "by a Chinese family that came to this town." Fred suggested that this was the kind of opportunity that would not have been available in the previous town. He said the same about a hackathon in which his son participated.

Similarly, Melissa, a white mother of two who coached her sons' robotics team, told me that "90 percent of the parents on our robotics team—and there's twenty kids involved on different levels—have one immigrant parent. . . . I don't know if they have come towards us because we are, you know, we have a half-immigrant family [Melissa's husband is an Asian immigrant], or if it's because they see that my husband and I have been very successful in business, and therefore they kind of are simpatico." Melissa and her husband both hold doctorates in STEM fields. Their children went to private schools when they lived in a different nearby suburb, but later the family moved to Woodcrest so their older son could attend Woodcrest High School. She said simply: "He went to Woodcrest High School. We moved here for that. That's the reason we moved here."

While Melissa and Fred were unusually tied to Asians in Woodcrest among white parents I met, their perspectives are an important reminder of the role of profession in what parents emphasize and prioritize with their children. These parents seemed to appreciate the STEM focus of many Asian residents in Woodcrest. As we'll see, they were the rare white parents who considered Asians in town to be an unequivocal benefit.[1] I got the sense that parents like Melissa and Fred in other communities might frequently identify as misfits, or stereotypical science geeks. But the growing Asian community in Woodcrest, most of whom worked in STEM fields, provided a community to parents like them. Still, as I read and reread transcripts of my interviews with parents, I realized that parents like Melissa and Fred were not as common as you might expect, even though one in four white parents I met worked in technology, science, or engineering jobs. The weight of Asian American students' academic achievement seemed to cloud other white parents' abstract appreciation for diversity, as we'll see.

For many parents of color, diversity also played a role in their move to Woodcrest. Studies of upper-middle-class Black parents find that in addition to schools' reputations, they also tend to consider race, leery of schools in which their children might be the only Black student.[2] And in Woodcrest, some Asian parents—especially those born in the United States—also expressed appreciation for the presence of a significant co-ethnic community when choosing where to live, or for diversity more generally. This included Bernadette, a Chinese American mother married to a US-born white. She described their home search many years ago when they moved to the area which included, among other things, looking "at what towns in the area had more Chinese people." Priya, an immigrant Indian mother, explained similarly:

> We wanted a town which was diverse. We didn't want to go too far from the city. . . . We wanted yard space. . . . We wanted a decent school system. . . . It should be safe. What we didn't want was our kid to go there and explain every day why he looks different. And you know, if kids come [over], "What are you eating?"

Priya's explanation of diversity is telling—it is related to her children having peers of the same ethnicity. In fact, before Priya and her husband bought their home in Woodcrest they had an offer accepted for a house in another town that had less than 10 percent people of color at the time.[3] She said,

> We slept on it. In the morning we said, "We can't do it." Just the [lack of] diversity of [that town] worried us at the time. This was fifteen years ago. Because of the diversity of Woodcrest, even at that time, we chose it.

As with white families, however, the paucity of Black and Latinx families in Woodcrest did not come up when Asian families spoke of diversity. While the presence of Asian families was enough for most white families to claim Woodcrest was "diverse," most Asian families themselves were simply looking for neighbors who came from the same country as them.

Once they arrived, immigrant parents tended to have at least one set of friends—usually their closest friends—who came from the same country as them. Chinese parents often met them at the local Chinese church, through the town's two Chinese American organizations, or through school events when their children were young. Others connected with a larger Chinese community through various groups on WeChat (a social medium used primarily by the Chinese diaspora) for parents in Woodcrest and beyond. Some then signed their young children up together for activities such as speech leagues or math clubs, and developed close friendships through those. Indian parents made Indian friends through religious organizations, the Woodcrest Indian Association, and through their children's schools. Some connected with graduates of their same college in India, and some were even classmates. Woodcrest High School hosted an Indian culture school on weekends, which drew families not only from Woodcrest but also from many surrounding towns. All of these networks helped parents feel Woodcrest was a town for them.

A small number of Asian families I met moved to Woodcrest not from a different town in the same metropolitan area, but from another area entirely, explicitly for the schools and not because of a parent's job change or any other reason. Two Chinese American students and one Indian American student told me that one or both of their parents quit their jobs to bring them to Woodcrest. Neesa, the daughter of Indian immigrants, told me, "My dad was researching the best schools to go to for their children. So it was either this or Thomas Jefferson High School in Washington [a science and technology magnet school]." Her father could not find a job in the area, so he lived in another state and came to see his family on weekends.

Abigail, an immigrant Chinese student, told me that her parents did not like the pressures of the Chinese school system, which led them to bring her to Woodcrest. Her father continued to work in China while her mother lived with her in Woodcrest. A high school junior, Abigail attended an art studio for eight hours weekly and was preparing an art portfolio for college applications. She planned to attend college in the United States. She reflected on why her parents brought her to Woodcrest: "My mom, she always wanted like a different life for me. Like she wanted me to do whatever I want. . . . They obviously want like very good education for me, so I have a better future. And plus, I think they just don't like the education in China right now." Abigail's description of her parents' desires—for both a rigorous academic curriculum but one that allows for her individuality—resonates with Pei-Chia Lan's interviews with college-educated Chinese parents in both Taiwan and the United States.[4] Lan describes the global influences on parents in both places; they can consider places to work and live not just within their own country, but around the world. While many in Woodcrest saw families like Abigail's as driving ever-higher levels of academic performance, Abigail's story is a reminder that all burdens are relative; for her parents, the intensity of Woodcrest felt like a relief, and an escape from China's rigid and competitive standardized education.

Principal Smith, a white resident of Woodcrest, told me this was not uncommon among immigrant families:

> My understanding now is there are international marketing firms whose job it is to find a family home in one of these communities. So as the principal in recent years, I probably get four or five times a week an introductory email, "Here's my child's resumé. We're moving to Woodcrest. We're coming for the schools. . . . When can we come for an interview?" . . . And they like to send a resumé as if we're a private school.

Like well-off parents around the country, Asian and white parents alike in Woodcrest carefully considered schools as they searched for a place to live.[5] Most spoke with friends and colleagues at work to find out the "best" school districts. As other studies have shown around the country, this process frequently leads white families to school districts with high academic achievement, and, frequently, low numbers of students of color. Increasingly, however, this advice leads families to towns like Woodcrest, in which whites can express appreciation for the diversity driven by the large presence of professional Asian immigrants and Asians can find other families that share their cultural background.[6]

ACADEMIC EXCELLENCE

High levels of academic achievement are the norm in Woodcrest schools. Over half of the students in a school-wide survey reported spending three or more hours a night on homework; more than a quarter reported four or more hours per night.[7] Forty percent of all students take at least one AP exam in a given year, and one in four takes more than one.[8] In contrast to other school districts where many students who are enrolled in AP classes do not go on to take the exam for college credit, in Woodcrest it was the opposite: students and teachers in Woodcrest told me that many students not enrolled in the AP-level class, whether for scheduling reasons or because they were not placed in that level by the school, will go on to take the exam. They prepare outside of school and in rigorous non-AP classes.

Classes at Woodcrest High School are heavily tracked. For example, in eleventh grade chemistry students have a choice of four tracks: remedial, college prep (the default track), honors, or AP. In tenth grade, the teachers recommend a track for the students, though students can appeal the recommendation. Principal Smith told me that appeals were usually for placement in higher levels. About one-third of students took AP chemistry, one-fifth took honors, two-fifths took college-prep, and less than one-tenth took remedial. For US history in eleventh grade, students had three choices: remedial (taken by less than 5 percent), college prep (taken by almost two-thirds) and AP (taken by one-third).

Rather than honors or AP courses being seen as what the exceptional students took, for many at Woodcrest they were the default—and indeed, in chemistry over half of students took honors or AP. Neesa, the daughter of immigrant Indian parents mentioned above who moved from another region to attend Woodcrest High School, took the "regular" level (college prep) of math because "I'm not that great in math." In Neesa's social world, being weak at math doesn't mean needing a remedial course; it means not taking honors. This was true of white and Asian kids alike. Rory, a white mother active in town politics and who previously had a career in education, expressed frustration when her daughter said, "I'm not very good at math," despite earning an A+ in her college prep math class.

Some may assume that in a school in which more than half of students take at least one AP class, those classes must be watered down. That was not the case at Woodcrest. Despite high enrollment in honors and AP classes—on average students take four to five AP exams in high school—many reported that "regular" college prep classes at Woodcrest would be honors-level in other districts. Rory said,

> If we moved to another community. . . . Let's say we moved to Lincoln, Nebraska, right? . . . I would say to the school, during scheduling, "Okay, so she should be in calculus." And they'd be like, "She didn't take honors math, so there's no way." I'd be like, "I know. Just give her a placement test." And then she'd take the placement test and they'd come back like, "I don't understand."

Shloka, an Indian American teen who moved to Woodcrest from a neighboring state at the start of eighth grade, confirmed Rory's view: "A regular class here is like an honors class somewhere else. . . . And everyone still feels the pressure to take the highest-level classes in the school, which is like really, really hard." Shloka spoke of her transition to Woodcrest at the start of eighth grade:

> I [previously] was a big fish in a small pond. And I didn't really have to try that hard to get the perfect grade. You know, just like stand out academically. And then coming into Woodcrest was like a truck full of bricks coming at you at like 300 miles an hour. Because it was just like all of a sudden, I'm mediocre.

Nevertheless, Shloka was taking multiple honors-level courses and seemed to thrive at Woodcrest High. In addition to her high-level academic classes, Shloka spent considerable time on music, including her acapella group (which rehearsed more than eleven hours a week), and Western and Indian classical voice lessons (which took over three hours each week). She spoke in a noticeably upbeat tone and seemed to thrive in the diversity of Woodcrest. Her tone was surprising given all that she did every week—I felt exhausted just speaking with her. Still, perhaps Shloka appreciated the diversity of Woodcrest so much because her previous school was less diverse. She described being told there that because she was Indian, she should "stick to math" rather than try to join the school chorus.

Nearly all other students who had started school elsewhere and then moved to Woodcrest described the same experience as Shloka. They were strong students at their previous schools, but their move to Woodcrest deflated them. Daniel, a Chinese American student, said, "I moved here from [another suburb], which is nowhere as competitive as here. I mean, I think fifth to sixth grade was a big culture shock, because back then I was like, 'Oh, I think I'm the smartest kid in the school.' Came here, I was just a normal kid."

Parents agreed. One mother, Jaya, moved to Woodcrest from a larger, less wealthy, more diverse suburb in the same metro area when her only son was in sixth grade, eager for him to go to the better schools in Woodcrest that fellow Indian parents spoke of.[9] Jaya said about her son's transition to Woodcrest,

> He struggled. Because he was doing very well. Everybody knew him as the best student in that school system. And suddenly [when we moved] he realized that there were many other smarter kids. It was very difficult for him to keep up. And he kept complaining that he couldn't keep up.

Still, these harsh realizations did not make parents regret their decisions to move. Nearly all the parents I talked to said they would move to Woodcrest if they had to do it again. Jaya said, "The other option, if we didn't go to Woodcrest or [neighboring town with similar characteristics], is to stay back in [our previous town]. And I still don't prefer that. . . . It is important that your friends, schoolmates—you shouldn't learn bad behaviors. You should have motivation in life. I don't know if I'm right or wrong, but I wouldn't stay back in [that town]."

When it came to high expectations, all the parents I spoke with were like Jaya—they simply did not see another viable public school option. Other towns, even those with above-average resources and educational achievement, were simply not good enough places to raise their children. They wanted to surround themselves with, to extrapolate from Jaya's words, kids they assumed had better behaviors and motivation than those in other towns.

In fact, for many, other towns, especially towns that are not suburban, did not even appear on a list of towns they could have considered. One evening after I interviewed Priya we chatted in the library's parking lot long after it had closed. As many parents did, Priya asked me where I live. When I replied that I live in Cambridge—at the time I was a professor at Harvard—she expressed genuine confusion, naming multiple suburban towns near Cambridge and asking why I didn't live in those. I quickly tried to manage her impression of me, and shared that one of my children attended a private school, but that I am also very happy with the public schools my other two children attended. To parents like Priya, a Ph.D. Indian American like me simply would not choose an urban district for her children; it needed explanation, despite the fact that Cambridge spends more than 50 percent more per pupil to educate children than does Woodcrest. Parents like Priya deliberately sought a place in which their children would be one in a sea of high achievers. This may seem counterintuitive—after all, parents wanted their children to outshine their peers, and that is harder in a town like Woodcrest. But parents felt that Woodcrest would provide a context in which their children would feel compelled to achieve not just by their parents, but also by their peers and school expectations. Indeed, the investment in Woodcrest paid off for most.

College was the implicit—and sometimes explicit—goal of this academic achievement. In one of our first conversations, Principal Smith told me that "you'll hear elementary kids in the car, parents are saying, they're talking about what college they're going to go to. Fourth and fifth graders. That's in their fabric as they're driving to playdates, you know?" One white student, Eliana, when I asked about her goals, said simply, "College." She elaborated:

> I really want to get into either an Ivy League or MIT or Stanford or some other like really, really good school. And that's just like where all the attention is going in classes. Like it's not, "Oh, no, I got a B on this test. That's bad." It's "Oh, no, I got a B on this test. That's going to affect my GPA, which is going on my college application!"

Her perspective was commonplace. It seemed like everything these students did was a means to an end, and that end was college admission.

I was surprised again and again at how kids talked about college the same way their parents did. Far from our (frequently confirmed) assumption that teenagers innately tend to disagree with their parents just for the sake of disagreeing, here adults and teens seemed to speak as if in lockstep with one another. The most elite colleges were the goal, the topic of endless discussion.

Families routinely identified top colleges in the United States—residential four-year colleges that accept less than one-third of their applicants—as mediocre. For example, Melissa, the white mother who coached her son's robotics team, lamented the inability of one white teen on her robotics team to gain admission to MIT. I paused, nodded, and waited for the bad news to follow. "He's going to Notre Dame instead," she said, with a hint of both lament and judgment in her voice, despite naming a college that accepts less than one in five of its applicants.[10] Shivani, a US-born Indian American mother, said of her eldest child, "He . . . didn't get into any of his colleges. Either was waitlisted or didn't get in. He didn't apply to places like Tufts or New York University [colleges with admit rates less than 30 percent]. He kind of aimed high." To place these views in perspective, consider that less than 100 of the 2,700 four-year colleges in the United States are this competitive.[11] Furthermore, even when including less-selective colleges that admit up to three-fourths of applicants, only 15 percent of college students in the United States attend this broad swath of colleges.[12] Still, students and parents were disappointed when they didn't get into an even smaller number of top colleges.

What about the students not in multiple honors and AP classes, those for whom "aiming high" might actually mean a Tufts or NYU, or the flagship state school? Beyond the highest achievers at Woodcrest, there are many students who are not striving to be the very top students in their school. Just as low-performing urban schools sometimes get defined by their lowest-performing, highest-need students—as places that serve children living with drug-addicted parents, in extreme poverty, or close to violence—schools like Woodcrest are defined by the culture of the top-performing students—as places where competition is high, and students work extremely hard both in and out of school. During a focus group discussion, Tom, a white eleventh grader who had just returned from a college tour, described the different cultures in class levels:

> I think the competition definitely goes up like the higher level
> class that you're in. Like in an AP everyone wants to do really

well. And then like as you go down the levels, it's not as competitive. Just because the caliber of student that's attracted to those high classes is more competitive.

I was intrigued by Tom's description of different students' "caliber," so I asked more questions when we sat down for a one-on-one interview. Tom mostly took honors and AP classes, but seemed very aware of kids who did not. He elaborated his views: "There are kids who have potential and could do well, but they just don't care for whatever reason. And they could be like outside in the smokers' corner, smoking." Though I looked out for the smokers' corner after speaking with Tom, I never found it. Either the group was well-hidden, or he meant a metaphorical "smokers' corner" as a placeholder for kids who were not the highest achievers.

Tyler, a white eleventh grader, might have been one of the kids in the smokers' corner. Tyler yawned almost continuously during our interview—I almost felt guilty about taking him away from a nap he might have had during study hall instead. He wore all black, from his leather jacket to his black jeans to his black hoodie that he seemed to recede into. Unlike Tom, Tyler took mostly remedial classes. When asked about competition at school, Tyler said that he is "not in the higher-level classes, so I don't notice it." He understood that the levels had different cultures, even if he was less judgmental than Tom about those cultures. Tyler said, "Say you're in the easiest math level, versus someone in an AP math class. Everything could be different, from levels of stress, to math homework, to how the teacher is in general." Still, Tyler had a keen eye on college—he had recently joined the school track team in anticipation of applying to college: "Because some of the colleges I want to get into, they do have like certain athletic standards, so I thought that might be helpful." Tyler was interested in attending a military academy, following in the footsteps of his father. Even the lowest-achieving students at Woodcrest aimed high and had the supports at school and at home to help them move toward their goals.

EXTRACURRICULAR EXCELLENCE

Extracurriculars—organized activities outside of the required school curriculum that mostly take place outside of school hours—are an important part of life in Woodcrest. Nine in ten students participate in some extracurricular activity, with most participating in multiple ones.[13] Just over half of students at Woodcrest High School participate in an academic group or club, six in ten are on sports teams, either in or outside of school, one in three are part of a music ensemble, one in four engage in a service club, and one in four in a religious youth group. All this organized activity outside of school has real benefits. During extracurriculars, kids learn to work collaboratively, resolve conflicts, deal with challenges, and identify and pursue goals together.[14] Participation increases confidence, self-image, and even academic performance.[15]

Families in Woodcrest seemed to intuitively understand the benefits of extracurriculars, and many students excelled in them just as many did in academics. Extracurriculars rarely seemed to be a casual affair at Woodcrest; it seemed the only option was excellence. This was true of Asian American and white youth alike. Sports teams, robotics teams, and debate teams routinely won regional and sometimes state and even national championships. One young woman won a multistate Miss India contest in the teen category. Emily, a Chinese American eleventh grader, told me:

> We have a lot of people that are literally the top of their field. Like the skating team in Woodcrest is really good. They go to the world championships and whatever. I have people in my class that disappear for like weeks because they're going on the skating trip. And I know somebody in my grade is a top fencer in the US. And I remember in eighth grade, there was this kid that was nationally acclaimed in math. And then somebody's brother is a piano prodigy. And all these random people that are just really good at everything.

I sensed frustration in Emily's description, and I empathized with that. How does someone enter into a field in which everyone is already at a high level? So I asked her what she thought of the excellence all around. She said, "It makes people feel like they're not doing well. And in fact if you look at it, you *are* doing well." Still, I was pleased to see Emily taking risks and trying new things—in tenth grade a friend suggested she come to the bhangra (Punjabi Indian dance) team's practice, and after that she kept going because it was "fun," even though she wasn't a top performer: "the technique, I still don't have that down." I was struck by Emily's participation in bhangra. Aside from her not being Indian American, I also realized that I was beginning to take the high levels of excellence in extracurriculars for granted. Her testing a new activity at age fifteen was not the norm in Woodcrest.

When excellence is the norm, the expectations for preparation shift too. Helen, an immigrant mother from Hong Kong, told me that her daughter "doesn't practice much" on her viola. "How much?" I asked. Helen said, "She practices pretty much—maybe not *every* day—but when she does, she's about half an hour to forty-five minutes." Confused, I asked Helen how that compares to other kids. She replied, "They do easily like two hours. And then if they really want to get into conservatory, they do like three, four hours a day."

Just as Woodcrest has up to four tracks for individual academic subjects (remedial, college prep, honors, and AP), extracurriculars are also leveled. Varsity sports teams have competitive tryouts for which teens prepare seriously. There are, for example, six soccer teams (girls' freshman, junior varsity, and varsity teams, and the same three for boys). The school has three levels of concert bands and orchestras as well, all of which require auditions. Students typically begin their preparation for these tryouts well before high school begins. Xin, a Chinese mother who moved with her family from a different suburb to Woodcrest when her older child was starting middle school, reported that their arrival was too late for her son to be in the music program:

My son never joined the instrument program during his elementary school. Because that's very optional in [my previous town]. . . . So once we moved to Woodcrest and my son joined the middle school, he couldn't join any of the orchestras or bands because he's a beginner. To join the school bands or orchestras, you have to have at least have one or two years' experience. So it ends up that my son, the whole middle school, high school and college, everything, he doesn't have anything related to music. And that's a miss for me. I did not know that if I miss the elementary school level, then he would miss out on the opportunities.

Considering that Woodcrest High has three orchestras and three bands, I was surprised to hear Xin report that even the lowest-level ensemble in middle school required experience before joining. Middle school was already too late to express an interest in music performance. And this was not simply one parent's perception. One school leader told me that to participate in music ensembles in Woodcrest's middle schools, families were required to enroll their children in private lessons outside of school (at their own expense).

How did teens in Woodcrest get so good at what they do? Private coaching was common, and not just for musical instruments. Students and parents not only reported private tutors for academics and college admission, but also private coaches for singing, art, sports, and even skills within sports. And extracurricular coaching as a means to get ahead was not limited to academically high-achieving students. Melvin, a white eleventh grader, had a private baseball pitching coach. He told me he gets mostly C's in his classes, none of which were honors level. He admitted, "I know I can try a lot harder than I do. And I don't get the best grades. But I get good enough to pass. Because I'm not worried about getting all A's." Melvin was growing up in the house his mother grew up in, and told me that his parents too are not concerned about his earning top grades, reporting that "they just want me to try as hard as I can. . . . So as long as I try as hard as I can, my parents are happy." In contrast to his laid-back stance on academics, when it came to baseball Melvin was intense. He played on the varsity Woodcrest team, which practices or has a game six days a week during baseball season. In addition, in the off-season Melvin played with a private club team, alongside teammates from many surrounding private schools. The club team plays in the summer, but also has weekly indoor practices during the winter. Finally, twice a week Melvin worked with his private pitching coach, who is a coach at an elite college nearby. Melvin hoped to play baseball on a college team after high school. If anyone typified the "old Woodcrest" experience in my research, it would have to be Melvin. His parents' laid-back attitude when it came to academics, his mother's job as a secretary, and his family's intensive focus on baseball—a sport unfamiliar to most Asian parents in town—together struck me as a world away from the experiences of his Asian classmates. Still, as with Tyler above, Melvin set his sights on a selective four-year college—and a prestigious one that recruits athletes, at that. When I visited his college prep chemistry class, Melvin and another student spent most of the period working with a paraprofessional in class who was there to assist the teacher, because he had trouble understanding the classroom teacher. With support like that, I got the sense that Melvin's college dreams would work out just fine.

These dynamics—an early start, long hours, and private coaching—meant that dabbling in extracurriculars was usually not an option. Coaches reinforced these expectations. Sally, an Indian American student, told me that when, during the summer after tenth grade, she decided not to enroll in the residential debate summer camp attended by most of the Woodcrest debate team, she decided to quit the team altogether. She said, "This year [eleventh grade], I know a lot of people went to camp. And I was like 'Oh, everyone's going to be better than me.' So I didn't know if I wanted to really do it. And it was just so competitive." I assumed that a teacher might encourage Sally to persist, to tell her not to worry about what others were doing. But when Sally told her teacher she was considering quitting, her teacher seemed to agree. According to Sally, her teacher told her,

> "You can move to public forum," which is another more relaxed type of debate where there's not that much prep. But that conflicted with a lot of my classes. . . . I was like, "What if I really want to come back to this?" And then my teacher said that I could be in the class senior year, but she can't guarantee that I get placed in it. So there was always that kind of risk of dropping and not being able to get back in.

Early involvement and sustained commitment were also crucial to the award-winning robotics club. In Melissa's case, the resource she provided was her own time, rather than money spent on a coach. She shared with me the development of the team:

> We started [our older son], I think, in kindergarten. . . . By the time he was six years old, he was already doing Lego robotics [at home]. We just bought him a kit. . . . We recognized exactly what he was doing. And so we were like, "This kid is phenomenally talented in mechanical systems." . . . I said, "Well, I want to do this Lego robotics. Let's take basically all the kids who are interested home to my house on Friday nights and we'll teach them Lego robotics, which I'll have to figure out along the way."

Melissa devoted fifteen to twenty hours to the team per week during robotics competition season, and team members spent anywhere from six to thirty-five hours per week. She described her son. "He's at thirty-five. It's like a job for him." Her flexible part-time work and background as a scientist enabled Melissa to coach a group of children from third grade to a national championship in high school.

Overall, an early, firm commitment many years before high school was required for students to engage in most popular sports and extra-curriculars in Woodcrest. Parents were critical in getting kids started on the path to extracurricular excellence. Once they started, sustained focus on the activity, often with the support of a coach or a parent, pro-pelled many to excellence. In these ways, Asian American and white families in Woodcrest shared a culture of extracurricular excellence.[16] Still, as we'll see in chapter 3, which extracurriculars they emphasized and the hours they devoted to them varied, with clear patterns by ethnicity.

COLLEGE ADMISSIONS

One goal loomed over all the achievement in Woodcrest, whether academic or extracurricular: college admissions. Parents were less likely than children to say this overtly, perhaps because of a growing moral stigma against being seen as too focused on achievement in a town with a growing emphasis on emotional well-being. Still, students felt the pull of elite colleges. As Emily, the Chinese American student mentioned above who participates in the school's bhangra team, said:

> Everybody's subconsciously prepping for college. Some of my friends started clubs this year. And I'm like, "Why did you start three clubs in junior year?" And they're like, "Oh, it looks good on college apps." I don't think they care that much. . . . People are like, "I don't have enough on my college resumé!" Like, "I do a sport, but I don't do two sports!" Or like, "I take an AP, but I don't take three APs!" I feel like they feel they need to be better than everyone else.

Emily's comment points to a frequently unspoken understanding about the purpose of extracurricular participation and advanced-level coursework—college admission. Teens had to demonstrate "passion" and "interest" in their activities, while also understanding that partic- ipation would support their college applications, and a lack of demon- strated interests and engagement beyond the academic curriculum in school would hurt them in the college admissions game.

Several students reported that they were working with a private col- lege admissions counselor to bolster their college prospects. Lakshmi, a daughter of Indian immigrants, said, "I have a college counselor. And they suggested that I should do a summer job to get experience be- fore college starts." Eva, the daughter of Chinese immigrants, said her mother found her a Chinese college counselor on WeChat. When we met in the winter of her junior year, Eva and her counselor were "building my resumé." Tom, a white student heavily involved in the Boy Scouts, told me that his parents hired a private counselor after Tom's older brother "got messed up by the college process. He got waitlisted at seven schools and rejected at a bunch." Tom's eldest brother ended up at the flagship state school, while his middle brother got into an elite private college with the help of the same private counselor now working with Tom in his eleventh-grade year. Robert, a Chinese American stu- dent, felt sheepish about his counselor, but also recognized the stress reduction it allowed. He told me that his parents expect him to attend an elite college:

> They hired a college counselor for me. I used to be kind of
> ashamed of that, because I felt like I should be able to do it by
> myself. [Now] I actually take it more as a blessing, because it
> frees me up to not worry as much about it. He guides me through
> everything so thoroughly.

Even parents who spent considerable energy on reducing academic pressure seemed to have a laser-like focus on the college application process. Patricia, a white parent, did not allow her children to take more than one AP class a year because she worried about their emotional well-being. Still, she took on the college search for her children:

> So what [my daughter] wants is to have a school [where] she
> could major in theater or musical theater that she doesn't have
> to audition for. So not a BFA, but a BA, that's a good size, that

has a football team and the whole "Yay rah rah!" spirit. And she doesn't want to be too far away from home. Okay. So with all that information, I kind of used all the resources that I have and came up with this list. And then we talked about it. And she's like, "Yeah, those all sound good."

The tension between reducing their stress about college and providing security to her children led Patricia to this seemingly contradictory stance. That same tension manifested itself differently in different families, based on their understandings of the college admissions process, the extent to which they cared about their children finding a passion, and how tied students were to their extracurricular preferences.

INVESTMENT AND PAYOFF

The excellence I saw in Woodcrest and the money spent on college counselors paid off in the college admissions process. In just one year nearly three dozen graduates were off to study at Ivy League colleges. Even more got recruited by selective colleges to play for their sports teams. Altogether, over one-third of students went on to attend the most selective colleges in the United States, including schools like Berkeley, Northwestern, and the Ivy League. In addition, when you include slightly less selective schools like Mount Holyoke, the University of Michigan, and Rochester Institute of Technology—mostly schools that accept less than half of their applicants—you account for four in five graduates of Woodcrest High School.[17] And nearly half of adults raised in Woodcrest go on to earn in the top 20 percent of US incomes.[18]

Amidst the endless discussion of achievement in Woodcrest, it is easy to conclude that parents there simply expect more of their kids than parents in other communities. Maybe they just care more about education than the rest of us. I certainly had that thought on more than one occasion during my interviews, as I started to think about how many times in the last week I had turned on a TV show for my kid just so I could finish plowing through my emails. However, it is important to remember that the desires of Woodcrest parents are far from unique. A belief in the importance and power of education is nearly universal among parents in the United States and, indeed, around the world.[19]

Kids too usually express a desire for academic excellence, even those who are in danger of failing.[20]

Still, the fact remains: Woodcrest was different. The kids at Woodcrest High School were surrounded by parents and neighbors with extraordinary levels of education, many of whom held degrees from top universities in the United States and Asia. And that was completely normal—taken for granted by nearly everyone in town. This makes a degree from the Ivy League part of a teen's cultural repertoire: one of several possible—and feasible—"strategies of action" for what they'll do after high school.[21] Going to a good college is just something that happens for Woodcrest kids; the whole town is orchestrated so that it is just *what you do.* The utter normalcy of that path is perhaps where the gap between Woodcrest kids and teens in more economically disadvantaged areas is most noticeable. For kids living in economically disadvantaged areas, attending an elite residential college might as well be like traveling to Mars. It is something many may long for and dream of, but still something that is unfamiliar given the lack of graduates from those kinds of colleges in their social networks, and given the distance between their lives and the lives of most students on those campuses.[22]

When families arrive in Woodcrest most find themselves surrounded by similar families—mostly white, Chinese, and Indian, frequently working in STEM or technology, and with abundant resources to support their children's achievements, both academic and extracurricular. Indeed, this is what draws most families to Woodcrest in the first place. In addition, families are able to provide abundant opportunities to their children beyond the public schools—tutoring when they struggle, whether in a remedial or honors class, private coaching and club teams in sports to give them an edge in high school varsity sports tryouts, and hours spent coaching their children's teams, whether baseball or robotics. In these ways, the immigrant Asian and US-born white parents I met were not all that different from each other. The similarities, on first glance, might lead a casual observer to assume that the boundary between white and Asian in Woodcrest had dissolved—most kids and parents came to Woodcrest for similar reasons, and they seemed to achieve excellence in academics and extracurricular activities in roughly the same ways. This, after all, is what we might expect of highly skilled immigrants.

But as we'll see in the next chapter, parents go about deploying their resources in support of their children differently, leading to ethnic tensions. Perhaps these tensions are inevitable—all this focus on children's achievements creates a competitive tinderbox. Given the intensity with which everyone was pursuing excellence, differences in *how* parents pushed their children became sites of contention, clearly delineated by race.

Tensions over the "Right" Way to Achieve Academic Excellence

TERRY WAS A US-BORN CHINESE American mom of two who spent much of her career working with Asian American youth. Over lunch we spoke about life in Woodcrest, her work, and her family. She met her husband, an immigrant from Hong Kong, at church. Sometimes they differed on what was best for their children, which she attributed to his childhood in Asia, where testing determines so much of one's future. "Sometimes I say [to my husband], 'I want the kids to go out and play now!'" Still, every year she went along with "dad's summer camp" of academic work for their kids. One summer they learned the computer programming language C++.

Stewart, Terry's older son, was aligned with his parents in his desire to take the most rigorous courses and not miss a single academic opportunity at Woodcrest High School. When Stewart was diagnosed with a learning disability in middle school, the school suggested he replace the usual foreign language class with a special learning support class. But Stewart told his mother, "Mom, I want the foreign language. Because I'm going to be behind if I don't learn a foreign language." Terry agreed to speak to the school, and Stewart ended up doing quite well in Latin. "It surprised me. I was like, 'He really can learn a language!'" In high school, "he fights for the school to allow him to do APs. Because they say, 'We don't think you can do it.'" I asked Terry who drove the push for honors classes, to which she replied, "He wants to. . . . He says,

'Mom, can you go in and talk to the teacher with me? They won't let me. I know I can do it. I'll work really hard.' And he does."

When I met Stewart, he was taking AP chemistry and told me he mostly gets A-'s on his report card. Like most Asian American kids and parents I met, Stewart and Terry were united in their emphasis on taking as many rigorous classes as possible (even when told not to by his teachers at first) and working hard to do well in those classes. And Stewart's learning disability did not deter them. While Terry was acutely concerned about mental health, particularly among Asian American youth, this did not preclude supporting her son's academic ambitions. As we'll see, Asian parents in Woodcrest, like Terry and her husband, emphasized striving for the highest levels of academic achievement possible; they were less concerned about the workload associated with high-level classes than were white parents. This was especially true for immigrant Asian parents like Terry's husband. And it was true even among parents who were concerned about emotional well-being, like Terry was.

PARENTS PURSUE ACADEMIC EXCELLENCE

Nearly all parents share a desire for academic excellence in their children. And a majority of the parents that I talked to in Woodcrest moved there so they could send their children to its excellent public schools and thus push their children further up that ladder of excellence. But that's where the similarities ended. Immigrant Asian parents and US-born white parents in Woodcrest tended to approach achievement differently. They came of age in different reward systems, as I described in the introduction, and tended to focus on cultivating the skills most rewarded in the system they understood best. In this chapter I highlight the different cultural repertoires that parents held—the different strategies with which they acted in the world.[1] Childhood experiences in school and on the job in China, India, and the United States, messages from their own parents, observations of siblings, cousins, and neighbors, and so much more together contribute to the cultural repertoire each parent holds.

Parents in Woodcrest did not easily forget the pathways to their own success, and that knowledge very much guided their parenting. In Asia, standardized tests are the sole basis for entrée to elite colleges, and elite degrees are critical in Asia for getting an elite job.[2] As a result, most immigrant parents held a laser-like focus on academic achievement. They frequently implored their children to focus on academics over athletics, to enroll in supplementary math education and to spend summer vacation on academic pursuits. Many also felt that they lacked the social networks and cultural references that open doors for children of American elites. That is, even within the United States immigrants may rely on elite college degrees to succeed more than the US-born does.[3]

Unlike elite Asian universities, US elite colleges do not just look at academic assessments when selecting students. US-born parents knew and understood this difference, so they had internalized more desire for pursuits beyond academics for their children. Further, even if a degree from an elite college does help in the United States, it is not as critical for success as it is in Asia.[4] Given their own experiences in the US labor market, US-born parents tended to see more pathways to success. This led many to want limits on academic pursuits, in part to make room for excellence in extracurriculars, especially sports. In Woodcrest, these differences, patterned by ethnicity, were constantly on display.

Of course, there is no single "Asian cultural repertoire" when it comes to parenting, or anything else, just as there is no single "white cultural repertoire," even among parents of the same social class and ethnicity, born in the same country, living in the same town. These groups are too varied and parenting is too complex. For example, whether someone from China grew up in a rural or urban area, or in a working-class or upper-middle-class family shapes their cultural repertoire.[5] And migration inevitably shapes the cultural repertoires of immigrants. US-born Terry and her immigrant husband had overlapping but not identical cultural repertoires.

And college admissions and job prospects are not the only drivers of parenting. Parents also expressed desires to raise morally upright, happy children.[6] And they wanted to help them find their passions too. But in a time of economic anxiety and declining admission rates to top colleges, college admission plays an outsized, if sometimes unspoken, role. And there were remarkable similarities within each of these groups, as we'll see.

Asian Parents

Immigrant Asian parents in Woodcrest, like parents everywhere, wanted success and happiness for their children. In their experiences, academic achievement, especially in math and science, was *the* pathway to success. Tutoring, supplementary math classes, and long hours of homework were familiar to them—these were common when they themselves were children in Asia. Parents expected rigorous standards in math and homework assignments to practice their skills and keep them busy. A frequent question at Indian and Chinese parents' social gatherings and in their social media feeds was not *whether* they would send their children to math classes outside of school, but *which one* to choose. In those circles, parents also discussed which level of classes high school students took, and more often than not, a child was choosing honors or Advanced Placement. Among immigrant families in Woodcrest, supplemental math and honors classes are just what one *does*, the default, rather than something for a child particularly precocious in math or particularly interested in a given subject.

Many immigrant parents explicitly compared their experiences in Asia to those of their children in Woodcrest's schools, concluding that even Woodcrest's schools fall short when it comes to science and math. Helen, a Chinese mother who first came to the United States for her undergraduate studies in engineering, sent her children to an advanced math club. She explained, "I like that training. And that's why I send [my daughter] to those programs. She can get an edge on things. So I think like, because we came from Hong Kong, we know, we've been through that system."

Parents like Helen used their own experiences growing up as a benchmark—this is just what kids are supposed to do. They didn't see extra math as unusual or particularly striving, as many white parents did. This was true of Chinese and Indian parents alike. Saumya, an immigrant Indian mother, said,

> We grew up in India. Math was much harder in elementary
> school than here. . . . We Indians see math as the foundation for
> a lot of things. You need to be good at math for anything you do
> in life. In second grade, we started my daughter with RSM to get

more challenge, to learn more. And then we had some friends who were doing it. And they're like, "Yeah, it's great."[7]

Saumya also points to the importance of social networks. Given that her friends routinely sent their children to RSM (Russian School of Math) classes, she did so too. Once a quorum of parents in a social group decided to enroll their children in RSM classes, it became part of the "normal" cultural repertoire for how to be a good parent in their network. In Saumya's experiences both in India and among fellow Indian parents in Woodcrest, extra math is just what one *does*. White parents were not part of these conversations.

Like Saumya, Anjali was disappointed with the math standards at her children's elementary school. Anjali saw her daughter's enrollment in RSM as teaching her children to work hard, despite the low standards that she perceived for math in school:

> One of the challenges for us is to keep her challenged enough. . . . Because when the kids are small, if they get things easy, they don't know how to work hard. And when they come to middle school when other kids have caught up, then they're lost. . . . As a parent, we need to keep them challenged so they know how to work hard. Because after a while, hard work is what makes you. Not your smartness . . . It's a homework ritual for her.[8]

Overall, Asian parents tended to expect more homework from school than white parents. Shivani, a US-born Indian American parent, mentioned a Facebook group in which mostly moms in Woodcrest posted: "There's all the Asian parents saying, 'No, no, give them more, we want more homework.' And then the Caucasian parents are like, 'No, no, we don't need to do that. It's too much stress.'"

As I started this research the school district had just implemented a new, gentler homework policy: homework was entirely done away with at one elementary school and banned for middle and high school on all religious holidays, school vacations, and long weekends, an explicit attempt to reduce academic pressure. I asked Fan, a Chinese immigrant mother, about the policy. She said, "I think the homework is not enough. I think that they need to give more homework to my son.

He just finishes his homework very fast! . . . I don't like that. I think that they should have homework on holidays and the weekends."

Some immigrant parents—mostly those who had spent decades in the United States—felt ambivalent about the push to excel academically. Ruby, an immigrant Indian mother who had lived in the US for over twenty years, explained about her kids, "I want them to be all-rounders, not just doing what they're told." Still, Ruby noticed different standards between Indian and US schools, which concerned her:

> I think the major difference between the education systems in India and here . . . is in India, they put in more effort. . . . When I go back and I see my brother's kids studying and studying and just doing that, it scares me. Because my children, I don't know if they're doing enough.

The transnational influence of her brother's children weighed on Ruby. While she had immigrated to the United States because of the abundant opportunities for herself and her husband, she worried that even the very best schools in the United States paled in comparison to elite schools in Asia. When she thought about returning to India, her brother told Ruby that her children may not fit in because of the academic rigor:

> My brother just says, "Yeah, you can come back, but your kids are not going to fit in. They're going to have the hardest time. And all they have to do is study and study." And my nephew actually, he sat for the exam for engineering. And he got like 99.999 to the sixth decimal . . . And then if he clears this, then he sits for the second one. They take best of the two. And then he goes for the advanced, which is like the IITs.

Ruby's eyes grew wide as she talked about her nephew's talents, and the possibility of getting into the IITs, the Indian Institutes of Technology. Still, I sensed deep ambivalence in Ruby. Even her brother seems ambivalent—he tells her that "all they have to do is study and study." On the one hand, the academic focus of her nieces and nephews "scares" her and convinced her to sign her children up for RSM classes in the summer. But on the other hand, Ruby reminds herself, "I say, 'No, I want them to be all-rounders.'" Ruby was likely influenced by parenting in the US—autonomy in parenting and holistic college admissions are key features of the American landscape. I related to her ambivalence—I imagined it was the same feeling I had when interviews with some parents in Woodcrest made me feel as if I was not doing enough to propel my own children to success, even if I too wanted to develop their own autonomy and well-roundedness more than my own immigrant Indian parents did for me. My parents planted extra math beyond the school curriculum into my own cultural repertoire as well. Still, Ruby's children were high achievers. When I met Ruby, her son was about to start ninth grade in honors math—the highest level. Ruby's cultural repertoire was shaped by her schooling in India, her experiences in the US, and her brother's parenting, which led her to emphasize achievement while also rejecting the Indian system in favor of wanting them to be more autonomous.[9]

Bernadette, a later-generation Chinese mom of two, also had a broader understanding of excellence than most immigrant Asian parents. Her children were deeply involved in the music program at Woodcrest High School, and the elder had recently completed a college degree in jazz. Bernadette was one of the founders of an organization focused on Asian American students' mental health. She told me that when her children, now adults, came home for Christmas recently she told them, "The only thing I wish for you guys is that you fall in love with the right person." In fact, she and her husband were supporting their son's music career by paying his rent, with the stipulation that he produce a song every month. She said, "The price of our partial support is, we're buying songs. That's basically what we're doing. In order for him to get his monthly allowance from us, which basically covers his rent, he has to deposit a new song into his SoundCloud." Still, like many Asian American kids, Bernadette's children did projects for the school's science fair, and Bernadette herself admitted, "I started [my son] on piano when he was four. I started [my daughter] on violin when she was six. I mean, I'm still a pretty Asian mom in that regard." Both Bernadette's childhood outside China along with her ethnic Chinese parents' cultural repertoire likely played a role in her parenting.

Michelle was raised by Taiwanese immigrant parents in Woodcrest at a time when not nearly as many Asian families lived there and few classes like RSM were available. She and her husband moved back to Woodcrest to raise their two children there. Her immigrant Chinese mother-in-law seemed puzzled by her granddaughter's dance classes, and offered instead to pay for RSM classes:

> She was like, "How much are you paying for these dance classes? [laughs]. Is that worth it?" And really sort of questioning that. I'm like, "Of course it's worth it! [laughs]. She loves it. Look at her face when she's dancing!" Starting elementary school, his parents saying, "Hey, we'll pay for Russian School of Math, or Kumon, if you want her to do that." I was like, "No. She's only six or seven. I don't want her to do that." So they offer every now and then.

Michelle's cultural repertoire was different from that of most immigrant parents, and from her mother-in-law, probably because of her experiences growing up in the United States, even in Woodcrest, and perhaps also because of her experiences as a teacher in another school district.

Yan contrasted her own upbringing with her husband's, both in China. Yan's parents were engineers who frequently moved based on their work-related projects. In contrast, her husband came from a working-class family:

> He showed strong interest with his studies when he was in fifth grade. . . . So eventually he got his Ph.D. in physics. I was on the path to get my Ph.D. And then I decided, you know, in our household, we don't need to have two Ph.D.s, so I will just work. . . . And when he was in middle school, he probably was the number one for the whole county. . . . His mom only had maybe elementary education. Dad probably had a similar education. And his parents, especially mom, worked very hard. [While he was] studying every night, she would stay up late, she would cook dinner even at ten or eleven, just make sure his supper's on, he had enough nutrition. So he was very focused with his studies. And at the time in China, going to study physics, that was a very popular and highly competitive major.

Yan's husband's academic accomplishments, despite his parents having little education themselves, make her three master's degrees seem unremarkable by comparison. While the experiences of Yan's husband may have been particularly unusual in China, it was precisely these kinds of backgrounds that landed Chinese and Indian families in Woodcrest. Most immigrant parents I met did not have the very humble beginnings that Yan's husband did, but they did share experiences of educational success, usually through extra focus on STEM subjects, tutoring, and long hours of homework outside of school.

Given the extra math classes and tutoring even when a student was not struggling in a class, was it any wonder that a disproportionate number of Chinese and Indian American students ended up taking the highest-level classes at Woodcrest High? The frequency with which Asian students in particular were in advanced classes at school could make it even harder to make decisions *not* to take the high-level classes for Asian American students. Saumya acknowledged that "it's really hard to find a balance between not stressing the kids out and keeping up with stuff. . . . I do more focus on her kind of relaxing. I don't know if everybody does that. I don't tend to push them too much." Saumya told me that her daughter did not want to take Advanced Placement biology in tenth grade, and she agreed, but this created some anxiety in Saumya: "I'm in so many meetings where my kid is the only one who's not doing AP bio, especially amongst Indians." Those experiences make her feel "scared," because she thinks, "Oh my God, what if my kid is left behind? Others will get into the colleges of their choice, and she won't. Or her application won't be competitive as the other kids'." Like Ruby, Saumya did not want to push a relentless focus on academics. But they both were embedded in communities—Ruby mentioned her brother across the world in India, and Saumya mentioned other Indian parents in Woodcrest—that provoked anxiety about decisions *not* to push for the most rigorous coursework or extra math outside of school. As we'll see, white parents usually did not feel the same concerns about their children's achievement. Their cultural repertoires for success were different.

White Parents

Most of Woodcrest's white parents placed a higher priority on making time for extracurricular activities than on taking the most rigorous academic courses possible. This meant, too, that they also hoped for less homework to make room for those activities. They were more likely than Asian parents to worry that too much schoolwork would cause undue strain on their children and were careful to maintain what they felt were reasonable expectations of achievement. They wanted "balance" in their children's lives. And they reserved summer vacation for fun, job experiences, and developing noncognitive skills. White parents usually saw academic work outside of school (besides homework) as important only if someone needed remedial help and AP classes as designed for the minority of students who have a particular interest and aptitude in a particular subject. Most of all, they often contrasted themselves to *other* more unreasonable parents, as they perceived it. Those unreasonable parents were sometimes labeled explicitly as Asian, but more frequently the association was implicit. Of course, they too expected academic excellence—after all, that was what brought them to Woodcrest in the first place. But many felt academic excellence had spiraled out of control in Woodcrest. Supplementary math, academic pursuits in the summer, and multiple AP classes in one term were decidedly *not* in their cultural repertoire for what to suggest for their children, and often it seemed white parents defined their parenting in terms of what they did *not* do more than by what they did.

Patricia and her husband were one couple who chose Woodcrest for its academic reputation yet limited their children's advanced schoolwork. Patricia is the parent in chapter 1 who took on the college search for her kids. She said:

> We wanted to choose a town that had really good school systems. . . . We only allow a child to take either one AP or one honors every year, because our kids have always been very, very involved in music and drama. . . . That's where they really excelled and really spent all of their time. We made sure, obviously, they did well in school. . . . But we also made sure they had time to really do all the other things that they liked to do, because I think it's really important to have as much balance as possible.

I heard the word "balance" from parents of all ethnicities, but it was most common among white parents—they used it more frequently, and it appeared in more of their interviews.[10] Patricia mentioned "balance" for her children on eight different occasions in our interview. It wasn't that parents like Patricia didn't care about academics—their move to

Woodcrest suggests they did and that they deployed their resources to help their kids achieve academically—but they were more likely to also want balance between academic achievement and other things for their children—extracurricular achievement, time with friends, sleep, and more. Promoting balance through limitations to the amount of academic work was a main element of their cultural repertoire for parenting.

Lisa was another US-born white mother who, along with her immigrant Chinese husband, chose to live in Woodcrest because it was a "high-achieving town" yet worked to convince her child to reduce his course load in high school:

> When he was in ninth grade, he wasn't always doing his homework. He'd be disorganized. He would start homework and forget he had completed it. So we said, "I don't think you should take Advanced Placement classes in tenth grade, because you don't seem ready, because you're unorganized. You're not going to take AP bio." And then he came to me and he said he wanted to take AP history. And I was like, "Alright, you never said you were interested in history. Where is this coming from?" And he was going to have to petition for permission because he has a B, and you need an A. . . . So I was like, "Look, if you really tell me that you're going to be happy about reading the history textbook, because it's going to involve a lot of reading of the history textbook, I'll write that letter for you. But I have to understand why you want to take this." And he said, "Well, I feel bad because all my friends are taking it." So I said, "That's not a good enough reason. When this is AP, that means it's college level. And you're fifteen and it's totally okay that a fifteen-year-old is not taking a college class." So then he got over it.

The irony of parents overruling peer pressure to take advanced classes did not escape me. Many white parents got more than they bargained for when they moved to Woodcrest—they wanted a place where their children would encounter high-achieving peers and families, to surround them by excellence with the hope that their children too would excel. But for some that influence was much too profound, and they found themselves having to reel in that influence on their children. Some white parents actually saw the influence of highly motivated peers as a negative influence.

Fred, a white father we heard from in chapter 1 expressing appreciation for the influence of Asian families in Woodcrest, still contrasted his own parenting with those of some of his son's Asian American friends. Fred said that some of the immigrant parents put too much "pressure" on their children. He then gave me an example of his son's Asian American friends: "They didn't do as well on the SAT as their parents wanted them to. So one of them's getting angry texts from their parents, and they're both getting heat from their parents about their SAT scores not being adequate." Fred contrasted those parents to his and his wife's style:

> We try to find the right balance between not making him miserable, and trying to get him to get stuff done. Like we're definitely on his case every day to practice the cello and get his homework done. . . . And my feeling is, it's legitimate to lean on your kid when they're not trying hard. But it's not legitimate to lean on your kid when they're trying hard and not getting results. If they're making a good-faith effort, I think you should be happy with that.

On the one hand, Fred appreciated the Asian families in Woodcrest for creating an environment in which his family could thrive. He had a lot in common with a sizable number of his Asian neighbors—he was a software engineer parent of a child who liked computer programming. He was one of a handful of white families that seemed to experience a stronger pull toward Asian families—rather than reject their emphasis on STEM fields and academic activities like computer programing classes, Fred's son joined those Asian-dominated activities. Fred even expressed appreciation for the focus he observed in Asian families: "There's a changing mix of cultures and ethnic backgrounds in the town, which I view as a positive in terms of making it a more exciting and interesting place to be. A lot of the newcomers come with a strong work ethic." On the other hand, Fred disapproved of some of those same parents for pushing their children too hard to excel in school. But he did so gingerly, comparing early Jewish stereotypes to those he sometimes heard about Asians in Woodcrest:

I had a conversation at the gym with a guy who does local real estate. And he expressed some concern about the Chinese moving
in, like they're going to take over. And he felt like this is an alien
invasion or something. And that just felt creepy to me because as
someone Jewish, there's a long history of bad things happening
to Jews.

Just as I sensed ambivalence in Ruby's comparison of her children's
amount of schoolwork to that of her brother's children in India, so too
did I sense ambivalence in Fred. He seemed to appreciate the things that
Asian families do and strongly rejected overt racism toward the growing
presence of Asian immigrants in town, and yet his voice had an edge
of judgment as he told me about the Asian parents of his son's friends
scolding their children for their SAT scores. He contrasted that parenting to the balance he and his wife strive for in their own parenting,
in part by considering their child's emotional state—not making him
"miserable" when communicating academic expectations. Reducing
academic pressure, as we'll see in chapter 4, is part of white parents'
cultural repertoire for maintaining emotional well-being.

Jennifer was a white mom who got involved in town leadership because of her concerns about student stress related to the amount of
schoolwork students in Woodcrest were doing:

The kids who get to college from here, they go to Carnegie Mel-
lon, it's less stressful. They go to Princeton math department, it's
less stressful. They go to Harvard and Yale, piece of cake. That's
a sign that perhaps our teachers are taking the college-like AP
classes too intensely. It doesn't need to—it's not *actually* college.

Why did white parents not push their children to meet the highest
academic levels as many Asian parents did? Many drew on stories of
successful individuals in the United States who had not been academic
superstars. Furthermore, unlike many of their Asian neighbors, they
considered pathways to success only in the United States. One such
parent was Sarah, who said: "I have a lot of work experience in human
resources because I've been in that for a long time. And I have seen it
doesn't matter. It really doesn't matter where your degree is from."

Avery, a white mother of five, said she and her husband are

fairly strict with our kids, expectation-wise. But we've never paid our kids to get good grades. We figure it's enough for you to be happy with what you do, and to do the best that you can. If you're a C student, be a C student, don't be an F student. . . . You're not necessarily going to go to school at Harvard when you get out. Maybe it's a vo-tech. I love creative, artistic people who don't always get it with academics. And I am fine with that. But fly with that artistic side of you. Do your best. I'm not going to push you into making A's in calculus if that's going to make you stressed out, have a nervous breakdown, that kind of thing.

I wondered, too, if Avery also believed that there are C students who should not try to be A students. In other words, like the AP classes described by Lisa, A's were for outstanding students according to Avery, rather than something most students should strive for. But both felt that A's and AP classes should not take kids' lives out of balance.

Of course, white parents had basic academic standards that they wanted their children to meet, and they paid for tutors when they felt their children needed extra support. Balance also meant maintaining a basic academic achievement standard—higher in Woodcrest than in most places. Coach Rebecca lived in a town close to Woodcrest that she frequently compared to Woodcrest when she spoke. She contrasted her children's use of tutoring to the enrichment of their peers:

> We've paid for tutoring. . . . In a town like mine, and in a town like Woodcrest, we're not trying to get ahead; we're trying to stay where we are. And the sociodemographic changes have pulled the curve so far in terms of academic achievement that my kids need tutoring to stay in the classes that they're in. . . . When I say I'm spending money in academic resources, it's not necessarily enrichment. It's tutoring, it's a preparation class, it's a study skills management sort of class.

Rebecca's example demonstrates the value white parents did place on tutoring—but only when their child was falling behind. Rebecca eventually moved her son to a local elite private school. She described her son's struggles with mental health to explain why she decided to move him. This was not uncommon among white parents, as we'll see in chapter 4. Like most parents, she skirts the question of ethnicity—she does not name immigrants or Asians explicitly—while still making her view clear, describing "sociodemographic changes" as the reason for her children needing tutoring.

Like Rebecca, Lisa, the mother who implored her son not to take AP history, also expressed high hopes for her children's achievement. She said:

> One of the benefits of going to someplace like Stanford or MIT is that they talk to their students about like, "You are the best." There's a positive thing to that, because it does really help them achieve. They really do think they're the best. . . . I have friends that are from MIT. If I hear them talk about engineering, they really think, "If you're not from MIT, you're not a good engineer." . . . It's so powerful to have that confidence. I lacked that confidence and I think that if I'd had that confidence in me, you know, I would have done something else, would have achieved more. So it's very powerful.

Lisa was unusual in the explicit desire she expressed for her children to attend elite universities. These ambitions may have been driven by her modest upbringing compared to most other white parents I met—she attended public school in an urban district where, she shared, "we had no concept of applying to the Ivies" and went on to a state college where she grew up. Her high ambitions, however, did not change the cultural repertoire with which she guided her son to reconsider his desire to take AP history.

Lisa's seeming paradox—her Ivy League ambitions despite pushing her son to forgo AP history—is one illustration of many that shows how our actions tend to be guided more by our cultural repertoire rather than by our values or ambitions. For Lisa, that meant she was used to thinking of AP classes as being for high-achieving, organized students particularly interested in a subject. In contrast, for many Asian parents in Woodcrest, taking as many advanced classes as possible—and clearing one's schedule to make room for those classes—was the usual thing to do; this was what they observed in Asia growing up, and what they heard from fellow parents from the same country when they socialized in the United States. In this way, white and Asian parents landed on different emphases for their children. But how did those emphases, messages, and requirements shape what their children actually did?

STUDENTS PURSUE ACADEMIC EXCELLENCE

Given the myriad influences on teens, how did their parents' messages and cultural repertoires shape what they ultimately did? As parents we sometimes wish we were the sole influence on our children. We worry about negative influences on them, especially from their peers. Sometimes we gently nudge them in a different direction—toward particular kids, classes, or activities that we think they have a chance to excel in. But before all of that, those who have the resources plant themselves in communities where they think the influences outside home will be to their liking. Did Woodcrest parents succeed in imparting their cultural repertoires onto their children?

Asian American and white students alike seemed to heed the messages from their parents, with ethnic differences that paralleled those among their parents. Peer influences reenforced those differences. Friendships were shaped by the level of classes a student took, and those mattered for the extent of their hours on homework and for their striving for the highest levels of achievement. Ethnicity also shaped friendship networks—when your peers at Sunday school are also enrolled in extra math classes you are likely more willing to go along with it than if you are the only one. Overall, I found significant differences in Woodcrest between white and Asian American students' perspectives on academic achievement, with implications for what they actually accomplished.

Asian American Students

Despite high academic achievement and hard work across all groups at Woodcrest High School, on average Asian American students put in more hours on homework, took more advanced classes, and achieved higher grades than their white peers at Woodcrest.[11] Asian American students were also more likely than their white peers to spend their summers on academic pursuits. This was true of students in honors and nonhonors tracks alike. Their parents' strong focus on academic pursuits seemed to pay off in their children's accomplishments. Partly this was a result of the activities parents signed them up for when they were young—taking supplementary math classes in elementary school set them up to take honors and AP math in high school, for example. And then, in honors and AP classes Asian students were more likely to encounter peers who were spending long hours on homework and other academic pursuits, making those long hours seem more common than if they were surrounded by peers in the college prep track. Those hours usually led to higher grades too.

Indeed, overall in Woodcrest, Asian Americans were doing better academically than their white peers. In the year that I observed eleventh-grade chemistry, six in ten Asian American students were enrolled in Advanced Placement, the highest of four levels, compared to two in ten white students. And, Asian Americans taking the highest-level classes were not limited to STEM subjects. In the same year, Asian American students were also more likely to take Advanced Placement US history (43 percent) than their white peers (36 percent).

The higher-level classes taken by Asian American students did not preclude strong grades. Woodcrest High School does not "weight" grade point averages—that is, unlike many schools, an A in an advanced course counts the same as an A in a standard or remedial-level course toward a student's GPA. Despite their overrepresentation in harder, higher-level classes, Asian American students still earned higher grades than their white peers. While one-third of students were Asian American at Woodcrest, nearly half of students in the top fifth of class rank were Asian American. Asian American students were more likely than their white peers to take AP exams, and of the fifty students who took five AP exams in one academic year, three-fourths were Asian American.[12] Indeed, the only place that Asian Americans were underrepresented at Woodcrest was on the other end of the academic spectrum: they made up just one-tenth of students in remedial-level courses, and were just one-fifth of students in the bottom 20 percent.

Asian American and white students alike noticed this pattern. Caitlin, a white student who took some remedial classes, said, "If you look across the school, the races and like different classes that you're taking, I feel like you'd probably find different races taking higher classes and lower classes. . . . If there is an Asian person in a remedial class, I feel like they are out of place." And Karthik, an Indian boy taking mostly honors and AP classes, agreed: "There's always the stereotype of Asians being

TABLE 2.1. Student enrollment by race in eleventh-grade chemistry (by percentage)

	REMEDIAL	COLLEGE PREP	HONORS	AP	TOTAL
White	8	49	22	21	100
Asian	2	25	15	59	100

Source: Woodcrest school data 2017.

more overachieving than others. . . . When people talk to me about my GPA, they assume it's like a 4.0 or above. . . . It adds to the stress that's already put on me by my parents. I always feel the need to fit in. So I'm always trying to improve my grades, get that B+ up to an A."

Time spent on homework explains at least some of the difference in grades. While over half of white students at Woodcrest High School reported spending two hours or less on homework on an average weeknight, over 60 percent of Asian American students reported spending over three hours on an average weeknight.[13]

When asked about their goals, Asian American students were more likely than their white peers to set specific target achievements, such as a particular GPA or SAT score. Josh, the son of Chinese immigrants, said his goal was to "get 1500 on the SAT," and Chinese American William said he wanted to "keep a good GPA . . . around 3.5." When I asked William about his plans for the weekend, he made clear that he couldn't do anything else because the chess tournament he was competing in would keep him busy from morning until night, though the soft-spoken young man also loved gaming. When I wished William "good luck" on his chess tournament as he left the room, his soft voice became animated in his insistent reply, "It's not luck!" I replied, "Then what is it?" to which William replied, "It's dedication and hard work!" For many Asian American students, like their parents, long hours of dedicated hard work was worth the payoff of winning that chess tournament, or improving that SAT score or GPA. Their parents' cultural repertoires for getting ahead clearly had become a part of theirs by the time they were in high school.

Students seemed to heed their parents' preferences for summer activities as well. Asian American students were much more likely than their white peers to report that they spend time during their summer vacations on academic pursuits. Many took advanced academic classes and worked with academic tutors during the summer (as well as during the school year). These classes were not the remedial classes that many readers will be familiar with—required classes taken by students who failed during the school year. Rather, they were enrichment classes designed to propel the student ahead, whether to skip a class in school, to prepare for what promised to be a challenging class the following year, or to learn additional material not taught in school. Lakshmi, the daughter of Indian immigrants, said when we spoke in early May that she planned to take two computer classes during the coming summer at a local private school, on the recommendation of her private college counselor: "I was thinking of being a computer scientist. So I wanted to try some classes out before I obviously went to get the major. [My counselor] was like, 'There's these two classes.'" The summer before she had taken robotics and chemistry at the same school. The chemistry class was in preparation for the AP chemistry class she was acing when we met. The alignment between her college counselor's recommendation, the cultural repertoires for getting ahead among most Indian parents in Woodcrest, and what many Asian American students did during summer vacation together made academic summer classes a part of Lakshmi's own cultural repertoire. So the recommendation was probably not a hard sell.

Lakshmi had also started an Indian club at Woodcrest, and, with all her commitments, had taken her mother's advice to quit running on the track team when she got to high school in order to focus fully on schoolwork. While many children might rebel when a parent asks them to quit an athletic activity, I sensed no tension in Lakshmi's decision. She seemed to agree that the commitment was too much: "My mom wanted me to focus more on my education than on track. . . . Also, track met six times a week, so I had to go on Saturdays as well." Lakshmi continued with a weekly Bollywood dance class: "I've always loved dance in general. And we watch a lot of Bollywood movies. So that just kind of fused together." As with Lakshmi, I heard surprisingly little tension between most students and parents when it came to their academic and extracurricular pursuits. It seemed that by the time they got to high school, most kids had fully internalized the cultural repertoires of their parents related to academic achievement.

Pooja, a gentle eleventh-grade Indian American girl, told me about her summer plans as a local professor's research assistant:

> I found a research opportunity with a professor. So I'm going to help write a research paper with them over the summer. . . . I want to get lab experience too. So I've been looking around and hopefully I'll find something for that. . . . I also want to do science fair research.

I attended the school science fair that year, which was the year before Pooja's intended submission. Close to half of the submissions were by Indian American students, and another quarter were by East Asian students. This was a strikingly different crowd from what I'd seen just a few days prior at a school concert of show tunes, in which the student performers were predominantly white. As I walked around at the science fair, looking at the displays and talking with students, I quickly realized I was in over my head. I could not understand the complex projects students had undertaken. One student told me she got into her project through working in a lab, and another through volunteering at a hospital. I wondered if Pooja had met them and gotten the idea for her own summer plans through those students. If not them, perhaps a different student at the science fair. For Indian American students in particular, summer lab work culminating in a science fair project was a part of their cultural repertoires for summer planning. Even if a minority of Indian American students ended up at the science fair, I was struck by the complete absence of Black and Latinx students. I guessed that of their parents, neighbors, siblings—none had had the opportunity to participate in one in the past—and most probably did not have the social networks to find a position in a science lab. It was not part of their cultural repertoires.

Asian American students not enrolled in honors and AP classes also tended to engage in intensive academic work. Neesa took the college prep level of chemistry and math, forgoing honors and AP. Still, she spent one to three hours on homework every night and earned high grades. With a sister already at an Ivy League college, Neesa had big boots to fill. Neesa told me her goal is to attend an Ivy League college, and that she is preparing for college by "doing SAT classes to get a good grade on that, and doing more extracurriculars, because it looks good on your resumé. And I'll do like hackathons, because that also looks good if you win medals. And I'm trying to look for an internship."

Smriti was another Indian American student in the chemistry college prep track. During eleventh grade when I met her, she was working with a college counselor and planned to take classes for high school students at a local college that summer. One class, as she described it, was "a health science program, [in] which you get a deeper look into what it's like to be a doctor," and the other was college essay writing. Like most eleventh graders around the country, Smriti was thinking about college. But unlike most others, her parents' financial resources and their cultural repertoires for getting ahead led her to work with a college counselor and take summer classes to help make that happen.

Luke, a Chinese American student in the chemistry college prep track, said he spends four to five hours on homework every night and that his goals are to get into a "good" college, which he described as "like MIT or Harvard. Ivy League schools are really good colleges." Similarly, Luke said his parents' goals for him are simply "Good grades. Good college. Good job."

These examples show that even Asian American students not taking the highest-level classes spent considerable time outside of school on homework, worked with college counselors, and did summer activities involving academic work. And they aspired to the very top colleges, just as many of their peers in honors and Advanced Placement classes did. Furthermore, I did not hear Asian American students complain about their parents' emphasis on academics or suggestions of doing academic activities after school or during summer vacation. Rather, they seemed to have internalized the cultural repertoires for success that their parents held, even when that pathway was not the same as their white peers.

White Students

We saw that Asian American students at Woodcrest were more likely to take advanced classes than their white peers, in both the sciences and the humanities. They also were more likely to have top GPAs at Woodcrest, despite the lack of weighting grades by level of courses. White students were much less likely to focus on academic pursuits over the summer than their Asian American peers. A majority of the white students I interviewed had plans to work over the summer instead. Indeed, the one white student who was considering an academic class, Hunter, also planned to continue his job at a local restaurant, spend time at his family's lakehouse, and play football with the Woodcrest team. Other white students planned to work as counselors in summer camps they attended as children. Ilya was typical: "The summer camp that I'm working at for the first time this summer is a Boy Scout summer camp that I've been going to for a long while. . . . I'm skipping the last two days of school. It runs from then for nine and a half weeks."

Many white students described the message I also heard from white parents: that high academic achievement isn't necessary for success in life. Carly, Avery's daughter, said, "A lot of kids at school have a lot of pressure on them to be getting really good grades and to go to a really good college. And I think a lot of people have the thought that if they don't do that, that they're going to be a failure. But I don't really think that way." I asked Carly why she's different, to which she replied, "My parents don't put that pressure on me. And also I've watched my [older] brothers go through stuff, so I understand how you don't always have to have everything perfect for you to be doing okay."

I imagined Avery would have been pleased to hear her daughter echoing her perspective. While schools were one reason that Avery and her husband chose Woodcrest when they were moving to the area eight years before we met, she also felt the academic emphasis in town was too high. Hunter, the white football player, said, "My dad always says he's seen a lot of guys who might not get all A's, who aren't the smartest, but if they work hard, they're like very successful." Ilya heard a similar message from his father:

> There are people who get into Ivy Leagues who didn't do all APs and tons of extracurriculars. I'm not even trying to get into an Ivy League. Because for the most part, people care more about the diploma that you get than they do about where it came from. . . . Theoretically, the education could be better from certain schools. But it's not enough to really change your chances of success. . . . . My dad when he graduated from high school, was doing al-. right. . . . And he has a Ph.D. now. . . . And he's like three away from the top of the director of the lab. And in high school he was

getting B's and C's and not really doing his homework and stuff like that.

I don't know whether the parents of Carly, Hunter, and Ilya were simply trying to assuage their children's worries when they were not the top performers in their schools. I know that when my children are stressed I sometimes convey the same message: "It's okay to not know what you want to do in life, I never took a sociology class in college— didn't even know what sociology *was*—and now I'm a professor of sociology!" and "Your dad didn't get top grades in college, and now he's a successful entrepreneur!" even while I still hold high achievement expectations. Yet none of the Asian American students I spoke with shared this kind of specific message from their parents, even if they sometimes did tell me that their parents were not as demanding as *other* parents (a common refrain from students and parents alike across groups, as we'll see in chapter 5). Like their Asian American peers, the white students had internalized their parents' cultural repertoires for getting ahead.

There may be some truth to the message about academics being less important than they think, especially coming from white, upper-middle-class parents. Other research has shown that getting a degree from an elite college makes a difference in your future earnings only for students who are underrepresented minorities (Black or Latinx), whose parents lack a bachelor's degree, or whose parents have low incomes.[14] In other words, families of color may need to rely more on elite college degrees than their white neighbors.

Colleen, a white eleventh grader taking honors chemistry when I met her, told me about a shift in her friendship circle in high school, from a "mostly Asian—Indian, Chinese" group to a "predominantly American, like their parents were born in America" group. Colleen told me that her earlier group had too strong a focus on academics for her taste:

Whenever I hung out with them, it was always just school. It was always studying. Or if they got like an 87, they'd freak out, because that would be like an awful grade. So I think I kind of put those standards on myself too. And my parents don't really push me that hard. They don't get mad if I don't get an A. I more push *myself* to get good grades. But I think when I was in that group, I was always comparing myself to these other kids who were constantly studying and worrying about school, and taking as many honors and APs as they could. I don't think that was the right fit for me. It stressed me out.

Colleen described the stress she felt about academic achievement when she hung out with her previous set of friends, which she attributed to their parents' influence on them. She contrasted her own mother's approach to that of her peers' parents: "My mom, she grew up in [nearby suburb] which is also a pretty academic town. So she grew up in the same situation as me. And I think that she didn't want that for her kids. That's why she doesn't push us super hard." When the cultural repertoires of her peers and parents did not align, Colleen made a conscious effort to find a new set of friends.

In many ways, the cultural repertoires of both white students and white parents were more defined by what students did *not* do rather than by what they did. And striving for the highest academic achievement by spending summer hours on academic pursuits, taking the highest-level classes, and spending long hours on homework were *not* part of their or their parents' cultural repertoires. Like Asian American students, their perspectives seemed aligned with their parents' perspectives.

The starkest difference in academic focus I found between Asian American and white students was among those who were not enrolled in honors or AP classes. In contrast to Asian American students in college prep chemistry, white students I met in college prep tended to have a more relaxed attitude toward academics. Many described feeling satisfied with lower grades as long as they were trying their best, a message reinforced by their parents. For example, Caitlin told me that her goals are "getting good grades and staying on top of everything. Trying my hardest." When I asked Caitlin to clarify what grades she is happy with, her response revealed a difference from most Asian American students I met,

It depends what subject. Like math, I'm awful at. So I could get like a C in math and be like, "Okay, I tried." And then I could get a B in English or history and be like, "This isn't a good grade for me," because I know I could have gotten better. But mostly if I have above a B, I'm satisfied.

In contrast to her satisfaction with B and C grades depending on the subject, Caitlin was ahead of her peers in basketball, a sport she played since age five with her father and brothers. Her father was a former college basketball player and sometimes was hard on Caitlin when it came to her effort in basketball: "When I was younger, he would just be like, 'You're not trying your hardest,' and like, 'I know you can do a lot better.' And it was like a lot of pressure." In contrast, she told me that her parents want her to "get A's and B's" in her academic subjects at school. The only pressure she mentioned was related to sports. I spoke with Caitlin just before the winter school holiday, when the team would be practicing every day except Christmas—including New Year's Day.

Eleanor, another white student in college prep chemistry, explicitly distanced herself from her Asian American peers in terms of academic emphasis and seemed to repeat the message I heard from many white parents: that academic excellence isn't the sole—or even main—driver of success in the United States:

> A lot of Asian kids hang out together. Because they tend to be in like the same AP classes. And they tend to have the same values of focusing on class a lot. . . . It's silly to me because . . . I know that like the grades you get in high school aren't a big determinant of your future success. It's a lot about resiliency and networking and stuff like that. Sometimes I wonder why people put so much time and effort into something that isn't going to make that big of a difference. And I feel like you're only like a teenager once. So I feel sad when they miss out on doing fun kid stuff that they're not going to be able to do later on.

While the families of Eleanor and Caitlin had been in Woodcrest for generations—both were growing up in a parent's childhood home— many white students whose parents had come to Woodcrest more recently shared their perspectives. Cody was one such student. We have met his father, Fred, who works in tech and appreciates the Asian influence on tech opportunities for kids in Woodcrest, but distanced himself from the pressure he perceived Asian parents place on their kids. When I met Cody, he was taking college prep chemistry. He was also doing honors math and honors in two electives. He contrasted himself with— and seemed to express disdain for—peers who took several advanced-level classes:

> There's kids that are just like, "How many ways can I kill my-self?" [laughs]. There are kids that I know that take AP history, AP chemistry, and then honors everything else. And I think that's pure suicide. And then in addition to that, they usually do something athletic. And then also they're usually on debate. And so these people usually get home at like nine PM every night, or later. And usually get very little sleep. So I see these people. And I'm just glad I'm not one of them, because it does not seem like a healthy way to live.

Cody's description may be an exaggeration—I did not meet students that fit the bill he describes, even when I visited AP classes. In particu-lar, multiple AP classes and varsity sports were usually not paired. Still, Cody's general point that others overload themselves with commit-ments and strenuous classes did resonate with what I sometimes heard. Later, Cody told me that his friend group was an "Asian-ish group":

> If you wanted to put me in a social group, that would be this group of Asian kids that do fencing and they also play League of Legends and video games and stuff like that. But they're always talking about their grades. A lot of them are struggling to main-tain their A averages. And I'm listening to them talk about their like honors and APs and how they're just barely making A's in them. And I'm thinking about "Well, I'm not nearly that good." A lot of them have already taken SATs, and thinking about how they can get into Harvard or whatever.

I asked Cody to clarify what he meant by "Asian-ish," to which he re-plied, "Work hard. Get into a good college. Press yourself insanely to do well." Still, Cody was a strong student, telling me he earned mostly B+ and A- grades. I was surprised that Cody did not mention Asian American students when asked to explain "Asian-ish." Over time in Woodcrest I learned that most did what they can to avoid talking directly about race or ethnicity. I guessed that this group was predominantly Asian, though clearly not exclusively so, given Cody's membership. Interestingly, he also seems to distance himself from the desire to "press yourself insanely," despite that description of his friend group.

During a focus group discussion Cody shared his experience of shifting from Advanced Placement US history down to the college prep level:

> I actually started off in AP US history this year. I ended up dropping down shortly after the school year started. And the difference was huge. If you look at the AP classes, like almost everyone is talking about test grades almost all the time. Whereas if you go down a level, to what's referred to as "normal" history, people are a lot more interested in actually learning the material and just enjoying the class than they are in getting the best test scores and scoring well on the AP exam.

Cody's comments suggest a moral judgment of the culture in high-level classes, where, he suggests, students are there to achieve rather than for intrinsic learning. While he does not mention race, the school data tell us that Asian American students are overrepresented in AP classes in Woodcrest. I guessed that his comments were influenced by racial stereotypes of Asian Americans as excessively and mechanistically focused on achievement.[15] The contradiction between his characterization and what I observed and heard—I found that Asian American students in college prep classes were just as intensive about academics as their peers in honors and AP—suggests this may be the case. And Cody's boundary making to distance himself from a group of students normally valorized—those taking advanced classes—may provide a much-needed sense of confidence for students attending school in a high-achieving community like Woodcrest. While Cody seemed to associate with Asian peers more than most white students at his school, he nevertheless distanced himself from them in other ways, perhaps a defensive response to their higher achievement. While Cody hinted at moral judgment of a group of students that was "Asian-ish," many white parents I met were more direct, as we'll see in chapter 5.

BEYOND WOODCREST HIGH SCHOOL

Immigrant professionals come to Woodcrest in search of academic excellence, just as many of their white neighbors do. However, their understanding of how to promote their own children's excellence often differs from the understandings of their white neighbors, leading to tensions over achievement. Asian and white parents drew from different cultural repertoires to guide their children. White parents tended to see diverse pathways to success, whereas Asian parents tended to rely on academic achievement as the key strategy to put their children on a pathway to success.[16] And their children tended to heed these messages, especially when their peer networks aligned with their parents' messages.

Do the differences between Asian American and white student academic achievement behaviors even matter? From the little data available on outcomes in Woodcrest, we can see that while growing up in Woodcrest is advantageous for everyone, Asian Americans do even better academically than whites. While nearly every graduate of Woodcrest High School goes on to college, Asian Americans are more likely than whites to go on to selective four-year colleges.[17] While this does not point definitively to the influence of parents' cultural repertoires, it suggests that Asian American parenting in Woodcrest may be even more helpful than the parenting of their white neighbors, at least for future college selectivity. While many have assumed that Asian Americans seamlessly integrate into the dominant white group in upper-middle-class suburbs, I found little to suggest Asian families were adopting ways of getting ahead from white families.[18] Unlike the white parents I met, no Asian parents talked about limiting the number of advanced classes they would allow their children to take, for example. On the contrary, Asian families relied on academic achievement as the best option for future success.

Are Asian Americans actually forging a new pathway to socioeconomic success in the United States? And will white families start to emulate Asian Americans? I did not find evidence for this, even when white parents recognized Asian American achievement and parents' influence in that achievement. In fact, as we'll see, some white parents rejected Asian parenting as bad parenting. But first, we need to understand life for Woodcrest teens after the last school bell of the day rings.

CHAPTER 3

The Racial Divides of Extracurricular Excellence

THE AMERICAN COMMITMENT TO EXTRACURRICULAR activities, especially high school sports, runs deep. Most US schools spend more per pupil on sports teams than they do on math education.[1] In contrast, in both India and China, high school sports teams are rare.[2] These priorities are likely related to college admissions: Chinese and Indian universities pay little attention to activities beyond academics when admitting students. In contrast, being a top athlete can get you into a good college in the US even if your grades aren't stellar.[3] At Harvard, just 6 percent of applicants who are not athletic recruits are admitted, compared to 86 percent of recruited athletes who apply.[4] At the nation's top liberal arts colleges, one in five students admitted is a recruited athlete—at Amherst College more than one-third of admitted students come through sports recruiting.[5]

As with cultural repertoires related to academics, Woodcrest parents' cultural repertoires related to extracurricular activities were often aligned with their childhood experiences in college admissions. In addition, they were also shaped by the activities of their friends' children, and what was available to them, both logistically—if a town doesn't have a crew team, no kids will become rowers—and financially. Their cultural repertoires in turn shaped what activities they encouraged, and how much time they thought their children should spend on those activities.

Most parents in Woodcrest engaged in some form of what Annette Lareau describes as "concerted cultivation" of their children's extra-curricular talents, exposing them to multiple activities at a young age and insisting they cultivate talent in *something*.[6] But that was where the similarities ended. Asian parents tended to encourage their children to participate in STEM activities and to join the debate team. They also were less committed to intensive sports than white US-born parents, prioritizing academics over athletics. They especially disliked the intensive commitment required for participation on varsity sports teams: students I met who participated in sports did so for an average of twelve hours per week, with half the athletes reporting fifteen hours per week or more. In contrast, nonathletic extracurriculars typically required fewer hours of commitment every week, with an average of less than six. Regardless of their children's activity of choice, white parents in Woodcrest prioritized time to devote to an extracurricular pursuit, especially one their child excelled in or expressed a passion for. As I described in chapter 2, this sometimes meant curtailing their academic ambitions to make time for sports, theater, or other time-consuming extracurriculars.

The differences between Asian and white families related to sports in particular were the reverse of what I saw in academics: white families tended to prioritize sports, sometimes signing up for private coaching and elite teams outside of school to give their children the best shot at making it onto varsity teams in high school, and sometimes lower-ing academic ambitions to make room for sports commitments. Asian families also cared about extracurricular excellence, but tended not to go the extra mile for sports. In the end, these differences led to ethnic patterns visible on sports teams, music ensembles, and other extra-curriculars.

There was another important aspect of extracurriculars: how par-ents balanced the twin goals of guidance and autonomy for their chil-dren. As parents, we all try to guide our children. Especially when they are young, this can mean strongly encouraging or even requiring par-ticular activities. Parents in Woodcrest told me about activities they required, usually when their children were younger: Russian School of Math classes, debate, baseball, Sunday school, and music lessons. Whatever the activity, any requirement a parent makes tends to wane by the time teens get to high school, when most parents move toward more autonomy for their children. Aside from nudging (or mandating) our children to particular activities, we also attempt to support their autonomy and self-expression by providing space for them to "develop their passions," especially as they grow older.[7] This was true for all parents in Woodcrest as well. They all felt the need to engage in this delicate balancing act—maintaining their children's autonomy (or at least, the illusion of autonomy), while also ensuring their children participate in activities that they felt would develop important life skills and make them competitive for the college admissions process.

But how parents encourage their children's autonomy is shaped by their cultural context. Upper-middle-class American parents place a particularly high priority on autonomy, which leads their children to a sense of agency and entitlement in the world, as Annette Lareau has shown in her study of class differences in parenting among Black and white American parents.[8] Large-scale studies show that Americans in general tend to emphasize self-expression more than people in India and China, and Indian and Chinese parents are less likely than parents in the West to emphasize children's autonomy.[9] This pattern holds after migration to the United States.[10] And again, these messages are successfully transmitted to children: children's autonomy seems to matter more for emotional well-being and motivation for white US children than it does for children in Asia or Asian American children.[11]

Indeed, in Woodcrest, Asian parents felt more comfortable explicitly steering their children to particular activities while white parents seemed to place more importance in their children choosing their activities. This difference was another domain in which white parents sometimes drew boundaries between themselves and Asian parents. In fact, here is where we start to see white parents in Woodcrest expressing a sense of superiority over Asian parents. They sometimes believed their choices and decisions simply made them better parents.

WHITE PARENTS

Avery and her family moved to Woodcrest for its good schools and its proximity to her spouse's job at an electronics firm. We met her in chapter 2, and heard about her message to her children about doing their best in school but not needing to take the highest-level classes, especially given their numerous sports activities. She said that Woodcrest

High School has "a reputation for being a pressure cooker, which we've tried to avoid with our kids." While Avery advised her kids not to take too many honors-level classes, they were more intense when it came to sports. We spoke most about her youngest child Carly, the only one still in high school. Avery explained Carly's vigorous participation— she played on two varsity teams (basketball and soccer) and did club sports throughout the year as well—as something innate:

> She was born that way. Absolutely. She's always been a very physical kid. . . . She taught herself to swim at three. She would swim across the swimming pool by herself. She was on a swim team when she was four. . . . She has these injuries. I'm like, "Get in a pool!" In that way I'm a little bit of a tiger [mom], because I know what's good for her body.

In a town in which many Asian parents are stereotyped as tiger moms, Avery's reference to herself as a tiger mom was a surprise. Mothers rarely self-identify as tiger moms—this is a label full of judgment, one to be avoided. I suspect Avery felt less stigma with the label for two reasons. First, Avery is white. Second, the stereotype judges mothers who are "tigers" when it comes to academics, but Avery's ferociousness is about sports. She self-identifies as "tiger" when it comes to developing her athletic daughter's physical body, despite her expressed desires for less stress associated with schoolwork and grades.

Avery's insistence that Carly's athleticism was innate may have stemmed from a preference for children's autonomy. When I asked Avery about her goals for her daughter, she deferred to Carly's goals for herself:

> She would like to be in sports therapy or criminology or something like that. . . . She wants to help people with prosthetics who lost limbs, using artificial limbs. She could be anything she wants at this point. I'm just fascinated watching. I don't really have any specific goals for her, except to support where she's going.

I was struck by Avery's deferral to her daughter, and her desire to watch things unfold, as if her influence played no role, despite her strong opinions about what would be good for Carly.

Still, Avery may have influenced her children more than she realized. Athletically built, Avery came to our interview dressed in sports gear, with "personal trainer" written on her T-shirt. While Carly taught herself to swim at age three, it was her parents who signed her up for a swim team at age four. In other words, Avery actively shaped Carly's early interest. Another family might never have been near a pool with their three-year-old, and if they did find their three-year-old swimming, many would have left it at that rather than seek a swim team that started even before kindergarten. Still, while Avery may have played an important role in cultivating Carly's skills as a star swimmer, the narrative by which she described her daughter's athletics emphasized personal interest much more than the narratives I heard from Asian parents. And as we'll see, these narratives often led to moral judgments about good parenting.[12]

Avery's parenting typified what I found among white parents in Woodcrest—she supported extracurricular excellence and varsity sports, and she emphasized her children's autonomy, even while subtly playing a role in what her children ultimately did beyond school hours. Parents like Avery took pride in the assertion that their children came to intense participation themselves, without needing to be pushed.

Coach Rebecca was similar. Her two children excelled in sports. Her daughter played on the US national basketball team for her age group. A former college basketball player herself, Rebecca beamed, "Both of our kids are very good athletes. They love it. At a very early age we said, 'We'll do [sports]. But if you ever complain once about going to practice, it will stop. Because *you have to want to do this*.' Like I am not into the kicking, screaming, dragging, 'you're going!' sort of thing." Still, Rebecca supported her daughter's love of basketball by spending tens of thousands of dollars on participation in various leagues and for travel to practices and games across the country and even abroad.

Perhaps to defend herself against potential criticisms that she may have pushed her daughter's high achievement in sports, Rebecca contrasted her daughter to her son. She told me her son joked about his sister's sport: "My son, we laugh all the time. He's like, 'Did I ever score?' I'm like, 'Honey, you never did.' He's like, 'I swear, like I must have scored at least once!' And I'm like, 'No. Didn't happen!'" The implication was that her daughter, unlike her son, had natural talent in her sport. Still, Coach Rebecca's son played three other sports at the varsity level, and one of those at the club level as well. That is, it may have been inevitable in a coach's family that a child would play sports, and do so at an elite level, even while they had choice about *which* sports in which they would excel, perhaps based on some kind of proclivity for particular sports or skills featured in those sports. In Coach Rebecca's view, her son was destined for the sports he plays given his talents and interests, his sister destined for hers given her talents and interests. I noticed a few years later that both of Coach Rebecca's children were recruited by multiple Division I colleges to play, well before the usual college admissions process. The contrast between the expressed beliefs in autonomy of parents like Rebecca and Avery versus the more subtle ways in which they guided their children also shows the importance of paying attention not only to what parents *say* but also to what they *do* when considering the influences on children's achievements, extracurricular and otherwise.[13]

From Avery and Coach Rebecca's accounts it should be obvious that high-level athletics took incredible resources—time and money. And many white parents seemed willing and able to expend them. Ashley, another white mom, told me that her daughter played varsity soccer for four years at Woodcrest High School, and her son played as well. Ashley explained the complexity of soccer in Woodcrest:

> [My son] actually didn't play [varsity] one year because he played academy. Academy soccer is year-round, and it's kind of more focused and intense. So he played that for a year, so he couldn't play at Woodcrest that year. . . . You start out in club soccer and then you try out and supposedly the best kids play academy. . . . It's a lot of driving, a lot of travel. And a lot of money.

I asked about the costs associated with academy soccer:

> I think it was $2,500 to be part of the club, $250 for the kit, and then you were traveling every weekend to [other states]. Typically you could do that in a day, though not always. So whether you had to pay for a hotel or not. And then there were [college] recruiting tournaments. So, Florida, or Virginia, or California, there's Las Vegas. Or ID camps. . . . If you want to go to a certain college, you go their ID camp for two or three days.

As Ashley described her son's soccer, I found myself confused about all the different levels—beyond the usual JV and varsity at school, there was club, academy, tournaments, and ID camps (ID camps are residential summer camps that involve training in front of multiple college coaches, who come to identify students to recruit to their teams in the future). I had to stop her midsentence more than once to clarify.

In the United States varsity sports teams regularly play for over a dozen hours every week. And for most sports at Woodcrest High School, intensive varsity teams were the only option. Parents who remained committed to varsity sports (or other time-intensive extracurriculars), mostly white, advised their children to adjust their academic levels of classes accordingly. Insisting that their children not overload their schedules with all advanced classes was part of their cultural repertoire for balancing academics and extracurriculars.

Of course, not all white families are the same, and many white students were not athletes. Jennifer, a white mother who met her husband at the Ivy League university they both attended and where their children now go to college, was different from most white parents I met. She signed her children up in elementary school for two different competitive problem-solving programs and required both children to join the debate team during ninth grade. Jennifer described the other children in problem-solving competitions and the debate team as almost exclusively Asian: "Often our kids were the only white person on a team." She felt some affinity with the immigrant parents of children on those teams: "They share a value around raising their kids that seems closer to our family's values. . . . It may have to do more with maybe a shared value around education." Jennifer grew up working class, and was the first in her family to go to college. Unlike the few other white parents who seemed to integrate more with Asian families in Woodcrest, she did not train in a STEM field. Still, her preferences resonated with more Asian than white families. While she did not connect her working-class background to her requirement that her children try debate in ninth grade and signing them up for academic extracurriculars early on, I did wonder if she connected with immigrant families because of their shared lack of history in the white upper-middle class in the United States. Jennifer was not an athlete, so I assumed her academic achievement in high school was what landed her in the Ivy League university she attended, a experience similar to many immigrant Asian parents whose academic achievements landed them at top colleges in Asia, eventually leading to opportunities that enabled them to move to Woodcrest.

ASIAN PARENTS

I did not meet any Asian parent or student who spoke of taking fewer honors classes to make room for sports, or of the possibility of being recruited for a college team. Asian parents tended to see sports as a means for physical fitness rather than as a domain for excellence, leading many to place lower priority on sports than white parents did. Sometimes this led Asian parents to press their children to quit sports teams, especially intensive varsity sports teams. Sharmila, an Indian mother of recent Woodcrest High School graduates and a teacher herself, was one such parent. Sharmila described her message to her children when they were in high school,

> I didn't tell my kids to go to a certain school. But definitely to study. That's your first priority. . . . If you have to leave certain activities, you leave. I told my son so many times to leave swimming because he was not doing his homework. But he said, "No, I want to do swimming." So he was doing all that and I was worried about him. He was doing too much. . . . Asian kids definitely know that studies are their first priority.

Sharmila should not have worried—her son went on to a top university that admits less than 10 percent of applicants. Sharmila's language around her son's course load paralleled the language Coach Rebecca used to describe her children and the sports they played. Sharmila said, "My son took a lot of AP courses. He was just that kind of person. . . . He took it upon himself. . . . So yeah, there was a lot of work. . . . Many times I said, 'If it's too much for you, don't do it.'" Despite her message, Sharmila's Ph.D., coupled with peers who also took high-level classes, likely made academic excellence a key element of her son's cultural repertoire.

Nandi, an immigrant Indian mother, had a son who loved sports, despite his mother's ambivalence. Nandi tried to stop Anish from joining the freshman football team in ninth grade: "I didn't want him to try football. . . . I literally, I said, 'I'm not signing you up.'" She worried about injuries from football, describing her son as "not like a big boy or anything. He's a skinny guy." Eventually Nandi was overruled by her husband who signed Anish up, but after a month Anish quit anyway. Anish also swam for the high school team. And he loved baseball, but Nandi preferred he not join another team:

> In the spring, he wants to play baseball. Last year he tried and he couldn't make it, because he is not doing baseball training throughout the year. But he loves baseball. And he has been play-ing since whenever little league starts. . . . So he's saying this year also, "I want to try out." He's asked me to get a pitch back for him, and he wants to go for some lessons. . . . He doesn't realize, like all the exams are during that time. The AP exams, and the finals will be in the beginning of June. And this is when he has allergies. So everything will add up. But if he really wants to do it, if he makes it, I wouldn't stop him from doing it. Like if he asks me in March or something, I definitely will make arrangements to take him to a couple of practice batting sessions and all. But we won't be like totally focused on getting him into the base-ball team. Because he does one sport, and that should be good enough.

Nandi expresses a desire to support Anish's interests, but focuses on his academic achievement and does not take deliberate steps to help him make it onto the baseball team. Perhaps his interest in baseball would surface early enough to put in the preseason practice along with talent to make the team—both talent and interest could outweigh par-ents' preferences—but the bar was higher for him to make the team. While one sport is good enough for Nandi, when it came to academics it seemed the more the better. Anish excelled in multiple subjects, taking AP biology, honors Mandarin, honors English, and AP statistics. He was a year ahead of even the highest level for his grade in math classes. This contrast was common among Asian American students—many were performing at high levels academically and taking advanced classes in multiple subjects, but when it came to sports, if they participated it was usually in just one sport. Contrast this lukewarm commitment to athletics to the same parents going out of their way—some moving from houses to small rental apartments and even moving jobs to come to Woodcrest—in order to avail themselves of what they understood to be an outstanding public school system in the realm of academics.

A small number of Asian parents lamented the dearth of less-intensive sports at Woodcrest High School. They wanted their children to have some kind of athletic experience, even if they did not appreciate the intensive varsity sports the school offered. The solution, for these Asian parents, was intramural sports. Two Chinese parents shared their interest in intramural sports with me. When I asked Mei-Ling, an immigrant mother from China, what the one thing is that she would want to change about Woodcrest High School, she said,

> I have proposed to the school one thing, but the school has not responded: recreational sports. People talk about reducing stress, having a healthy mind. And there's nothing better than sports. And here, sports is the privilege of a few. . . . Also, the sports teams here, they are all or nothing. When he first started, my son joined the cross-country team. And the cross-country team meets six times a week. You have to make all of them. So then the clubs started, like a month later. And then my son was more inclined to do some of the clubs, even though he would still have two or three days a week to do cross-country. I mean, he's out of the team just because he couldn't make the six-day commitment. So if you have a recreational option, you're just going to go out and run a couple of days a week. That would tremendously help the students reduce stress.

Mei-Ling's solution to student stress was informal sports, but, as we'll see, school leaders and white parents had different ideas about how to address student stress. School administrators told me about requests like Mei-Ling's. In fact, the outgoing principal cited the lack of intramural sports as one issue he wished he could have tackled during his time at the school, despite requests from multiple immigrant parents. Like Mei-Ling, many other Asian parents also felt physical fitness was critical, but for physical fitness teens simply needed a baseline level of activity that could wax and wane with the ebbs and flows of school projects and academic competitions, the same way that many adults tend to exercise more during particular times of year—when work is quieter, when the summer brings longer days to exercise after work, and in January in response to New Year's resolutions.

Asian parents were also more explicitly directive than most white parents. Shuyi, an immigrant Chinese mother, told me that she insisted her son sign up for debate in middle school despite his apprehension:

> In middle school, everybody said Woodcrest debate is good. There's an elective course, but there's a lottery. So I just said, "You should apply and see if you get it." At that time he was not into debate at all. Because he's quiet—he doesn't like to talk that much. He said, "If I don't get in, that will be perfect!" [laughter]. But somehow he got in. And then once he got in, I think the teacher, the group of kids, they do a lot of tournaments—he likes to win. You know, the feeling of getting a medal. So then he said, "Oh, that's good!"

Shuyi's prompting, based on shared community information, got her son in the door, and then luck got him a spot in the class, but his positive experiences, interest, and perceived talents kept him there. Overall, Asian parents more frequently told me they encouraged (and sometimes required) their children to sign up for nonathletic extracurriculars, like supplementary math classes and clubs, robotics clubs, and debate.

Hong, too, was explicit when it came to his preferences for after school-activities. Hong's eleventh-grade son played on Woodcrest's varsity tennis team, and outside of school he participated in both a public speaking club and a competitive math group. I asked Hong how his son got involved in those activities, and he was clear about his own influence: "Most of those are through us parents. Because we have lots of different channels to gather information. And we think, 'Okay, you've got to do something.' I think most of the time, they don't know what they want. . . . So my wife and I did a lot of driving of what to do." The influence of Hong and parents like him may have led to a tennis team dominated by Asian American students: twenty-nine of the forty-two players on his son's team were Asian American. While Hong's son was unusual for his participation in a varsity team in high school, his choice of sport was not.

Still, Hong was also flexible when giving direction. His twelve-year-old daughter loved dance, and took classes in multiple styles, including

Chinese dance and hip-hop. Beyond dance, she was involved in tennis, Chinese school, and advanced math outside of school. Hong said, "Definitely we know that's too much!" Hong laughed when he said this, but I couldn't tell whether this was a nervous laugh at realizing his daughter's hectic schedule might stigmatize him in my mind, or if it communicated his ambivalence about her dance, which perhaps he blamed for her overscheduled life after school. He said about dance:

> We don't think that will lead her anywhere. At the beginning, we didn't [support her interest in dance]. But then we said, "If she really loves it, then we'll give her a chance." . . . So that's why last year she only did twice a week. . . . But she really wanted to do more, so we said, "Okay, let's support you. It takes so much time and money, but it's okay." . . . Math, we said, "Okay, I don't want you to be in the competition level, but you've got to be good at it. That's a foundation." That's kind of a Chinese family [laughs].

Hong delicately considered his daughter's interests—he wanted to grant her some autonomy in her activities—but made clear his expectation that his daughter needed to be solid in math, beyond what she would learn in school alone. In Hong's social world, the baseline for math achievement was not simply doing well in the college prep level math at school; rather, it was doing additional classes outside of school. For him, children with a particular interest or aptitude for math would go to math competitions.

As for tennis, Hong negotiated a deal with his daughter:

> When they were little, I liked to bring them out. Did I want them to be a superstar? No. Because I'm not [laughs]. But I think it's a good activity and it's also good exercise. . . . So they became better and better. My daughter, she is pretty good at it. But unfortunately, she loves dance more, so we had to cut tennis to two times a week. I would rather her to do three times a week or more. But we don't have time. So our agreement is "At least you keep tennis. Don't drop it."

Most parents I met wanted to foster their children's autonomy, especially by the time they got to high school. But many Asian parents, like

Hong, felt comfortable sharing their expectations and influence on their children as well.

US-born Asian American parents seemed to be influenced by this Western focus on autonomy, even more so than immigrant Asian parents. Grace was one such parent. She mentioned that Asian American kids in Woodcrest were overrepresented in the school orchestra, and perhaps to stop me from seeing her son as a stereotype of Asian Americans, told me that she "really didn't want him to play. . . . I remember clearly announcing to all my friends, 'No way are my kids going to play a musical instrument.'" She then told me the story of her daughter, the elder of her children, begging to learn to play the violin at age three, and then her son joining those lessons eventually. After a few years her daughter quit but her son persisted. Her story of early interest is not unlike Avery's description of her daughter's swim team at age four. And yet it is probably not mere coincidence that Grace's Asian American children took to the violin and Avery's white child to sport. Still, beyond the orchestra, Grace's daughter was an outstanding athlete—she placed third in a national ice skating competition. To prepare, she spent twenty-five hours per week on skates, unusual for an Asian American student in Woodcrest. Grace's childhood in the United States probably shaped her own cultural repertoire, such that she was willing to allow her child to spend dozens of hours every week skating, while the Woodcrest environment alongside Grace's childhood in an immigrant Chinese family may have ensured that Grace's children still took interest in activities like string instruments more common among Asian American youth.

WHAT THE KIDS DID

Of course, parents are not the sole drivers of what teens ultimately do. There are students' peers, their natural proclivities and talents, a particularly inspiring teacher or mentor, and the activities available to them at costs they can afford and in locations and times they can get to. Still, parents did seem to influence patterns I found in what kids actually did. Nearly two-thirds of white students participated in some kind of sports activity, compared to just over half of Asian American students. At the elite sports level the difference was even more dramatic: over 40 percent of white students participated in varsity sports, compared to one-fourth of Asian students. Asian students were underrepresented in three-fourths of sports offered.[14] A small number of sports attracted a disproportionate number of Asian American players—tennis, volleyball, boys' swimming.[15] These are sports outside of the traditional American ones—baseball, basketball, and football, for example—which may have enabled immigrant families to gain a foothold more easily (see table 3.1).

On the other hand, more than 70 percent of Asian American students at Woodcrest High School participated in an academic group or club, compared to 43 percent of white students. Asian Americans were also more than twice as likely as white students to participate in one of the school's orchestras or bands, with nearly half doing so.[16] These patterns parallel trends in the US overall. Across the United States, Asian American kids tend to participate in school clubs more than their peers of other races; however, they are less likely to participate in sports.[17]

As with academics, I found more resonance and less rebellion when I compared how students talked about extracurriculars to how their parents did so. Earlier we heard from Avery about her athletic daughter Carly. I met Carly at school before I met Avery, right after the school day ended one day, during the time between the end of school and the beginning of basketball practice at four. Like many students, she was much taller and broader than me—she looked like an athlete. Wearing a sweatshirt, black leggings, Converse all-stars, and an ankle brace, Carly walked with confidence as we looked for a quiet space to talk.

With four older brothers, Carly could barely remember a time when she wasn't playing sports (recall that her mom got her onto a swim team at age four). She played for the varsity Woodcrest soccer team in the fall, and the varsity basketball team in the winter. Basketball met six days a week for practices that lasted at least two hours, plus weekly games. In the spring she played for an elite club soccer team, with some games played much further afield—she told me about an upcoming game that was going to take her family over nine hours to reach. That team also met during the late fall and winter seasons for off-season practices forty-five minutes away. Carly hoped to get recruited to play for a college team. Avery would have been pleased to hear that Carly told me that "my parents don't put pressure on me."

Avery would have also been pleased to hear that Carly too thought she

TABLE 3.1: Sports participation by race, Woodcrest High School

SPORT (sports with >30 participants included)	% ASIAN AMERICAN (overall: 36%)	% WHITE (overall: 52%)	% BLACK, LATINX, MULTIRACIAL (overall: 11%)
Boys swimming	70	24	6
Boys/girls tennis	68	25	7
Boys/girls volleyball	54	32	14
Ultimate frisbee	38	56	6
Track/indoor track	28	59	13
Girls swimming	26	70	4
Golf	22	78	0
Cross-country	21	68	11
Boys/girls soccer	20	72	8
Football	17	64	19
Skiing	13	84	3
Boys/girls basketball	11	72	17
Baseball	10	83	6
Boys/girls lacrosse	6	88	7
Field hockey	8	90	2
Boys/girls ice hockey	3	92	5

Source: Woodcrest school data 2017.

should limit her academic involvement to make room for sports. Carly was taking AP history when I met her, and she took honors chemistry:

> I almost did AP chem. But then I decided that would be too much. And I just didn't want to put too much pressure on myself to do everything. . . . I knew it would get a lot tougher this year.

And with all the sports, especially since I added on club soccer through the winter.

This struck me as just the opposite of what was reported by many Asian American students and parents, who tempered sports ambitions to accommodate their myriad academic commitments. And it worked, evidenced by Carly's solid grades, which she reported as "A's, some A-'s, occasionally a B+, but mostly just A's."

Many Asian American students explicitly told me about heeding their parents' advice about prioritizing academics over extracurriculars, especially time-intensive sports. Ajay, the son of Indian immigrants who previously ran on both the cross-country and track teams at Woodcrest before quitting, said, "My parents encouraged me to do track at the beginning [in fifth grade] because it's a healthy activity that takes up your time in a positive way." Later, however, Ajay's parents nudged him away from athletics: "Now in high school I think [my parents] are less excited about track and cross-country because it takes up a lot of time." In eleventh grade, the year I met him, Ajay quit track in order to save time for academics. Still, Ajay participates in other extracurriculars. He takes private trumpet lessons, plays in the top-level concert band at Woodcrest, and also plays for the audition-based Woodcrest jazz band. Ajay was also involved in a student organization focused on mental health. Still, together these commitments did not add up to the hours required by joining one varsity sports team. Beyond extracurriculars, Ajay told me he took "mostly AP and honors" classes and managed to earn a 3.95 GPA. His extracurricular and academic accomplishments suggested that Ajay worked hard and was willing to commit to high-level extracurriculars, yet shied away from the commitment required to participate in varsity sports during the most intense year of high school to date.

Sophia, the daughter of Chinese immigrants, has been swimming on the YMCA swim team since elementary school, and continued on that team in high school rather than join the school team because it was less intensive. She said:

During the school year, I actually don't go to practices that much. Maybe like once or twice a week. But I do it a lot over the summer. . . . The school swim team is more of a time commitment.

I think you have to meet every day and you have meets every week. And I really didn't have the time for that.

The casual YMCA swim team allowed Sophia to keep fit while accommodating her intensive academic schedule, which included AP chemistry, AP history, honors English, and honors math—these were the highest levels available to eleventh graders. While Sophia was casual about swimming, she did have one intensive extracurricular, debate, perhaps a recognition that she would need to show intensive commitment to something outside of school when she applied to college. Sophia attended debate tournaments and was about to go to nationals when I met her. The previous summer she attended a residential debate camp, and she planned to do so again the summer after we spoke. She got into debate on the recommendation of a Chinese American friend in ninth grade. Given her course load and racial differences by academic track and extracurriculars at Woodcrest High School, Sophia was more likely to make Asian American friends, and those friends were more likely to introduce her to debate than to varsity sports. In other words, students' social networks, influenced by academic tracking, enhanced racial differences in extracurricular participation, making Asian American students like Sophia even more likely to participate in nonathletic extracurricular activities, even beyond the influence of their parents.

One white student, Colleen, did complain about the competitiveness of soccer in Woodcrest. Colleen described the tryouts for varsity soccer: "I found it was very competitive.... So it wasn't a very fun environment. I loved soccer, but I didn't really like the competitive part of it." Being cut from the soccer team led Colleen to join the track team, rather than quit sports altogether: "I got cut from the team. So then I started track. I really like it.... It's not a sport you have to try out for. You join it and it's kind of like on your own level. You can be like super intense about it, or you can be very relaxed."

Colleen was the only student who described participation on a varsity team as more relaxed. Perhaps because track is more an individual sport than a team sport, it enabled greater participation, with a bigger range of performance levels among team members. Still, note that when Colleen wanted to quit soccer she did not give sports up altogether—rather, she simply switched to a different sport, one that Indian American Ajay quit to make room for rigorous academics. Carly, Avery's daughter who played soccer intensively, also imagined switching to a less-intensive team when I asked if she ever thought about quitting soccer. Carly told me that "I don't think I've ever thought seriously of not ever playing again. If I did, I would just go to a lower club or intramural or something like that."

The lower priority of sports among Asian families may have made it harder for Asian Americans to make it onto high school teams even if they wanted to play. Asian American students at Woodcrest High were almost 50 percent more likely than their white peers to report that they tried out for a sport (or other activity, where cuts were less common), but didn't make it.[18] Genevieve, a Chinese-born mother who attended a US boarding school for high school and has lived in the United States since then, contrasted her son's middle school experience with Woodcrest High School,

> I thought he had a very well-rounded experience in middle
> school. Not as much in high school. . . . What I observed is that
> because the school is much bigger, it became a lot more difficult
> to get into activities. And he . . . tried out for basketball, soccer,
> [but] he wasn't able to get on teams.

Eventually Genevieve sent her son to the same boarding school she attended, in part because the school "had sports for every kid. . . . You're required, actually, to do sports." Her own experiences at boarding school may have shaped Genevieve's priority placed on sports, in contrast to most parents I met who were born in Asia.

Paul, a Chinese father, reported that even after five years of swimming with club teams, his son could not make it onto the varsity swim team at Woodcrest High School. Saachi, an immigrant Indian mother, told me that her son "used to always play soccer. He couldn't get on the soccer team. Kids passionate about a sport cannot get in because it's so competitive. There are so many things, so many people. I think there are like 76 spots and 400-odd kids try out for it." Of course, white students also experienced competition for sports teams. Indeed, 17 percent of white students reported having tried out for something but not making it in high school. Still, this was significantly lower than Asian students' reports of not making it onto a team they tried out for.

These findings resonate with data on admissions to Harvard University, which became public in the wake of the ongoing lawsuit by Students for Fair Admissions. The data suggest that one reason for Asian American applicants' lower admit rates than whites' (when comparing students with the same grades and SAT scores) is the higher likelihood that white applicants are recruited athletes—identified prior to the admissions process as players the coaches want for their teams.[19] White students admitted to Harvard are four times as likely to be recruited athletes as Asian American students admitted to Harvard.[20] Overall, white kids in the US are far more likely to be recruited by college coaches to selective colleges than kids of any other race.[21] And at Woodcrest, in one year over forty students were "recruited athletes"—meaning coaches identified them as students to admit as long as they achieved a minimum academic level—yet just five of those students were Asian American. Sports recruiting was a significant path to elite colleges in Woodcrest—10 percent of students going on to top colleges from Woodcrest High School were sports recruits.[22] So sports may be an enduring area in which whites are able to maintain advantage over Asian Americans in college admissions.

RACE AND THE PURSUIT OF EXTRACURRICULAR EXCELLENCE

Many white parents did for sports what many Asian parents did for academics: pay for extra coaching, enroll their children in activities outside of the school system, and support their children's performance at high levels in multiple domains. Going into this research I thought that these differences would lead to critiques from Asian parents about sports that were parallel to those I heard from white parents about academics. I imagined that some Asian parents might even lobby for less extracurricular-related stress and shorter hours on the field, just as some white parents lobbied for a new homework policy to reduce schoolwork and academic pressure. In other words, I assumed they would advocate for their own children in ways similar to white parents in the realm of academics.

I also wondered if I would find some Asian families who were spending considerable energy cultivating athletic excellence in their children, just as they did to cultivate their children's academic excellence. That is, once Asian families realized that sports are an important avenue to college admission in the US, unlike in Asia, I wondered if some would shift their priorities away from academics and toward athletics, especially if they noticed serious talent and interest in their child. This is what theories of immigrant assimilation would predict—immigrants changing their behaviors to be more like established Americans, in pursuit of the American dream.

I was wrong on both fronts. Asian parents seemed to take a "live and let live" approach to athletic excellence. That is, most did not seem to mind when their children could not make it onto competitive varsity sports teams. The immigrant parents I talked to wanted to chart their own pathways to success, and despite being newcomers to the US, they felt quite confident in those pathways. They did not seem to feel the need to assimilate into the sports aspect of upper-middle-class white culture. In fact, some used white families' emphasis on sports to justify and defend their own emphasis on academic excellence, drawing a parallel between the two. Most Asian parents did not disapprove of the high sports standards at Woodcrest High School, and they did not criticize white families for limiting entrée onto high school teams only to those with intensive prior training. This was simply not a competition that they envisioned their children to be a part of.[23] Instead, they seemed to more fully embrace the meritocracy of academic competition in which they were embedded. They put all their eggs in the academic basket, perhaps in part because they felt it was their best shot at winning.

CHAPTER 4

Emotional Well-Being: Happiness and Status

JUST BEFORE I STARTED VISITING Woodcrest High School and speaking to students and parents, I attended a forum for candidates running for two new seats on the school board. The forum was held in a basement meeting room of Woodcrest's public library. I planted myself in a seat in the back. Soon, the room was full. I assumed I would hear questions about how candidates would ensure the most rigorous teaching, the latest technology in school, and high levels of excellence. In this town of suburban liberals, I also guessed that many would express support for the town's diversity and the busing program that made it even more diverse. But what I heard that night took me by surprise.

Every single question the audience asked was—whether implicitly or explicitly—about the emotional well-being of the kids. Parents wanted to know whether candidates thought student stress was an important issue, where they stood on it, and what they planned to do about it, asking: "Do you think there should be a limit on how many AP classes a student can take?" "Do you agree with creating limits on how much homework teachers can assign?" "How *should* the district address mental health?" "What is at the root of our children's stress?" While some parents were clearly looking for guidance about this tricky topic, others seemed to be using this hot topic to gauge a candidate's stance on particular policies. But regardless of their motivations, I realized that night—before I had even set foot in Woodcrest High School or interviewed any parents—that the emotional lives of students were a source of huge concern and significant tension. This was true for white and Asian parents alike (even if their cultural repertoires for addressing children's emotional well-being sometimes differed, as we'll see).

Fretting over one's children and their emotional well-being was a primary activity for parents in Woodcrest. Of course they worried about whether their children were doing well in school, but they seemed to worry much more about whether kids were getting enough sleep, whether they were having enough fun on the weekends, and whether the pressure to achieve was pushing them to depression and anxiety. And they raised alarm bells at the school survey data showing that one in six students at the high school had "seriously considered attempting suicide" sometime in the past twelve months.[1] And as with parenting in other domains, ethnic tension simmered related to what parents were doing and how the district should address their concerns.

I did not expect these worries to be so clearly front and center, but perhaps I should not have been surprised. After all, the concerns I found in Woodcrest clearly parallel worries that we've heard across the country.[2] A growing number of studies show that intensive parenting at home and high levels of academic rigor at school can lead to psychological strain in children, conflicts between teachers and parents, and family conflict.[3] These worries are not new—in fact, parents were concerned that homework could damage children's emotional health over a century ago in the United States, with many municipalities and even the entire state of California banning or limiting homework.[4] Others blame more recent heightened stress among upper-middle-class teens on competition for college admission.[5] Some even suggest a full-blown mental health crisis among American adolescents, with upper-middle class children particularly vulnerable to bouts of depression and anxiety that emerge from the dogged pursuit of excellence.[6]

This national (and century-old) conversation about teen stress seems implicitly to be about *white* upper-middle-class teens.[7] However, there is an additional and different conversation about so-called Asian tiger parenting for what some view as excessive pressure to achieve.[8] Some studies find that Asian American young adults report their parents to have very high educational expectations, leading those lacking stellar achievements to experience "feelings of shame, embarrassment, and depression."[9] These feelings often stem from weak relationships between Asian American youth and their immigrant parents, or a sense of obligation to parents to achieve.[10] Indeed, Asian American youth have higher rates of suicidal thoughts and attempts and lower self-esteem than white youth.[11] On the Harvard campus, six of the nine suicides from 2007 to 2017 were Asian American students, although they only made up 20 percent of the student population.[12] And yet Asian Americans are much less likely to utilize mental health services than any other racial group in the United States, even when they have a demonstrated mental illness.[13]

At the same time, parenting norms are changing in Asia. For example, Pei-Chia Lan, in a study of Chinese parents in the United States and Taiwan, found that upper-middle-class Chinese parents pay much more attention to their children's emotional needs than in the past, due in part to transnational flows of ideas about parenting between China, Taiwan, and the United States.[14] It was evident that concerns about emotional well-being had made it to immigrant Asian parents in Woodcrest too.

When it came to concerns about children's happiness and stress, sometimes it felt like Woodcrest families were playing "opposite day." The typical parent-child conflict story we are used to hearing is that parents are all about trying to get their kids to focus, work hard, and get A's. I remember as a child overhearing my parents express disdain for my classmates' parents who rewarded good grades with money (my immigrant Asian parents expected nothing less than A's, which weren't seen as exceptional in my house). Even local businesses did their part to try to motivate hard work and dedication to school: we could bring our report cards to the local arcade and get tokens for every A or B we earned. Across all of these particular "solutions," the overall picture is clear: the biggest problem parents have, it seems, is getting our kids to do more academically. And this is still the typical story in much of the country, and for me as a parent outside of Woodcrest. When my son's middle school sent home a letter alerting parents to the option of doing extra work to gain credit for accelerated math, my son sheepishly let me know he had already declined the offer, leading to a heated argument between us. But this was the exact opposite of what I found in Woodcrest. There, as we have seen, many parents of high school students were asking their children to put on the brakes. To do less homework. To take fewer APs. To quit varsity sports. Everyone seemed to be fretting about this ill-defined but increasingly important notion of mental health. Some parents even turned to teachers and the principal for help in conveying the message that the relentless focus on academic achievement was too much.

An overarching concern about teen emotional health dominated many community meetings I attended, as well as interviews with school staff and other members of the community, even those who didn't have kids at the high school. Of the five people I interviewed who had run for school board, two ran on a platform primarily aimed at reducing student stress, another two started to focus on student stress after hearing about suicides, and the fifth listed the issue as one of their top five priorities. Multiple town organizations addressing emotional health among youth provided a variety of services, including free counseling that did not require parental notification; events for parents with nationally known speakers offering advice on reducing student stress and fostering independence; and a suicide prevention program.

Most school staff and administrators in Woodcrest seemed to be aligned with parents in their concerns about students' emotional health, with coordinated efforts to reduce student stress. When a new superintendent was hired shortly before the start of this research, improving student mental health was one of five identified goals for the district. The high school principal's monthly letters to the school community also emphasized the need to dial back achievement and not make college admission the sole focus of high school. Multiple parents told me about how the principal, speaking at the high school orientation for eighth grade students and their parents, implored students to limit their number of advanced classes in ninth grade in order to maintain a reasonable workload, even if their eighth-grade teachers were recommending the advanced track in multiple subjects. Students and parents also reported that in that same meeting the principal had practically begged them not to talk about college at all in ninth grade.

Changes reflecting these concerns were everywhere at Woodcrest High. Soon after I began my research, a teacher told me about the school's relatively new Peace Space, a small room for relaxation and reflection, complete with couches, low lighting, and arts and crafts activities. I sometimes found a handful of girls chatting or snacking in the room when I passed by. Woodcrest had already decided to stop calculating numerical class rankings and did not weight students' grade point averages for AP and honors classes like most high schools do. The school did not name a valedictorian. All of these were attempts to discourage competition among students to be at the top of the class and to reduce the incentive for students to take more advanced classes just to boost their GPAs. The year that I began this research the school also implemented a school-wide study hall period three days a week, a change led by Mr. O'Brien, a school administrator. He said:

> Students have been saying for years . . . that they're stressed out. . . . So there was a perception of a need for some sort of flexibility in our schedule. . . . And the feedback through surveys is that that helped lower the stress for students. Students feel like they have access to the teachers, and they're getting more opportunities to get things done during the day and therefore spending less time at home doing schoolwork, which I feel has a huge impact on student well-being.

Woodcrest High School also tried to reduce stress by instituting an honors chemistry class two years prior to the start of this research, with the intention of pushing some students from AP-level chemistry to honors, a slightly slower-paced class but still appealing to students who would not be satisfied with taking the college prep track (unfortunately, this change resulted in even fewer students taking college prep chemistry, but the number taking AP barely budged). Overall, while school staff and parents alike were concerned about students' emotional lives, the actions the predominantly white school staff took at school to address emotional well-being most frequently aligned with the desired actions of white parents, as we'll see.

PARENT CONCERNS ABOUT EMOTIONAL WELL-BEING

As parents in modern society, worrying about our kids is just what we do, a marked difference from previous generations.[15] We parents can be unrelenting in our anxieties. Catharine Warner, in a 2010 study of middle-class parents and their elementary school children, found that parent concerns about their children's emotional well-being seemed so excessive that they were dismissed by teachers.[16] Warner noticed parents engaging in what she calls "emotional safeguarding," which includes habitual "intervening to protect a child's self-esteem, and expecting that teachers understand a child's unique personality"; on the flipside, she found that teachers viewed such behaviors as unnecessary expressions of parental anxiety.[17]

Warner hypothesized that as children grow older and academics become more central to their school experiences, parents will worry less. And that decrease in turn would make room for more worries about academic achievement. In Woodcrest, I found the opposite. Many parents shared with me concerns about their children's emotional health that *grew* as their children grew older. Hualing, an immigrant Chinese mother, said,

> I quit my job to be a housewife, to take good care of my kids and make sure they have a good education, go to a good school. That's the initial goal. But after a few years I realized this was not correct ... because I felt so stressed. Every day I would look at the tests. On exam day, I would worry about the exams.... So my parenting style changed. [Now] I'm not the normal Chinese parent that just wants their kids to go to the top school.

Hualing's early focus on tests probably had to do with her own upbringing—when she was growing up in China, after every test her school would publicly post a list of the students in rank order. She said, "This was really stressful. Even if you are the top student, you are afraid you cannot retain the top spot. If you are the last student, you are so ashamed.... I hope they have changed it by now." I found Hualing's mention of her own feelings of stress refreshingly honest. We often tell ourselves that we are worrying for the sake of our children, when in reality our anxieties often reflect our own insecurities about being good enough parents.

As Hualing's children grew, she considered their happiness. She told me that she hoped that as young adults her children would "enjoy what they're doing. Have friends. And then have impact on society, on the field they focus on. Have respect in the field they're working on."

Like Hualing, Rana, an Indian immigrant mother, told me she stopped pushing her kids after elementary school, though Rana's shift was related to extracurricular activities:

> There was a time that I would say "My child has to do this and this and this and this." I wanted them to be very busy.... Then I

kind of realized that I didn't want to do that anymore. . . . I really wanted them to find things to do that they really wanted to do with themselves, that they liked doing.

Like white and Black upper-middle-class parents of elementary school children in Annette Lareau's study of "concerted cultivation," Rana kept her young children busy with activities. But as they grew older, Rana seemed to focus more on their autonomy and a desire for them to enjoy their activities. Still, I sensed a hint of ambivalence when I spoke with Rana. She contrasted herself to "other parents" who, as she described it, "have been very good about persisting in keeping the kids on for all of these different activities." She seemed to wish that her fellow parents shared her desire to pull back from all the activities, or else that her son would have chosen to continue with all the activities she had him try. When fellow parents—especially, in the case of immigrants, parents from their same country—were intensive about achievement, it was hard to pull back. In fact, it took an active decision *not* to engage in the intensity apparent all around.

Molly, a white mother of two recent graduates of Woodcrest High School, described a shift between elementary and middle school in academic work that led to increased concerns about stress on her part:

My [children's] elementary school climate was loving and learning based, and exploration based. . . . Then comes middle school. And it hits you like a ton of bricks. Some of the teachers pile the homework on. Some of the teachers start the, "When you're in college, you can't slack off. When you're in college, blah, blah, blah." . . . I remember the homework. There were nights he wept. And I went to talk to the principal about the homework load. . . . Too much homework. Too many hours.

Rather than shift her personal perspective like Rana and Hualing did, Molly laid blame on the school when describing her increasing worry about her son. Some parents reported hearing about their children's peers who were suicidal, which led to increased concern as well.

Growing amounts of academic work, time-consuming extracurriculars, watching other children struggle with feelings of suicide, and personal reflection on what truly matters in parenting all came together to lead most parents of high schoolers to pay attention to their children's emotional health. By the time their children were in high school, most parents emphasized happiness and attention to stress, and the importance of balancing emotional well-being with academic and extracurricular success.[18] Perhaps by the time children were in high school, teens had so fully internalized their parents' and peers' emphasis on high levels of academic and extracurricular achievement that parents could feel confident that their children would pursue excellence without explicit messaging. This enabled parents to focus their messaging on taking care of emotional well-being—getting enough sleep, not being overscheduled, and enjoying life, among other things—without sacrificing achievement.

Parent Goals and Visions for Success: "Happy" and "Not Stressed Out" Children

Parents' goals for their children also often signaled their concerns about emotional well-being. When I asked parents about their goals for their high school–aged children, most reported, among other things, a desire for their children to be "happy," "joyful," or "not stressed out." Patricia, a white mother of three, said, "My goals for [my youngest child, a high school senior] are, number one, to feel happy and self-assured and content. . . . I want her to be happy." Molly, the mother who expressed frustration with the academic work in middle school, told her children that what was crucial was to "find your joy." She shared her message with me:

> You're going to be a human being a lot longer than you're a college student. I want you to be a human being first. . . . I want you to have healthy stress management, healthy outlets, healthy friendships, healthy sense of self. A sense of humor. Get a good sleep. Be around joyful people. . . . You're a person a long time. Every age has stress to manage. Every age has friendship to balance, and competing needs of competing friends to balance. I want my boys to learn balance and take pleasure in living.

I also asked parents what a successful life for their children ten years out would look like, as another way of gauging their priorities and goals.

When Avery imagined a successful future for her athletic daughter, Carly, she said:

> She is not stressed out. She's not having a nervous breakdown. She's happy with the work she does. . . . She gets up and she goes, "I love my job." I don't care how much money she makes. I don't care if she's married or not, if she has kids or not. I just want her to wake up and say, "I really love what I'm doing."

It is worth noting that Avery, like most parents, did not express any specific concerns about her daughter, suggesting that her words were not in response to particular emotional difficulties her daughter faced, but rather reflect what was important to Avery overall.

Dads had similar goals. Fred, a white father, described his goals for his high school–aged son in very simple terms: "emotional development, building and sustaining relationships." James, a white father, served on a town-wide mental health committee. He described the committee's work as "trying to help students come to terms with whatever emotional issues that they have, and advocating for social-emotional learning in the schools from a young age."

Each of these parents had children who were thriving in school academically. Perhaps their children's success in school enabled them to focus on happiness and the importance of balance.

Most Asian parents also spoke of their children's happiness when articulating their goals for their children. Still, they were more likely than white parents to talk explicitly about happiness and educational or material success as going hand in hand. Betty, a Chinese immigrant mother of two, said, "Going to college is a goal. . . . And the other is to be happy." Akshata, an immigrant mother from India, said this about her goals for her son Aarav:

> To get into a good school, yes. And be happy with what he's doing. I always feel that if you're happy with what you're doing, the money will follow. So of course I want him to have a comfortable life. And you do have to work hard to have a good life. Nothing comes for free in this world, right? But whatever he does, he should be happy with it. That's what my goal and wish for him is.

For Akshata, material success and happiness seem to go hand in hand—one cannot be achieved without the other.

Shu heard about pressure at Woodcrest High School back in China when she researched schools online in anticipation of moving to the States; her husband's work brought them to the area, and initially they settled in a different town in the same metro area. She said, "I read a lot of comments, and a lot of people said, 'It's a pressure cooker.'" Two years later, however, Shu's family moved to Woodcrest for its strong STEM focus. Shu described her ideal school as "very caring, very loving." Shu's move in particular highlights the competing interests of parents to cultivate both emotional well-being and excellence, especially as children grew from the elementary up to the high school years.

Saumya, an immigrant mother from India, spoke explicitly about her desire to maintain the right balance between pushing her children to achieve and maintaining emotional health:

> I think it's really hard to find a balance between not stressing the kids out and keeping up with stuff. So I will tell my daughter, "Fridays don't do homework, just chill. Go hang out or watch TV." But then at the same time, come Saturday, [if] she's still chilling out I am like, "Get on with it. Don't leave it for Sunday night." So I think I do more focus on her relaxing. . . . Like she didn't want to take AP bio this year. You know, like "Fine."

One US-born Indian American dad, Salil, also pointed out this tension, but at the level of college admissions. He said about his goals: "What I always say is I just want to optimize for happiness," and then quickly pivoted to college admissions in the next breath: "So ideally we'd love him to go to a Harvard or MIT or whatever." Later in our interview Salil elaborated: "If you think your kid has a shot at [getting admitted to an Ivy League or MIT], you want to encourage them. But you also want to say, 'Look, it's not a big deal.' It's a catch-22. Because you want to say 'strive,' but also, 'don't worry if you don't make it.' Which is conflicting to be honest, right?"

Some Chinese parents, both immigrant and US-born, drew on their Christian faith to express broad goals for their children. Eric, a US-born Chinese American dad who grew up in a working-class family, was one such parent. He contrasted his laid-back style to the pressure his son puts on himself: "My philosophy is as long as you learn to give it your best, you don't have to get all A's. You don't have to be the top of the class. It's a matter of personal learning and personal growth." Eric's son still took honors and AP classes and earned A's and B's. But he told me that his son's friends "are getting all A's and getting into multiple AP classes and honors and so on. So for him, he doesn't think that he [stands out]." Eric went on, "I try not to give them too much pressure, because I know everybody has a different calling in life. From a spiritual point of view, I'd like them to remain faithful to the same faith that I share."

While most parents responded to questions about their goals and definitions of success for their children by mentioning some form of emotional well-being—happiness, fulfillment, lack of stress—six parents, all of whom were Asian, did not.[19] Hong, an immigrant Chinese father, was one such parent. In response to the question about goals for his children, he said, "I think ideally we want them to find something they like to do. And also, at the same time, it can at least sustain their lifestyle." Hong's definition of success in ten years also did not include "joy" or "happiness" like others, did: "My definition of success is that you can provide whatever service or products to benefit more people. That's my definition. You help more people." Note that even while he does not bring up affective dimensions in his goals or definition of success, Hong focuses on work and service, not simply achievement and individual success.

Even while most parents did bring up some aspect of emotional well-being, Asian parents were less likely to identify problems related to emotional well-being as a serious concern in need of solutions. Beyond the six parents described above who did not identify emotional well-being as a goal or aspect of success for their children, other Asian parents did not perceive teen emotional well-being as a problem, even if some of those parents did express emotional well-being as an important goal.[20] Hong, the father focused on work and service, mentioned discussions of "pressure" in Woodcrest schools, about which he said, "I don't think that's a big deal. Stress is anywhere you go. You want to excel but you can't. . . . So that's what I say. It's not a big deal. . . . You have to live with it." Hong described a changing population in Woodcrest that is increasingly Asian, which, as he described it, led to more competition. I asked what he thinks of that competition, and he replied,

I think competition is a positive thing. We're not fighting each other. I think the reason the town itself is getting so much better is because . . . you attract more good students, good families. And then they provide a good environment. And then your kids hopefully will benefit from that environment. . . . So we hope in this environment, everybody wants to do better, everybody wants to work harder. . . . And in that environment, hopefully your kids, they may not be the best, but at least they will go with the flow.

Hong identifies an influence in Woodcrest that social scientists call social capital—the ways that who we know and encounter regularly brings us advantages.[21] His perspective on the value of living in Woodcrest was common—recall all those parents in chapter 1 who moved to Woodcrest in part to be around Woodcrest's well-educated, professional parents and their children. Still, Hong was a minority, even among immigrant parents, in his perspective that pressure is not a big deal at Woodcrest's high school.

Hualing, the mother above who described her shift in parenting as her children got older, worried that all the talk of emotional health in Woodcrest could make problems worse: "I think maybe the kids can overcome [mental health problems] by themselves. . . . But they [educators at school] overemphasize it. I feel it's a negative impact. . . . If nobody talks about it, maybe some people may suffer. But maybe they can overcome by themselves." She felt that even some of her friends overemphasize mental health concerns about their children.

The perspectives of Hong and Hualing were not the norm in Woodcrest. Chinese, Indian, and white parents alike tended to identify goals tied to happiness and reducing stress for their children, and most expressed some desire to address those goals. They wanted to balance their desire to promote excellence in their children with their desire for their children to feel happy inside. Still, parents differed in their views on how the school and community should assist them in doing their jobs of raising simultaneously high-achieving and emotionally healthy kids. While Asian and white parents were aligned in their concerns about emotional well-being, their cultural repertoires for addressing those concerns were different, as we'll see next.

THE BATTLE OVER HOMEWORK

A town battle over homework was already brewing when I started this research in Woodcrest. In a school-wide survey, over half of students reported that homework caused them "a lot" or "extreme" stress. White students reported even more homework-related stress than Asian American students did (despite Asian American students reporting more time every night on homework). Some parents were adamant that reducing homework was a crucial way to reduce student stress; others felt homework was an important part of learning, and some parents even felt that Woodcrest students didn't get *enough* homework. Parents advocating for less homework tended to be white. Often their children played on one or more sports teams, whether for varsity Woodcrest or private club teams; practices and weekend games could easily eat up more than a dozen hours a week, leaving what seemed like impossibly narrow windows for homework. Parents who appreciated the chance for their children to enhance their learning at home tended to be Asian; those who had immigrated to the States as adults had spent even more time on homework when they were children in Asia. Their children tended to have fewer commitments outside of school (and as we saw in chapter 3, some of their kids quit sports to clear space for more academic work after school). Parents across the board were invested in their children's emotional well-being, yet reducing homework as a mechanism for maintaining that well-being was a controversial move.

Some parents brought their concerns to school staff and school board members. For example, Molly, the white mother who implored her children to "find your joy," relayed one of her children's experiences with stressful amounts of homework in middle school. She said, "I went to the principal and said, 'There shouldn't be homework before a school vacation. There shouldn't be three projects due in three classes that are large projects due on the same day. This boy is weeping.' . . . The principal said to me, 'I have parents coming in here telling me there's not enough homework.'"

Molly and other parent advocates were successful in pushing for a new homework policy aimed at reducing the amount of homework in Woodcrest's schools, which was implemented just as my research got under way. The new policy passed by the school board banned homework on religious holidays, long weekends, and during school vacations at Woodcrest High. One elementary school eliminated homework altogether. (That choice was framed as a pilot project that would be used to help decide whether a similar policy should be enacted for all the elementary schools in the district. Eventually, it was adopted district-wide.)

By calling for reduced academic work, these white parents argued for deemphasizing a domain in which their children were outpaced by their Asian American peers. Perhaps it is unsurprising, then, that some immigrant parents disagreed with the new policy. Priya, an immigrant Indian mother, disapproved of the new policy and the decision-making process that led to it: "There was a single voice that was taken into account when this policy change was made. . . . There are many, many parents I've talked to—immigrant more so. They're wondering, 'Why was this change made?'" Priya noted, finally, "It's the majority [vs.] minority." The alignment by ethnicity, with more Asian parents disagreeing with the homework policy and more white parents embracing it, made district leaders less likely to listen to her concerns, as Priya saw it. She said she attended district meetings about the homework policy: "But there was some rolling of eyes, like 'Oh, another immigrant telling us.' . . . When you say, 'That's not stress,' now you're feeding into the same thing they believed about immigrants, that we don't see stress."

Priya pointed out that many white parents advocating for less schoolwork had children very active in sports. She said, as if speaking to a white parent, "Your child was playing sports till nine, so didn't have time to do homework, so your child was stressed. And my child wasn't playing sports, so he was not stressed." In other words, parents could choose to allow their children a hectic sports schedule, but if they did not, the school should assign homework for them to do.

Priya also suggested that school board members did not understand the impact of the policy. She told me that immigrant parents sent their kids to Russian School of Math more frequently as a result of the policy change: "There are many, many [after] schools which have opened up. . . . Their child comes home. 'Do you have homework?' 'No.' So they'll check it. What are kids doing, then? Kids are on devices. It's not that kids are being productive or they're socializing. If that was the intent, that's not happening."

Priya was unusual among Asian parents in her civic engagement. Beyond the sports-academics racial tension she identified, she complained to the superintendent about the way she addressed happiness:

> The superintendent said, "I want the kids to be happy." I said, "What is happiness? Is [there] a singular definition?" So I did challenge her. Her take was, "Look, I went to [low-ranked state school], and I'm happy. I'm superintendent." I said, "Well, that's okay. But maybe that's not happiness for somebody else." So my point to her was, listen to the voices which are saying—the immigrant population. They don't have any bank balances they come with. . . . They start with a hundred dollars, sometimes a thousand. And they create a house. They give their kids education. And the only path to success for them is education.[22]

The unfettered faith in American meritocracy of Priya and others like her was striking. Priya describes Asian families as the true believers in the American dream—being newcomers to the United States, their only way up is through academic achievement, as many described it. While American meritocracy was designed to benefit upper-middle-class whites, Asian Americans in Woodcrest had mastered some of its measures, especially the academic ones. They were, ironically, advocating more for this system than the group it was intended to benefit did.[23]

Asian parents also tended to believe that individual families, not the school, should make decisions about how much academic work to take on. In their view, if a child was stressed about homework, that was the family's fault for not having the child take the appropriate number of intensive classes. Akshata, the Indian mother who shared her desire for both financial security and happiness for her son Aarav, said: "I know people talk about a lot of stress at Woodcrest High School. . . . But a lot of that stress is brought on by the parents. And the students. I personally feel the school system doesn't tell you to take fifteen APs. . . . It's the kids and the parents who are driving that." Sharmila, another Indian immigrant, said,

> We are thinking kids are stressed out. They're not getting enough sleep. And we are hearing all these complaints about "Oh, there's so much homework and there's so much stress on kids." But I

feel like the kids or parents, they're taking it on themselves. Like, nobody asked them to take four AP courses. Obviously in an AP course there will be more homework.

These parents adhere to a very American belief in individualism identified by Alexis de Tocqueville centuries ago.[24] Akshata and Sharmila also seem to believe that some kids are capable of handling copious amounts of homework, while others are not. And those who are not should not hold back those who make time in their schedules to do so and are up for the challenge.

Why did Asian parents tend to advocate for family rather than schoolwide responsibility? While I was sympathetic to parents like Priya, Sharmila, and Akshata, I also noticed that they were trying to protect opportunities to shine in the domain where Asian American students tended to shine already: academics. Both Asian and white parents held cultural repertoires for dealing with emotional health that protected their status. White parents advocated reducing schoolwork, which had the potential to reduce academic achievement at the top, where Asian Americans were outperforming whites. Simultaneously, Asian parents did not want to limit how much students could take on—an absence of limits that enabled top-performing Asian American students to spend as much of their hours outside school on homework as they chose.

Ultimately—and unsurprisingly—the parents advocating for limiting homework prevailed. Other research has shown that white, upper-middle class parents are often skilled at bending schools to their will, sometimes at the expense of students of color attending the same schools.[25] This happens for many reasons. First, they can draw on professional expertise in their advocacy.[26] Second, they can use their social networks to build support for their perspective.[27] Third, their shared racial identity with most school staff—90 percent of teachers and school staff in Woodcrest schools are white—means they are also more likely to share similar cultural repertoires for addressing students' emotional health, such that their repertoires are more likely to align with those of school staff.[28] Finally, minority parents may not have as much of a sense of agency to advocate for change at school as white parents do.[29]

Indeed, this is what happened in Woodcrest. White parents were more actively involved in their children's schools, as volunteers, PTA members, and members of hiring committees, than Asian parents. And they frequently shared the perspective of school staff. One white parent, Jennifer, was on the committee to hire a new school superintendent. She reported that the hiring committee was in agreement about wanting someone who would prioritize socioemotional learning over academics: "We [members of the hiring committee] wanted the same things. We wanted someone who cared about social-emotional learning. We wanted someone who didn't need to be number one [academically]." While all parents may have cared about socioemotional learning, it was white parents who were more likely to prioritize it over academics.

Asian parents mostly kept their views to themselves. For example, when Radha told me about her frustrations with Woodcrest High School, I asked her, "Did you bring any of these things up with the school?," to which she reluctantly, almost apologetically, replied, "I did not. Maybe I should have." Helen, an immigrant Chinese mother, when asked about the homework policy, replied, "I think, not so good. I know a lot of parents talking about, 'Oh, we pay that much money for the houses here so that our kids can get a really good education. And then now you say there's no homework.'" Yet, she also did not bring her concerns to any school staff to advocate for her perspective. In fact, the school principal told me that his main interaction with Asian parents, in contrast his more frequent interactions with white parents, was around their children's class placement: "Wanting to skip a full year of math. It's mostly math and science, STEM. That it's a personal affront to their child's intelligence if the teacher has not recommended their child for AP. . . . [They say,] 'I know my child best. My child can handle it. It's not your job to say that's too many AP classes for my child.'" Mr. Smith, like any good principal, always backed his teachers' decisions and deferred to them to work with families to come to an agreement. He told me that, in contrast, many more white families come to him with a variety of concerns, including related to homework. But when white parents brought up course load, it was most often for the opposite reason: white parents wanted Mr. Smith to convince their children to take on fewer AP and honors classes.

The Asian parents' lack of advocacy was obvious even when the district explicitly invited families to give feedback on the homework policy. Three years into my research the school district tweaked the relatively new policy, opening opportunities for families and school staff to weigh in again. The tweak changed the "no homework" days to make them more predictable, and also expanded the elimination of homework to all elementary schools. Given the strong views many parents expressed in my interviews, I expected a large turnout at the meeting I attended at which parents could voice their perspectives. Instead, I found the school board facing a room of less than twenty in the audience, all but one of whom appeared to be white. The one Indian parent who spoke was the lone voice questioning the wisdom of the policy. At first he did not speak, only walking to the microphone when the board chair announced last call for audience members to speak. The parent then told the board in a quiet voice that without homework his fourth grader was not developing a sense of responsibility, nor getting the "simple repetition" necessary for learning. In contrast, two white teachers spoke forcefully early on in the meeting, and expressed their support for the policy. One white student also spoke earlier, and began her prepared remarks by listing the myriad extracurricular activities in which she participates—student council, volunteer work, a varsity sports team, and more. She then described a schedule in which she had little time to herself or to socialize with her friends. She expressed hope that the school board would take into consideration the hectic schedules of kids like her when they decided whether to keep the homework policy.

I was struck by the paucity of voices, whether at the meeting or in my interviews, suggesting that activities rather than academics be forced to reduce their commitments. Why did no one suggest a new extracurriculars policy, establishing a maximum number of hours on the field or in the robotics lab or days off from extracurriculars, to reduce students' committed hours outside of school to make room for homework, rather than homework making room for hectic extracurricular schedules? I was particularly surprised that only one Asian parent ever suggested this, whether in public meetings or in our one-on-one interviews.

That sole Indian parent was Harleen. Harleen was born and brought up in Ireland, and moved to the US for work. She did express disapproval of the long hours of sports teams in our conversation. When I asked Harleen what she would change about Woodcrest High School if she could change one thing, she shared a strong opinion,

> [I] found the emphasis on sports to be ridiculous. . . . [My daughter] was doing cross-country at one stage. She was doing it four days a week, five days a week. Why do you need to do that? And

then the counselors are like, "Oh, the children are under so much stress here." Yeah, hell, yeah. Cut back on some of the sports, guys!

And when she was playing school soccer, it was like, soccer, soccer, soccer.... Your child doesn't come home till, say, 7:30, 8:00 from school, from soccer. Then they've got homework. Then they've got to have a shower.... What are you putting these kids through? If you're going to do sports, do it every second day. Give the kids a break in the week. They don't have to do it four, five days in a week.... I think that perhaps when the school says that their kids are all very stressed, all the parents should help, the parents should do this. Yeah, but you know what? You guys should also stop and think; what is your sports department expecting of these kids?

Harleen had a warm demeanor. I went to the wrong Starbucks for our meeting, and when I finally found the right one twenty minutes late, I was nervous that she would be irritated. Instead, she greeted me with smiles and a hug. Though we'd never met, she walked up to me and said, "I'm a hugger, I'll give you a hug!" And then she tried to buy me coffee. Still, her outrage about the emphasis on sports was clear, and even more surprising given her positive affect about pretty much everything else. When I asked if she ever brought her concerns to anyone at school, Harleen said, "I think with the counselors, once or twice we talked with them. You know, people shrug their shoulders, right? I don't think the change comes. Perhaps it's this country, the greater emphasis [on sports]." Despite her passion, and her success in a career that required her to speak up and confront colleagues, even Harleen did not take her concerns beyond one or two conversations at school. I also did not hear about this issue in school board meetings I attended or viewed minutes for or in other public discussions among parents in Woodcrest. Harleen's solution was to implore her daughter to quit sports (she wasn't successful). A combination of lack of cultural know-how and the alignment between white parents' perspectives and the perspectives of school staff and leaders made views like hers fall on deaf ears, if they ever made it to school staff in the first place.[30] Overall, it seemed the very American cultural practice of expressing views and concerns to school officials was not part of Asian parents' cultural repertoires for what to do when one disagrees with a policy at school.

EXITING FOR PRIVATE SCHOOL

As far as I could tell, families never left the Woodcrest public schools in order to attend another town's public schools. They either shifted to a private school, or moved because a parent's job took them to a different metro area altogether. No one in Woodcrest—parents, school staff, or local leaders—could name a family that moved away from Woodcrest so their children could attend a different public school. In addition, when I asked parents whether, if they could go back in time, they would have moved to Woodcrest again (or stayed there, for the few who grew up in Woodcrest), nearly all said they would. One exception was a white mother who said she "might have" stayed in the same urban district in which she lived prior to Woodcrest, giving the caveat that if her family hadn't moved, "our kids probably would have ended up in private schools at some point." The only other parent who expressed a preference for other public school districts was Shivani, a US-born Indian American mother whose daughter struggled with mental health–related illness. In a high-performing district like Woodcrest, the only imaginable alternative for most parents was private schools.

Woodcrest parents sought private schools mostly to provide a less stressful environment to their kids. Parents seeking less stress in private schools is not unusual: a study conducted by the National Association of Independent Schools found that one of the four main reasons parents enroll their children in independent schools is dissatisfaction with a school that "is focused almost solely on test scores and academic curriculum." These parents seek "a school that will focus on [their] child's social and emotional development."[31]

Almost all the Woodcrest parents I met whose children attended private schools were white. Robin, a white mother of two who moved to Woodcrest for its schools before her children were born, pulled her younger child from Woodcrest public schools after eighth grade for a private high school. She claimed to be "not your average parent in Woodcrest. I try not to be." She went on to contrast herself to "other" Woodcrest parents:

> We haven't pushed our kids. My daughter who went to school
> here, we encouraged her not to take a lot of APs and all that. She

did take one AP a semester or a year, which is unusual in Woodcrest. You would think that would be a lot. But we really didn't
push her to take a lot of those classes, because we just didn't
think it was healthy for her.

After that daughter's anxiety was exacerbated by the environment at
Woodcrest High School, as she perceived it, Robin sent her younger
child to a private high school: "I think they're not as high pressure.
The focus is not so much on 'How many APs and honors are you taking?'" The tuition at that school is over $50,000 per year and graduates
attend numerous elite colleges, including, in the past five years, four
Ivy League colleges and multiple liberal arts colleges around the country, from Smith to Carleton to Reed. Other private schools attended by
Woodcrest students whose parents I interviewed listed similar tuition
rates and college representation among recent graduates. They also all
included lower percentages of Asian American students than Woodcrest's schools. These were schools designed for white elites decades
ago, and even today white elites were the families most likely to send
their children to those schools.

Bill, a white self-described "laid-back" stay-at-home dad with a
"deep emotional involvement" with his kids, described the pressure at
his children's public middle school in Woodcrest as more intense than
the pressure at the private high school they ended up transferring to;
that pressure was his primary reason for opting out of the public high
school. Bill said, "I call Woodcrest a factory that makes college applications." In contrast, he described a more personal experience in private
school. "It's much more humane in terms of the way it interacts with
students and parents. There are adults who are really engaged personally with your kids." Bill and his wife moved to Woodcrest after their
children were born, with the intention of sending them to Woodcrest's
public schools. His and his wife's separate experiences attending private schools as children likely made private schools an obvious move for
them when they felt dissatisfied with public schools. These experiences
made transferring to private school a part of their cultural repertoire.
Still, the opportunities available in a smaller private school community
were not lost on Bill. He said, "The fact that you can do whatever you
want to do. . . . If you want to play soccer at [private school], you can play
soccer. I mean, my daughters played soccer. They both played soccer as

kids. But there's no way either of them would have played varsity soccer for Woodcrest High School."

Bill's assessment of greater opportunities to shine in private schools is generally correct. Private schools tend to have fewer students than public schools, and indeed, Woodcrest High School educated well over four times as many students as any of the private schools attended by children of parents I met in Woodcrest. Smaller size makes for fewer peers with whom to compete and better prospects in the college admissions process, as Mitchell Stevens shows in his study of college admissions at a selective private college.[32] Stevens also shows how stronger relationships between college admissions officers and private school guidance counselors than between admissions officers and public school counselors give private school applicants an edge.

While comparisons of students' academic levels between individual public and private schools are hard to come by, one Asian American parent suggested that math and music were more advanced in Woodcrest than at the elite private school her children attended. Grace appreciated the smaller class sizes and the emphasis on writing in private school, but noted that "if you're really interested in orchestra and math team, science, Woodcrest is actually a great place to be." She shared the example of a Woodcrest family she knew in which the two children had comparable scores on a math assessment at the same age. But one child attended the same private school as Grace's kids for middle school and was ranked number two in the school, while the other stayed in public school and did not even make it onto the middle school math team.

For Carol and her husband Charles, both white, racial dynamics in achievement also played a role in their decision to move their children to private schools, and they said that explicitly. They sat down with me together in their spacious living room for an evening chat. In a conversation where they seemed to complete each other's sentences, together they described their eldest child's transition to private school:

> She was struggling a little bit with identity issues. . . . Like in math club, she was feeling demoralized, because there were very few girls in math club. And there were maybe two Caucasian kids in math club. We'd say, "How'd you do on the test?" and she'd say, "Well, for the Caucasian kids, I did really well."

She had Asian boys in her grade who were extraordinary. One of them was a nationally ranked math guy and the other one was a pianist. These were savants. Prodigies. . . . And then after them, there were just many super competent, driven kids. . . . She was starting to give up on her intellectual identity.

I sensed that Carol and Charles wanted their daughter to feel successful and special, almost as if she were entitled to a position at the top of the academic hierarchy, but that hierarchy was spoiled by Asian American peers. Given their financial resources, private school was a viable solution to this problem for them.

It is hard to say how much increasing college prospects played a role in the switch to private school for parents like Carol, Charles, Grace, Bill, and Robin, since they never talked about those advantages with me. In the end, many made choices that ultimately would help their children achieve conventional success in the world of achievement and college admissions, but in the name of preserving their children's emotional well-being. This was probably not simply a happy coincidence.

These white families' exits from the public system as their children grew older were not anomalous. A higher percentage of children at Woodcrest High are Asian than the percentage of children in the town, and a lower percentage of children at the high school are white than the percentage in town.[33] In the past five years the number of white students at Woodcrest High School declined by 12 percent, while the number of Asian students increased by over 40 percent.[34] In contrast, while in the town the Asian population overall had increased by just over 40 percent, the white population had decreased by just 10 percent, suggesting both that fewer white families with school-aged children were moving to Woodcrest over time and that some were shifting to private schools.[35] This pattern is not unique to Woodcrest. In the United States overall, white children are more likely to attend private schools than Asian American kids.[36]

ASIAN AMERICAN CULTURAL BROKERS

Most parents in Woodcrest agreed that paying attention to their children's happiness is important. Still, a persistent narrative in town was that immigrants pressure their children too much, leading to poor mental health outcomes among Asian American students in particular. I was most surprised to hear this narrative among Asian parents themselves. A few Indian and Chinese parents, many of whom had adult children they raised in Woodcrest or were born in the United States, acted as "cultural brokers" to their respective communities, conveying messages about the importance of paying attention to their children's emotional well-being, and of easing up on academic expectations, making room for their children's autonomy, and more.[37]

Multiple residents pointed me to a handful of Indian and Chinese immigrant community leaders who established the town's ethnic organizations, encouraged dialogue between their communities and the town's government, and more. These leaders acted as cultural brokers. Suneel was one such Indian leader. He raised his children in Woodcrest and was now a grandfather. Suneel spent much of his spare time forging stronger ties between the established Woodcrest community and its Indian immigrants. Early in his interview, Suneel told me that he is "concerned about the stress" among students in Woodcrest schools. He later told me about a meeting with a candidate for state government: "This is what I was telling [him] the day before yesterday: 'You've got to have more counseling. Go and pass a bill that quadruples the number of counselors in the high schools.'"

Unlike Suneel, most Asian community leaders concentrated their efforts on changing parents rather than policies, sharing messages about the importance of attending to emotional well-being, and how to do so. Cultural brokers strove to shift parents' understandings of what it means to be a "good" parent through ethnic group workshops.[38] Some helped organize events for their communities related to mental health.

Kamala, an Indian immigrant parent with adult children who had lived in the United States for multiple decades by the time I met her, helped organize events specifically for the Indian community about parenting and stress. I asked her what advice she would give to younger Indian couples in Woodcrest. She replied,

> I just tell them, "Be smart about your expectations." And that
> is one focus that we [have] in those workshops, to reduce the
> pressure on the children. . . . I tell them, "You think it's the most

important thing to send your children to an Ivy League college. But I think it's more important to raise happy and healthy kids."

I attended an event Kamala co-organized, in which other Indian community leaders also implored fellow parents to focus on their children's happiness, interests, and passions, and to prioritize those foci over achievement. The event included a panel of Indian American graduates of Woodcrest High School. Parents who attended seemed eager to learn from the experiences of those speakers. The graduates and community leaders alike told parents and teens to expand their perspectives on viable professions and colleges, to support teens' exploration to find their "passions," and to focus on leading a balanced, happy life.

Terry, a US-born Chinese American parent who had worked with Asian American youth for many years, held a parent workshop at a local Chinese church. She told me that she spoke strongly to parents to convey the importance of emotional well-being. She asked parents, "What would you do different if you knew your behavior could drive your kid to attempt suicide?" Terry described some parents in the workshop as responding in tears, saying, "That's me, I could drive my kid to that."

These events usually tied parent pressure to ethnicity, with leaders suggesting that parents needed to move away from their ethnic cultures of achievement because in the Woodcrest context they were putting undue stress on their children. In some ways, these community leaders seemed to buy in to the tiger mom stereotype of Asian parenting and the damage such parenting can cause. Interestingly, I heard similar messages in community-wide events related to emotional well-being, without the tie to ethnicity. That is to say, in events organized around ethnicity, parent pressure was tied to being Indian or Chinese, but in events geared toward all Woodcrest parents, organizers attributed parent pressure to being in a high-achieving, high-income community that was, by all accounts, still dominated by white upper-middle-class families.

Still, events organized by cultural brokers, often in collaboration with town ethnic organizations, were more effective than town-wide efforts in convincing Asian parents to attend. Even when a town mental health organization invited an Asian American psychologist to speak about culture and parenting, about 80 percent of the audience appeared to be white. The speaker spoke about cultural differences between expressions of care in Asia and the United States, and asked attendees to reflect on questions such as, "When was your happiest moment?" In contrast, events organized by the town's Indian and Chinese organizations were attended almost entirely by Indian and Chinese parents, respectively, with turnouts from those communities much larger than in the town-wide events. The cultural brokers organizing ethnicity-related events were most successful in bringing Asian parents together to talk about how to manage their children's emotional health.

On the one hand, I questioned the wisdom of tying these discussions to ethnicity. After all, I found white and Asian parents alike caught up in their children's achievement, even while they sometimes criticized other parents for being too focused on achievement. I sometimes felt defensive of Asian parents, often seeing my parents reflected in their struggles to help their children succeed while also wanting them to experience joy. And I saw the ways that white parents criticized Asian parents while simultaneously enabling their own children to excel in sports through private coaches and club teams. The critiques felt unfair.

But another part of me wished that there had been an Indian organization in my town when I was growing up that organized events around reducing academic expectations, teaching parents how to express love to their children in the US context, and helping parents see the importance of increasing children's autonomy as they grew older. My parents' cultural repertoires *were* so different from those of my peers. When my best friend would kiss her parents goodbye and say "I love you" every time she jumped out of the car I questioned my own relationship with my parents: Why didn't they ever say "I love you"? Did that mean hers loved her more than mine loved me? My cultural repertoire or "love language" expanded in those encounters in the car, and perhaps my parents could have expanded theirs in workshops like those I attended in Woodcrest so that we could be better aligned. If I had grown up in India, of course, I probably never would have witnessed parents saying "I love you" to their children—instead, I would have seen expressions of love through food and hugs all around me. Cultural brokers in Woodcrest were part of the process of assimilation in parenting, sharing strategies for how best to attend to children's emotional well-being in ways that made sense in the Woodcrest (and broader US) context.

THE KIDS ARE (MOSTLY) ALRIGHT

What was the payoff of all the fretting parents did about their children's emotional health, and from the events organized by community leaders? If there was reason to worry, it didn't seem that worries about Asian American and white students should have been different. In the school-wide survey, students reported similar levels of sustained feelings of sadness or hopelessness across racial lines, with 26 to 29 percent of all groups affirming they had at least one period of sustained sadness or hopelessness in the past year.[39] In addition, 15 to 18 percent of both white and Asian students had "seriously considered" attempting suicide in the past year.[40] Aside from the similarities between Asian and white students at Woodcrest High, these rates were also similar to national studies.[41] So if there is a mental health crisis, it is not one related to ethnicity, nor to Woodcrest, but a national one. While many adults in Woodcrest attributed student stress and worries about emotional well-being either as related to Asian parenting or as endemic to Woodcrest, student data at Woodcrest and around the country suggest this was not the case.[42]

Still, Asian American students were a bit more likely to "strongly agree" that they face pressure from their parents to earn good grades (39 percent) than were white students (32 percent), even if a majority of students did not report this kind of pressure.[43] Beyond their parents, peers may have played a role in feelings of pressure to succeed academically, especially among Asian American students. Asian students reported more academic pressure from their friends than their white peers did, perhaps because they were more likely to be in honors-level classes. One-third of Asian American students said they strongly agree that they feel pressure from their friends to do well in school, compared to one-fourth of white students. Of course, this was the kind of influence many parents sought when they brought their children to Woodcrest. Those peers may have exerted enough pressure about grades that parents felt they could—and perhaps should—back off.

In our interviews students rarely blamed their parents for any achievement pressure they felt in school. In fact, they often told me that their parents were not like *other* parents—because they did not pressure them to achieve. Eva was one such student. Her parents went to college in China, then immigrated to the United States for graduate school before Eva was born. With a GPA of 3.9, Eva told me her goal is to get into a "good college" and eventually to become a pediatrician. She also dreamed of owning her own house or apartment, and having a dog. She described her parents, however, as having lower aspirations:

> They always tell me to not be too stressed out, to like bring home a C and get like good sleep instead. And they keep trying to convince me that becoming a doctor is really hard and it's too much stress. They want me to go to art school instead.

I didn't meet Eva's parents, so I don't know how serious the suggestion of art school or C grades actually was. Still, I do know they were serious about her achievement. They hired a college counselor they found on WeChat to guide her through the college admissions process. And they did take her art interest seriously, paying $70 per class for her private teacher.

Aarav, an Indian American student, told me that his mom Akshata, the mom who thought families should take responsibility for a sensible workload, and his dad are "not as strict as other Indian parents. They never force me to do any of these extracurriculars. I'm in a bunch of clubs, but that's more because that's what I like to do. . . . They're more hands off than other Indian parents." Like many of his Indian and Chinese American peers, Aarav's reference point was other parents who came from the same country as his parents. Living in Woodcrest enabled parents to back off.

Jonah, a white student, said: "Some parents force their kids to just like do everything in school perfectly, . . . but my parents want me to be happy as well, and not be stressed out of my mind."

I was happy to hear that most kids felt their parents were reasonable, though I sometimes felt as if students felt protective of their parents when they shared the view that their own parents were not as bad as *other* parents. It was clear that students' ambitions, whether in academics, sports, or other extracurricular activities, grew as a result not only of messages they heard from their parents when they were young, but also from what they saw their peers doing. And in a community of high achievers, children may not see parents with similar cultural repertoires as unreasonable. After all, that is how our cultural repertoires work; they become part of our everyday tool kit and not something unusual or a cause for rebellion.

Overall, the student data led me to question the prevailing narrative in Woodcrest that there is a mental health crisis in town owing to academic pressure from parents, especially Asian parents. The portrayal of Woodcrest as a place that leads children to depression, anxiety, and even suicide felt more like a manufactured moral crisis than anything else.[44] And I started to notice that parents seemed to advocate addressing emotional well-being in ways that protected their race's group status. Parents weren't ready to throw in the towel on their achievement ambitions, even when they expressed a desire for their children to feel happy and fulfilled. Rather, they were searching for ways to balance their goals of happiness and success. The overt worries about mental health may have even been displaced concerns about group status. Perhaps tensions between Asian and white parents over homework, limitations on coursework, and more were really just anxieties about status and children's success and worries about who was getting ahead. But from what I could tell in my meetings with students and their responses on school surveys, they were going to be alright—or at least as alright as other American kids.

HAPPINESS AND STATUS

Dorothy, an Asian American community leader, described a group of mostly—but not exclusively—white parents:

> When we ask parents . . . "What's success to you?" . . . Inevitably, the answers come out as they want them to be happy and resilient. . . . [But] behind that, there is more personal ambition for their kids than people admit to, or will come out and say. The people who speak the loudest about stress, and wanting the town to do something to reduce the stress, at the same time, they're pretty personally ambitious for their kids. They still want their kids to do everything needed to go to some top schools. So I think there is a lot of underlying ambition that doesn't jibe with what they say.

Dorothy's description reminded me of so many parents in Woodcrest who expressed great concern about emotional health—of their kids and of all kids in Woodcrest—but who also supported their kids in the pursuit of regional and national sports teams, multiple honors and AP classes every year, and more. Their behaviors, messages to their children, and rules with their children may suggest even greater attention to excellence than they themselves realize. And explicit messages about achievement when children are young may provide the space to step back and emphasize happiness as they grow older and have internalized the achievement message. Still, parents' words provide important context about how they define what it means to be a good parent, and how that meaning making differs by ethnicity, as we have seen. Much is to be learned by what parents say, even if what they do sometimes differs.[45]

But even in their responses to questions in interviews, parents tended to address concerns about emotional well-being in ways that emphasized their own group status.[46] It is no coincidence that white US-born parents were downplaying academic competition and schoolwork at a time when Asian American students at Woodcrest were thoroughly outperforming their white peers. When white parents noticed their declining status in the supposedly meritocratic domain of academics, they seemed to turn to emotional well-being as a different domain from which to maintain their sense of higher status than Asians in Woodcrest.[47] Furthermore, by shifting their children to private schools, white parents increased their children's chances of gaining entrée to selective colleges, even though emotional well-being was typically cited as the key reason for the change in schooling. For their part, many immigrant Asian parents disagreed with changes to reduce academic competition and schoolwork, domains in which *their* children excelled. And recall from chapter 3 that some Asian parents requested intramural sports opportunities as a means to reduce stress, which coincided with Asian American students' low representation on Woodcrest's very competitive varsity sports teams.

Overall, the various machinations of parents suggest that emotional well-being may be a new domain for gaining status, and for immigrant assimilation. Some students told me about their participation on the boards of town organizations devoted to addressing emotional health among youth, and others held positions as "peer mentors" for incoming students to Woodcrest High School—one of their primary jobs, they proudly told me, was to convince these new students of the importance of self-care. Students seemed well aware that these positions could be marshalled on the college applications they would be filling out in the very near future. Asian American students may be particularly keen on cultivating this self-presentation as students cognizant of emotional health given common beliefs that Asian Americans need to work against the stereotypes of them in order to have a chance at top colleges.[48]

Hearing parent concerns about their children's happiness was heartening. Despite all the conflict and competition in Woodcrest, parents seemed to have their children's emotional well-being at heart. White and Asian parents shared a desire to raise emotionally hearty kids. Still, as we saw, their cultural repertoires for doing so varied, just as they did for guidance on academics and extracurriculars. And all of this hand-wringing over emotional well-being and jockeying for status led parents to frequently draw boundaries between what it means to be a worthy versus unworthy parent, and those boundaries frequently were drawn along ethnic lines.

CHAPTER 5

The "Right" Way to Parent

ALL OF THE EMPHASIS ON pushing our children to excellence while protecting their emotional well-being and the pressure to be a "good" parent have endless consequences. We complain, we lament, we judge ourselves for not doing enough. But perhaps even more than all that self-directed judgment, there is another consequence that is even more common, and more pernicious: we judge other parents. We take parenting seriously, and we view others' parenting according to our own standards of worth. Beyond convincing ourselves we are good parents, we spend even more time judging other parents—for being too coddling, too harsh, too involved, too absent. We draw moral boundaries to distinguish ourselves from parents we feel are less worthy than ourselves.[1] In this chapter I dig deeper into the moral boundaries of parenting: What does it mean to be a "good" parent?[2]

Of course, the definition varies significantly, as I have shown throughout this book. Many parents in Woodcrest felt compelled to distance themselves from those who did things the "wrong" way in their quest to support their children's achievements, whether academic or extracurricular, or to support their emotional health. Parents often compared themselves to other parents, often those with a different ethnic background or birthplace. And parents of the same ethnicity even compared themselves to other parents from a different region of the same country of origin, all to make claims about their own, usually superior, parenting. They seemed to emphasize differences in order to cultivate identities as the good parents in a town where the supposed overemphasis on achievement by other parents was privately lamented and occasionally publicly shamed. Woodcrest parents were hyperaware of what the larger world was saying too; the growing discussion in popular culture about "helicopter parents"—often assumed to be white—and "tiger moms"—assumed to be Asian—was avidly discussed by the well-read population of Woodcrest, and parents frequently drew boundaries to distance themselves from those negative stereotypes. These claims frequently took on a moral tone.

Many white parents expressed disdain for parents who did not take family vacations so their children could stay home and study for the SAT, or who sent their children to tutoring to get ahead academically. This parenting, according to the critics, placed too much emphasis on academic achievement and too little on emotional well-being, did not valorize children's autonomy enough, and misunderstood what summer vacation was supposed to be for. The parents critiqued were often explicitly described as Asian, and at other times the association was implicit. These sentiments sometimes went hand in hand with worries about their own children feeling "average" or not special. These judgments helped white parents maintain a sense of superiority and greater moral worth, despite concerns that their children couldn't compete when it came to academics.

For their part, Asian parents were very aware of these critiques. Which is not surprising, since subordinate groups are often all too cognizant of how they are judged, misunderstood, and stereotyped by the dominant group. They responded in two ways. The most common response was assent. Many of the Asian parents I interviewed said that some Asian parents are indeed at fault: for having unreasonable expectations, for not allowing their children enough autonomy, and for not addressing their children's emotional well-being in the right ways. These parents were never critical of themselves; rather, they nearly always invoked some sort of intra-Asian distinction, claiming that Asian parents of a different generation, or of a different country, or even of a different region of the same country, were the ones that did the things that gave Asian parents a bad name.

A more tentative minority of Asian parents drew a parallel between white parents' attention to excellence in sports and Asian parents' attention to academics; these parents acknowledged different foci, but suggested that hyperattention to these divergent domains were acceptable, albeit different, styles of parenting. They did not judge white parents for their emphasis on sports in the same way as they were judged by many white parents for their own emphasis on academics. But they did judge the hypocrisy of whites criticizing Asians for similar behaviors in a different domain. Overall, perhaps because of their relative newcomer position in the US compared to most whites in Woodcrest, Asian parents seemed to be on the defensive when it came to judgments about parenting.

WHITE PARENTS: MORAL BOUNDARIES AROUND SUMMER PLANS, EXPECTATIONS, AND AUTONOMY

Rory's two kids, both white graduates of Woodcrest, were currently attending Ivy League colleges. Even though her kids had already graduated, she had no shortage of opinions. We met at the public library, where we found a spot to sit near the children's section. I worried about the background noise in that area, but I didn't need to. Rory's strong voice was clear and crisp. She did not mince words, even when talking about race, unlike many fellow white Woodcrest parents:

> One of my daughter's friends, she got a 1560-something on the SAT, right? . . . Her parents had her retake it. I was saying that to somebody and one of my friends said, "Let me guess. Her name isn't Sally Smith." And I'm like, "No, it's not." . . . [They are from] Korea. . . . They didn't go away on vacation because she had to study for the SAT2s. . . . As my friend says, it's never the blonde Norwegian [laughs]. . . .

Most of the white parents I spoke with were like Rory: summer vacation had a sacred quality to it. There were certain things that you and your kids were supposed to do: take vacations; get a job at the mall or volunteer at the local paper; sleep in. When other kids in the neighborhood didn't do those things and instead did additional academic work, it caused some consternation. The descriptions from Rory and others often came with nonverbal expressions of frustration and judgment—a sarcastic tone, an incredulous look, a search for affirmation as they made eye contact with me. Many tied the problematic behaviors they perceived to race or ethnicity, sometimes explicitly like Rory did ("Sally Smith" suggests both white and American, and blonde Norwegian distinguishes white from Asian immigrants), and at other times the link was more subtle. Rory went on:

> They are like, "In my country, in fifth grade, we were doing blah, blah, blah." I'm like, "Well, but you aren't in that country. You're probably here for a reason. Because your country is controlled by an authoritarian dictator. So let's embrace this" [laughs]. . . . So they're sending all these kids to Russian Math.

Rory's judgment was unmistakable from her tone. I found it hard to reconcile the likely reference to parents from China ("country controlled by an authoritarian dictator"), and the exhortation to "embrace *this*"— presumably her way—with her clearly liberal identity. During our interview Rory made a disparaging remark about President Trump, and later she said about Woodcrest, "people are very liberal," clearly including herself in that group. Yet she felt comfortable making a broad generalization about Asian parents. To Rory, the high expectations of immigrant parents who send their kids to Russian School of Math is, simply put, bad parenting. Parents having unreasonable academic expectations was one of the main aspects of Asian parenting that white parents frequently distanced themselves from and one they felt placed an undue toll on children's emotional health.

This perception of unreasonably high academic expectations, especially in math, led parents like Rory to disapprove of the overrepresentation of Asian American kids in honors classes. Rory told me about a tutoring class she heard about, independent of school, that was specifically for students in honors math. "Is it just me, or does anybody think there's something a little odd about the fact that so many kids in ninth-grade honors math—kids who are supposed to be somewhat good at math—need a tutor that this tutor has a whole class for honors math?" To Rory, students needing extra help was evidence that they should not be in the honors level in the first place.

Critics like Rory often assumed that parents, rather than children, were driving this insistence on high achievement and additional academic activities. But recall that most kids said that their parents don't pressure them like *other* parents pressure their kids, and kids often cited their peers, but not parents, as a source of pressure to take advanced-level classes. Still, Rory was skeptical about how much autonomy the children of such parents could possibly have. This was the third aspect of good parenting I frequently heard from white parents' judgments of the follies of other, usually Asian, parents. Rory said,

> If you got all the parents in this town and you said, "Raise your hand if your kid is passionate about math," . . . How many fourteen-year-olds do you think are passionate about math? I'm not saying none of them are. But I know what most fourteen-year-olds are passionate about. It's not math. They swear, "Oh, my child just lives and breathes math!" I know your kid! That's not true! [laughs].

Rory assumed parents forced their children to take advanced math or sign up for RSM. This time she did not name Asians, but from her previous comments I understood that this was who she meant. Indeed, as we saw in chapter 3, Asian parents did exert more direct influence on their children's activities than white parents, who also cultivated their children's interests but exerted more effort to maintain the impression that their children had autonomy.

Patricia, another white mom, also expressed disapproval of other parents related to summer plans, academic expectations, and autonomy. In chapter 2 we saw that Asian American students were more likely than white students to have summer plans involving academic work or research. Patricia told me about her observations related to ethnic change in Woodcrest as her three children grew older:

> I think the older two, they all had friends that were Asian or Eastern Indian. As the years went by, it became more and more. . . . My youngest—in her kindergarten and first-grade class, I would say it was probably 50 percent Asian and Eastern Indian. Which is again, perfectly wonderful. But you could tell as time went on, it was different. And specifically, when you go to graduation now,

there are very many names that are obviously not, quote un-quote, "born in the United States."

I will admit that I did not appreciate the characterization of names like mine as "not born in the United States." I frequently correct others—even my own children—when they use the word "American" as a stand-in for "white," excluding me from the country I have called home all my life. Despite highlighting things being "different," Patricia went on to express appreciation for the growing diversity in Woodcrest, calling it "really good." As she went on, though, she shared a downside she perceived: "In terms of the competitiveness of the school, I would say that it probably has become worse." I questioned just how much Patricia really appreciated the growing diversity of Woodcrest. It was as if she wanted the different cuisines and faiths without accepting other aspects of her Asian neighbors' cultural repertoires. Like Rory, Patricia specifically drew a boundary when it came to summer vacation plans:

> They're taking a summer bio class, and then they take AP bio [in school]. And they're doing that so they get the A in AP bio. . . . One of my daughter's really good friends, Leela, this summer took two classes at [local private school]. . . . My sixteen-year-old, the first half of the summer, we went abroad for a two-and-a-half-week trip, which was wonderful. [Then] she worked at [the town pool] for a week as a lifeguard and swimming instructor. And then she left and went to the camp that she's been going to for eight summers to go be a counselor. No biology. No math.

Patricia later told me that Leela's parents are immigrants from China. She sounded defensive when she described the impact of travel and work on her daughter during the summer:

> Did she grow over the course of the summer? Exponentially, because she had all these different social situations. She worked with kids. She figured out how to lead people. And I'd take that any day of the week over her taking a chemistry class over the summer before she takes her chemistry class. It makes no sense.

For Patricia, good parenting in the summer means taking children on vacation, encouraging a job, and building nonacademic skills. And not creating undue stress, which she assumed came with the "wrong" summer activities. She placed high value on maintaining a healthy level of stress, and contrasted her own style to others' parenting—"for our family, we really want to make sure that people are both physically and mentally happy. . . . And I see so many of these kids that are just being pushed. And creating such stress in their lives." While Patricia does not explicitly tie the behaviors to race or ethnicity like Rory did, Leela's Chinese ethnicity along with Patricia's description of ethnic change driving competition in Woodcrest suggests this was not a coincidence.

Emma was another white mom who believed in using summers to develop nonacademic skills through work. She had a particularly clear view of what students were doing outside of school because of her job at the high school:

> I see kids after ninth grade working in [hospital] labs. And on the one hand I say, you know what? That kid doesn't want to play basketball or maybe doesn't like arts and crafts. But school year-round? That's the equivalent of school. Maybe there's the very unusual, rare, truly brilliant kid for whom that is a great choice. But I frankly think that plenty of the kids who are doing that should work in Dunkin' Donuts part time. That's just a bias of mine. . . . I feel like it kind of robs them of a piece of childhood in a way that I frankly think is not so healthy in the long run.

Emma tries to signal no judgment, acknowledging her own "bias" about the summer activities she feels are most important. But like Patricia, her drawing of a moral boundary was clear. The children working in labs are being "robbed" of their childhoods, presumably by their parents.

Shannon drew a moral boundary about academic expectations. She and her family moved to Woodcrest when her older child was in first grade. Prior to moving, Shannon and her husband "did a lot of research and [Woodcrest] had an excellent school system. . . . So we chose Woodcrest." When I asked Shannon how the town has changed since she moved to it nearly twenty years ago, she said, "The population has shifted toward a higher percentage of Asian, that's very clear. . . . And the school district and the friends that my kids had, I would say changed over the twenty years from a small percentage of Asians to a large percentage of Asians." When I asked how the population shift has changed the town, she began, "It's hard for me to say this without—I don't want to sound racist. . . . I don't want to sound biased." I braced myself for what would come next—which Shannon indicated was likely to offend. She went on,

> But I do believe that with the influx of Asians, I think they choose Woodcrest because of the school's reputation. And I think they have different attitudes about education. . . . I think they push their children harder, and I think they have much higher expectations.

Shannon's lack of self-reflection here was notable given that she too had moved to Woodcrest for its "excellent school system."

Overall, many white parents expressed disapproval of these specific practices associated with Asian parenting: seemingly excessive academic expectations (which were assumed to stem from parental pressure), academic activities during summer vacation, and less autonomy than they thought was appropriate for teens. In a liberal town like Woodcrest most parents did not express overt disdain for a whole race group—they were too polite, too schooled in the harms of racial stereotypes to do so, especially in front of an Asian American researcher. Instead, their remarks were more subtle expressions about the right way to parent and the kind of parents they are *not*. Nevertheless, as I hope I have convinced you, the associations were clear and visible.

White Feelings of Displacement

How did white parents make sense of the consequences of the parenting they deemed problematic? Many pointed to the impact on their own children's emotional health and their sense of self, damaged by the relentless academic striving of their peers. I asked Shannon, the mom above who described Asian families as having different "attitudes about education," how that difference alongside the increased Asian population of Woodcrest had impacted her children. She led with a positive impact: "They had great friends who cared about education," she said without hesitation. And then she turned to the negative:

> On the other hand, my kids, and especially my older daughter, who was very bright and very motivated, felt like an average student, because there were so many geniuses and superstars and kids that are just off the charts. Whereas in any other school district anywhere else in the country, she would have been at the top of the class. . . . I think her self-esteem suffered a bit.

This sense of displacement was common among white parents in Woodcrest. Shannon seemed to feel entitled to her daughter feeling above average. There is no recognition here that those "geniuses and superstars" may have simply studied more. (Still, despite Shannon's worries, that daughter ended up at an elite college that admits just one in four applicants.)

Rory described a similarly negative impact, though she began with the negative impact she perceived on Asian American kids themselves:

> [After taking math classes] the kids come back to school. And then [parents] will complain, "Well now my child is bored." Well, your child is bored because you sit him for four hours in Russian Math over the weekend! Could have been better off playing out- side or doing something else.

Rory's moral disdain for the child's family quickly moved from the po- tential impact on *their* child to concerns about the impact on her *own* child:

> [Let's say you're] a parent who doesn't send your kid to Russian Math. You'd put a nail through your hand before you'd send your kid to Russian Math. But now he's like "Oh, but I can't be in hon- ors math, because all those kids—" and this did happen with [my son]. It was hard for him last year. Because he was like, "But all those kids, they already know how to do X, Y, or Z."

Rory blamed the parenting of Asian families for her son's loss of status and his inability to gain entrée to the honors math track she thought he deserved, based on her own estimation of his math skills. This was an unfair breach of the rules of parenting, as Rory saw it. Still, despite her disdain for parents sending their children to Russian Math, Rory did sign her son up for a math team in elementary school. And in the end, Rory's eldest child was attending an Ivy League college, suggesting her family still did well in the ongoing competition among Woodcrest seniors for spots at elite colleges.

The irony of Rory's child attending an elite and expensive college was not lost on me—like Asian families she critiqued, Rory pulled out all the stops when it came to her children's college application process. The only difference was the strategies they engaged. Rory did support her son in math, through an elementary school math team, but not the Russian Math more common among Asian families. And her daughter benefited from being a legacy to her college—Rory also went there—and smartly, she applied knowing that that would give her a boost in admission. Asian families, of course, were much less likely to have access to a legacy boost for US colleges, because most Asian parents did their undergraduate degrees in Asia.

Emma was another white mom who pivoted from the negative impact of bad parenting on Asian American kids to the loss of status for her own child. I asked Emma what the negative consequences are of the "academics year-round" approach she described. First she said,

> I really think that part of growing up is interacting with people over like stupid, silly stuff. Like . . . all week long, twice a day you've been going to McDonald's. A friend's saying, "Do we have to go there today?" That's not happening in a lab.

Then Emma pivoted to the impact on her own son, lamenting that he "self-identified as a nonstudent, not liking school very early on. . . . Because there are so many frankly cutthroat 'super students,' quote unquote." Parents of the kids she described, in other words, overstepped the boundaries of good parenting. At the same time, Emma too worked hard to ensure that her son got into the best college he could, in part by hiring a private college counselor for him and a private tutor to prepare for college entrance exams. Emma held a particular vision for what it means to be a good parent. In her view, hiring an individual tutor or college counselor was permissible, though a summer job in a research lab was not.

At times, Asian parents were publicly shamed for what others perceived as poor parenting. Sabrina, a white mom who was a strong critic of the ever-increasing academic achievements at Woodcrest, reported on a public discussion with a new district administrator:

> She was talking about how she really sees a major part of her job as to build connections and relationships within the town, between the different schools, between different groups within the school. And a Chinese dad stood up and said, "You know who you need to build connections with? The admissions officers at the Ivy League schools. You need to tell them that Woodcrest deserves a bigger piece of the pie. The reason it's so stressful at the high school is because we have so many kids that deserve to go to those schools. But because of quotas, they won't accept them."

Sabrina continued,

> A white parent said, "That's not where I want my superintendent's attention. That's crazy." And then I raised my hand and I said, "Here's the problem with that. . . . If you have only moved to this community thinking that it's a straight path to an Ivy League school, you have done your child a grave disservice. You've actually put them at a disadvantage. Because there are so many bright kids here."

In a town like Woodcrest, Sabrina could assume (and more often than not be right) that the schools brought a family to town, just like they brought her and her family to town. Like Shannon, she seems to resent Asian families following in her footsteps to the classrooms of Woodcrest. Still, she fails to fully grasp the privileges of living in Woodcrest when she suggests that doing so puts a child at a *dis*advantage in the college admissions process. Over thirty students from Woodcrest in one year of this research went on to one of the eight Ivy League colleges. To put this number in perspective, consider that in one recent year just sixty-seven high schools in the United States sent *any* students to Harvard, out of the over twenty-six thousand high schools in the United States.[3] Students coming from Woodcrest were much more likely to attend Ivy League colleges than students in almost any other school district in the country. Yet white and Asian parents alike, including both Sabrina and the Chinese dad she disagreed with, frequently claimed that going to Woodcrest High School made entrée harder.

Overall, white parents critical of Asian parenting seemed to lament their children's lost status. As they watched their children no longer feel above average, they grew resentful of the growing number of Asians in their community. Despite Asian American teens excelling academically, white parents did not emulate the cultural repertoires that they saw leading to that outcome, as might be expected when a group observes another achieving success. Instead, whites maintained their feeling of superiority by rejecting Asian families' strategies for getting ahead and describing the importance of children's autonomy, summers focused on nonacademic activities, and reasonable academic expectations, placing them outside the boundary of good parenting. Of course, this was not a conscious ploy. Still, what seemed to elicit the strongest feelings in my conversations with white parents were the things they believed Asian parents did that seemed to make achievement and standing out harder for their own children. Drawing moral boundaries around parenting— judging Asian parenting to be unworthy, even if it led to academic excellence—was one mechanism by which white parents could hang on to their sense of status and superiority.

ASIAN PARENTS: DEFENSIVE MORAL BOUNDARIES

Given the critiques I heard from white parents, I was surprised not to hear similar critiques among Asian parents about the different ways they tended to exert influence on their children. Instead, Asian parents more often than not simply excluded themselves from the behaviors that were judged morally suspect. Many were aware of the disapproval of parents like Shannon, Patricia, Emma, and Rory. In fact, the moral boundaries they described around parenting often seemed to involve a hyperawareness of those critiques. But instead of rejecting white parents' contrasting styles, perhaps unlikely given most Asian parents' marginal status in the US as immigrants, most Asian parents distanced themselves from the behaviors that were critiqued. In other words, they accepted the critiques but said that they themselves were not on the wrong side of the moral boundary, even if other—even most—Asian parents were. For example, Helen, an immigrant Chinese mother, told me that "Most parents, I think they want [their kids] to go to good schools, like Ivy League schools and then have a very good job. . . . I don't want exactly the same thing. I don't think [my daughter] needs to go to an Ivy League, or any of the prestigious schools." Like so many other Asian and white parents, Helen couldn't quite articulate what she did want for her daughter—just the boundaries around what she did not want.

Other Asian parents distanced themselves from those who were critiqued for not providing their children enough autonomy. Akshata, an immigrant Indian mother, contrasted herself to other Indian parents: "Most of the Indian parents that I know, I think for them, success is only through sciences. . . . We've left it to our son [to decide] what he wants to do." Akshata contrasted her and her husband's parenting with that of her sister-in-law who lived in another town:

> She has this idea in her head that her daughter should be a doctor. And she keeps trying to brainwash her. I tell her "You should not do that. . . . What if she doesn't want to? Let her decide. She's going into eighth grade now. And she has her own ideas. . . . You cannot decide for her. Don't do that."

Akshata also contrasted her desire for her son to get a summer job as different from most other Indian parents in Woodcrest. She and her husband felt that their son would learn the soft skills necessary to be successful at work in the future through a high school summer job:

> [My husband] started realizing that just studies was not everything. There should be an all-around development. You should know how to conduct yourself in front of ten people. How you meet and talk to other people is very important. And he saw that in the real world, people who are ahead of him or successful were not necessarily the brightest students when they were in school. But they were very good at selling themselves.

This realization resonates with the message we heard many white parents share with their kids in chapter 2—academics are not the sole avenue to professional success. Still, Akshata's son was a strong student—he told me his GPA is 3.75 and that he takes "mostly" honors classes.

Like Akshata, Nandi contrasted her own parenting with that of other Indian parents who were, as she described them, too directive. She said,

> I think the non-Indian parents, they give a lot of autonomy to the kids. . . . But Indian parents, definitely decide mostly for the kids. Very rarely do they let the kids decide. . . . So giving this freedom [to my son], at least he gets independent. He can decide for himself. Like when the language choice came, I personally wanted him to take Spanish. Spanish, I thought, would be more useful in the United States. And people say that it's an easy language to learn. But he decided he wanted to do Mandarin. So I didn't force him to take Spanish. . . . If he thinks he wants to do something, I think he should be able to explore that.

Parents like Helen, Akshata, and Nandi recognized the disapproval of some Asian parents' styles in Woodcrest related to expectations, autonomy, and summer plans. They responded by distancing themselves from those styles, thus insulating themselves from accusations of bad parenting. In many instances these were the same parents who acted as "cultural brokers" related to how to address children's emotional well-being, as I described in chapter 4.

Indira, a US-born Indian American mother previously married to a white American-born man, claimed that Woodcrest is "full of crazy parents." She explained her view with an example from her son's high school orientation in eighth grade:

> The principal goes through this whole little rigmarole of "Next week you're going to get the recommendations from your middle school teachers. Your kid's going to be recommended for up to three honors classes. . . . That's terrific. Take them out to dinner. Congratulate them. Celebrate your kid. Pick two." And he gives a nice talk about balance, and the importance of getting used to the setting, having extracurriculars and sports and whatever else your kid is interested in. And that two honors classes is really what they have found is the reasonable amount.

So I love this, right? I'm very happy about this. . . . And at the end of it, there's these parents who are like, "But if they only take two honors classes in ninth grade, how are they going to get into Harvard?" I'm suddenly panicked. I'm like, "Am I too relaxed?" And then I had this like, "No. I'm the sane one. *They're* the crazy ones!" [laughs].

When I asked her to clarify, Indira said that the "crazy" parents "tend to be more immigrant. . . . Of the friends I have, not so many of the born and raised in the US parents are quite so crazy." Indira aligns herself with the school principal, part of the dominant culture of signaling attention to emotional well-being by limiting academic ambitions. In doing so, she drew a moral boundary between her own parenting and that of immigrant parents.

Indira's son Ammar agreed that his mom seemed to get it right when it came to parenting. In a separate interview that took place at school, Ammar told me, "There's going to be like the extremely lenient parents who don't really care, and also like the really focused parents who micromanage every aspect of their child's life." He went on to say that his mom "is probably in the middle."

I imagined that Indira would have pleased to know that her son described her as "in the middle." Indeed, Indira's family were all high achievers. She met Ammar's dad at the Ivy League university they both attended. And when I met Ammar he was taking two honors classes and one AP class. He also was a part of multiple clubs and a varsity sports team. He also told me he was learning multiple languages on his own through the app Duolingo—Italian, French, Dutch, Portuguese, German, and Russian; this was in addition to the Spanish he was learning at school. Ammar told me that "I'm hoping to get proficient in all those, and then also add Arabic and Japanese."

While US-born Indira distinguished herself from foreign-born parents, some immigrant Indian parents engaged in boundary work in order to distinguish themselves from immigrants from China. Suneel, the Indian community leader who suggested legislators budget for more school counselors, described differences he perceived between Chinese and Indian residents of Woodcrest related to their degree of focus on academic excellence:

Back in China, they have the one-child policy. And here they want their child to really, truly succeed. So the tiger moms, that's what they do. And there are more tiger moms among Chinese than among Indians. . . . Once I was talking to a friend of mine. And he said, "I don't want my children to be friends with Chinese boys or girls." I said, "Why?" He said, "They just want to study, study, study."

Some North Indian immigrant parents even differentiated themselves from South Indian immigrant parents, whom they viewed as too focused on academic excellence, playing into a common Indian stereotype about regional differences in India.[4] Ruby, a Punjabi immigrant mother, said,

The southern part of India, people are more academically driven. Punjabis [northern Indians] in general, they're entrepreneurs, so they're more flashy, more outgoing as in just more fun in their lives. Not as academically driven. And that's where you see the difference here between the people from the southern part and the northern. . . . [South Indian parents] will have their kids in spelling bee competitions.

Ruby's children were high achievers, earning "mostly A's and A-'s." Her ninth grader took honors math as well. Still, she suggests the academic expectations of South Indian parents are even higher.

Overall, parents and kids in Woodcrest described lower levels of parental pressure than I expected when I began this research. I sometimes wondered if they were just telling me what they thought was the socially desirable answer, even if it wasn't what the parents actually do. In fact, other studies, based in New York City and Los Angeles, have found that adult children of Chinese and Vietnamese immigrants describe their parents' definitions of success when they were young as entailing extraordinarily high achievement levels.[5] But if parents and kids in Woodcrest were just telling me what they thought was the socially desirable response, it raises the question of why children of immigrants in New York and Los Angeles did not feel that same pressure. After talking with so many parents in Woodcrest and observing the busy lives of their children, I concluded that the social context in Woodcrest may have made those explicit messages unnecessary. Just as studies of youth living in concentrated poverty show how the lack of community members with steady jobs and college degrees makes those harder to imagine and sustain even when young adults desperately want both—there are few models to draw from on how to be successful in college, alongside a lack of resources to support that success—communities like Woodcrest may provide such abundant models of success that parents explicitly advocating high achievement may be unnecessary for success.[6] Asian parents living in places with a wider range of achievement levels (due in part to a wider range of educational backgrounds among parents), like those in previous studies of Asian American families, may feel more need to explicitly direct their children throughout childhood. In places like Woodcrest, the social context may make that influence unnecessary; everyone was achieving at a pretty high level, even if where exactly they landed was of course not the same. Indeed, on the school-wide survey it was African American students—most of whom were bused from the nearby city—who were most likely to say that their parents pressure them to do well in school.[7]

The defensiveness from Asian parents and kids suggested that they bought into the superiority of white ways of parenting. They took white parenting as the standard by which they should be measured. That is, to appear to be good, morally defensible parents, they needed to appear more like white parents. Still, a minority of Asian parents rejected the critiques. I turn to those parents next.

Asian Parents Critique Their White Neighbors

While many Asian parents responded to white disapproval of Asian parenting by distancing themselves from the tiger mom stereotype, some dismissed those critiques as hypocritical. Weren't Asian parents' high expectations in academics just like white families' high expectations in sports? For example, Shivani, a US-born Indian American mother of three, said:

> There's some nationally ranked ice skaters here. They skate hours a day. They get up at like five AM. . . . It's a lot of dedication.

And I think it's great. So I'm like, "'Do you complain about that?'" So if a kid wants to do math and loves math, so what if he goes to math camp every summer? If his parents aren't forcing him and he really loves that, there's nothing wrong.

Shivani pointed out the seeming contradiction in a board meeting of a local organization dedicated to teen mental health, on which Shivani sat:

White parents, they were like, "Well, but math is intense, and it's not recreational." I'm like, "No, it's the same thing. If they love it, and they have a propensity towards it, so what?"

Shivani said of teens in intensive sports that "it's great" and hoped for the same empathy for her own Asian American children's participation in more academic extracurricular activities. Still, she drew on the importance of autonomy in her critique. That is, she prioritized the importance of autonomy, similar to many white parents, but questioned white parents' refusal to admit that some kids may choose math camp.

Saumya, the Indian mother in chapter 2 who spoke of higher standards in math in her experiences in India than her children's in Woodcrest, also compared supplementary math to sports participation:

I think Indians are seen very negatively for putting the kids in Russian Math by non-Indians, and to me, it's just weird, because people do all kinds of clubs for sports. And I think it's the same thing. They are trying to get better in hockey or baseball or whatever, so they're doing clubs outside of school. That is not looked on negatively. But doing something extra in math is looked at negatively. . . . They're like "Oh, our kids can't get into honors math if they're not doing Russian Math, because it's too hard." . . . Which is probably true. But if my kid doesn't do a club team, he or she won't get into the JV or varsity teams. So what's the difference? It's just what you prioritize. And I think the Indians are prioritizing math over sports.

In other words, when white parents disapproved of Asian parenting for an intensive focus on academics some Asian parents, like Shivani and

Saumya, pushed back and suggested that they are simply focused intensely on different pursuits.

Sabrina, the white mother above who saw moving to Woodcrest as
dampening children's prospects of getting into elite colleges, explicitly
rejected arguments like those made by Shivani and Saumya. She responded to perspectives like Shivani's and Saumya's in her interview,
suggesting she had heard those arguments before:

> So a big argument that comes up when people do condemn the
> proliferation of academic enrichment: "Why is that any differ-
> ent from club sports or private coaching?" . . . And I understand
> the analogy. It's a little different, though. Nobody is required to
> do soccer in order to graduate. It's not a complete analogy. The
> academic enrichment stuff is co-curricular. . . . Whether a kid gets
> private coaching in baseball or soccer or whatever doesn't have
> the same impact on the kid's academic life.

Ironically, Sabrina justifies intensive cultivation of sports skills but not
academic skills by her prioritizing academics—suggesting academics are too important to provide enrichment beyond the school walls.
Indeed, Sabrina's children were active in sports both at the town and
club levels. While I guessed that I had some things in common with
Sabrina—I too never signed my kids up for academic enrichment outside of school—I found her justification perplexing. It was the homework policy debate all over again—attenuating academics to make room
for extracurriculars (especially sports), while placing no limits on the
intensity, hours, or private coaching in extracurriculars.

When I spoke with Dorothy, a US-born Asian American community
leader, it sounded as if she understood the perspectives of residents like
Sabrina all too well. She said:

> I think there's a sentiment from some people who feel that the
> Asian community is driving some of the academic pressure in
> the town. . . . I think it's out of fear that maybe the Asian kids are
> edging out some of the other kids. So you hear, "Well, they all
> send their kids to Russian Math and all these outside programs
> to give their kids a leg up. Why do they do that? That's not okay,
> it's a problem." And you hear that a good deal from some of the

people who, the wanting-to-dial-down-the-stress people. There are a lot of comments from them.

Still, Sabrina and parents like her seemed to set the terms of debate in Woodcrest. In public meetings and in conversations with school leaders I rarely heard arguments like Shivani's and Saumya's. This dominant narrative about the right way to parent meant that most Asian parents acted in response to it, often defensively.

Overall, when the dominant group, whites, defines the terms of worthy parenting, many immigrant parents seem to accept their judgments and respond by distancing themselves from the behaviors that whites reject. As they do so, some draw upon other lines of difference— generation, national origin, and region within national origin—to distance themselves from, as Indira described them, the "crazy parents" in Woodcrest.

I did not hear Asian parents expressing disapproval of white parenting, besides their critiques of white judgment of their own parenting.[8] As I considered the live-and-let-live approach of Asian parents in Woodcrest, I realized that their position as immigrants and racial minorities may have led them too to see white parents' cultural repertoires as the norm, even if they didn't share them, and hence see them as ineligible for critique. Much like working-class Americans who decry inequality yet often buy into systems of meritocracy that disadvantage them, and like women who critique men's sexism but less frequently the corporate workplace practices that make balancing home and work responsibilities challenging for them, so too Asian parents in Woodcrest sometimes called out the hypocrisy of white critiques of Asian parenting, but never white parenting practices themselves.[9]

THE FUTURE OF WOODCREST

Life is, of course, always uncertain; yet these days, that uncertainty feels all the more inescapable. From climate change to a global pandemic to financial insecurity, parents feel these burdens not just for their own lives, but for the lives of the children that they have devoted themselves to. Parenting, in turn, feels like an enormously important, and endlessly stressful, undertaking.[10]

Parents in Woodcrest, just like parents everywhere, grappled with everything as best as they could. They were determined to achieve the "right" balance in all aspects of their parenting: scheduling kids just enough but not too much, giving them freedom while still guiding them toward the best choices, finding the "right" summer plans, attending to their emotional well-being without sacrificing achievement. The list was endless. And for many Woodcrest parents, it seemed like a second job. No surprise then, that within a high-achieving community in the midst of global uncertainly, feeling like you are a "good," morally upright parent seems more essential, and harder to achieve, than ever.

In general, we don't want to brag, but we do want everyone to recognize how hard we are working and what a good job we are doing. Middle-class parents feel a moral obligation to pay for their children's college, despite the potential for high levels of debt.[11] Some well-off white parents of young children even feel morally obligated to provide test preparation classes so their children can have the "best" educational opportunities.[12] We also work hard to instill a sense of morality in our children. Wealthy parents often take great pains to raise their children to be morally conscious, despite their incredible privileges.[13] And we feel the need to show it. When we meet with teachers, we try to signal that we understand our children are imperfect, but nonetheless that we are good parents who take our parenting seriously.[14]

Of course, our perceptions about what makes a good parent vary. Books about parenting across cultures abound. Psychologists study the minutiae of cross-cultural differences in what parents say they value, the extent to which they emphasize their children's autonomy versus interconnectedness, styles of discipline, and much more.[15] This endless investigation is proof that parenting is one of the most vital, yet varied, things we do as human beings. At the same time, parenting cultures shift over time. In the United States today, we take for granted that everyone sees, and should see, their children as an important source of meaning. But this view on parenting developed only a century ago, with the shift from an agrarian society in which children contributed to household labor to one in which children became, as Viviana Zelizer has described it, "priceless."[16] With that shift came increasing worries among parents about whether they were doing the best for their children. Concerns about how best to raise our children have only grown more intense over time.[17] And of course, as we have seen throughout this book, the migration experience shapes ideas about parenting.[18]

Most parents in Woodcrest were adamant that they were raising their children the right way. But the terms of debate seemed to be set by white critics of Asian parents who cancelled vacations for SAT prep, did not provide sufficient autonomy for their children, and had children spending their summers in research labs and classrooms. The judgments of Asian parents as problematic, both for their impact on their children as well as on others' children, demonstrated that white parents' liberal sensibilities only went so far.[19] Defining the terms of good parenting enabled whites to label parenting practices more common among Asian parents as those that should change. They turned to morality to maintain their sense of status in the face of Asian American academic excellence. In doing so, they drew subtle moral boundaries between themselves and Asian parents, despite overt expressions of support for diversity.[20] At times, whites in Woodcrest sounded not so different from supporters of President Trump, buying into the narrative that immigrants are the reason for any lack of financial security they feel.

Asian parents often accepted these critiques, placing themselves on the right side of moral parenting as defined by the established white parents by distancing themselves from stereotypical Asian parenting.[21] They sometimes described problematic parenting in terms of *other* difference—generation, national origin, and region. While research on immigrant assimilation has assumed that achieving socioeconomic parity with the dominant group—middle-class whites in the US—will lead to a blurring of boundaries between the dominant and immigrant group, in Woodcrest I found the opposite. Parents turned to moral boundaries of good parenting to distinguish white and Asian parenting. A small number of Asian parents rejected whites' critiques, drawing a parallel between Asian families' emphasis on the highest levels of academic excellence with white families' focus on athletic skills.

It is important to keep in mind that the judgments I heard were rarely overt. They did not come to a head at any public meeting. No public officials made overtly racist comments about Asian parents. Rallies over proposed changes to homework or any other academic policy did not happen, let alone happen along racial lines as has been the case in New York City, New Jersey, Maryland, and many other places.[22] White parents in Woodcrest held strongly liberal sensibilities, and Asian parents did not push back against policies like the homework policy when they disagreed. Instead, tensions were just below the surface. Palpable, but often invisible. But those tensions make clear the enduring power of white upper-middle-class residents to set the terms of debate, even in a domain in which they were surpassed by Asian Americans, education. Still, I wondered what issue might light the tinder that lays in Woodcrest.

For some clarity on this question, I turned to Principal Smith. I thought that he, as someone who had lived and worked in Woodcrest for decades, might have some insight into the future of this complex town. We sat down for a long-overdue conversation as I was winding down this research. I was excited to finally have some uninterrupted time to talk with him without the endless distractions of the school day. We quickly dove in, and a recurring theme was ethnic tensions in Woodcrest, despite overt expressions of excitement about diversity. He said:

> There's been an increase in, among the families who are white, anger about perceptions about what's driving the schools. . . . You know, Asian American families coming in, . . . this feeling of "My child can't keep up with all of"—those stereotypical perceptions of the "smart" kids: "They're naturally smart. My kid's having to work too hard. . . . Who *are* those kids?" And there's just anger.

Mr. Smith described parents speaking much more explicitly about ethnicity than I heard in most interviews. In my conversations, white parents were much more polite about their unease with ethnic change— "anger" is not a word I would use to describe anything I heard from white parents. I guessed that Mr. Smith's white identity and long-term residence in Woodcrest may have made many parents assume he shared their perspectives, and hence made them more willing to share strong emotions about parents who look like me. His insight suggested to me that conflicts would arise sooner than I previously expected, even if they hadn't already.

In other places, issues like school boundary redistricting and changing admissions to magnet schools have led Asian families to participate in protests and to share their frustrations.[23] However, in these instances Asians were pitted against Black and Latinx families, not against white families. In college admissions, a small number of Asian Americans have blamed what they see as anti–Asian American discrimination on affirmative action for Black, Native American, and Latinx applicants to

Harvard as well. But the almost complete absence of Black and Latinx families living in Woodcrest and the limited number of busing students meant that the district never needed to implement policies that might challenge the privileges held by white and Asian American families alike in Woodcrest in favor of equity for less-resourced families. Still, I wondered how long it would be before the gap between Asian American and white students' academic achievement would grow so large that white parents and school officials would implement more dramatic changes that might spark flames, and in turn Asian families would push back forcefully. Would they try to implement limitations on the number of AP classes a student could take in a year? Would they de-level classes at the middle school and high school? Or would upper-middle-class whites simply stop moving to Woodcrest, choosing other, less diverse suburbs for their families?

The Anxieties of Parenting and the American Dream

WE ARE LIVING IN AN age of anxiety, economic and otherwise. Inequality in the United States is the highest it's been in half a century.[1] Working- and middle-class families increasingly struggle to make ends meet. These problems are rooted in the structure of our country—our adamant faith in a cutthroat version of capitalism and a stacked-deck version of meritocracy. Our undying suspicion of anything that aims to better the common good. Our unfettered devotion to individual rights. Our unwillingness to address the scars of racism.

Even families that seem rich to most of us still feel insecure. We live in communities segregated by race and increasingly segregated by class, so even well-off families can remain oblivious to their good fortune.[2] Those families that seem to have it all are often caught in a very particular kind of upper-middle-class culture—striving, hypereducated, hypercompetitive—in which having it all is not enough. This is the culture endemic in Woodcrest, and in a growing number of communities around the country. Many of these people "upscale" their standards about how much is enough.[3] They add to their list of needs, their list of concerns, their list of what is required to be good parents and to have the right life. The result is a spiral as predictable as it is vicious: more needs requires more money, which requires more work, which manifests as more stress, all of which justify the sense of precariousness.[4] And when parents feel anxious about their status, they spend considerable energy and resources on their children's education, because for American parents—US-born, immigrant, Asian, white, Black, and Latinx alike—getting a good education is the security blanket of choice.

There is a great irony here. We Americans believe in the promise of equal opportunity, and the idea that everyone can succeed in this country if they just try hard enough. People in most European countries are less likely than Americans to believe that hard work is and should be the key to getting ahead in life.[5] But we are also very aware of how much of that success is shaped by parents' strategies and resources. And so as parents, we hedge our bets. Well-off parents don't just invest in college savings accounts and hire financial advisers to secure their children's inheritances; they also invest in their children's excellence, buying or renting property in the "best" school district they can afford and paying for tutors, coaches, and expensive extracurricular classes and activities.[6] They also invest their time, volunteering in their children's classrooms, participating in school governance to ensure school policies align with their children's strengths, and teaching their children to advocate for themselves.[7]

As we have seen, what exactly each parent does can vary a great deal—parents do not all go about trying to secure their children's futures in the same way, and all of us are influenced by the various cultural repertoires that we have encountered in our lives. Our repertoires emerge from myriad sources: our parents and peers where we grew up, our neighbors, our colleagues at work, to name a few.

Having experienced success in hierarchical, test-based education systems in Asia, many Asian immigrants in towns like Woodcrest dive into American meritocracy with gusto. While others have suggested that Asian parents respond to worries about discrimination by emphasizing academics, I mostly did not hear about that kind of concern.[8] Nor did I hear about Confucian ideals or attempts to embody the tiger mom image among Asian parents. Rather, most Asian parents in Woodcrest, whether they were born in the United States or not, tended to draw upon the cultural repertoires that got them (or their own parents or grandparents) ahead in India and China—namely, an intense regimen of testing and ample public pressure to excel on those tests, especially in STEM subjects. Competition for scarce resources—in this case, seats at elite universities—makes those tests essential for future success in India and China, and this cultural legacy maintains its influence when families land in the United States.[9] For these successful Asian parents, there is nothing unusual in enrolling their children in supplementary math classes and summer academic classes, and in prioritizing academics over sports. In their own experiences in India and China, extra academics beyond the school curriculum was just what most kids *do*, not something exceptional for that unusually driven science aficionado or the slower learner who needs extra help to keep up with their peers. When these parents in turn worry about their children's emotional well-being, their instincts are similarly self-driven: they prefer solutions that ask individual families to make choices for their children, rather than school-wide policies that they see as limiting individual ambitions.

White parents, on the other hand, express a more holistic perspective on excellence, sometimes discouraging their children from taking too many Advanced Placement and honors classes, especially if they have busy sports schedules after school. Not surprisingly, this perspective is also the one favored by elite colleges in the US. Many white parents emphasize the importance of work experience and developing social skills as well. They more frequently emphasize a desire to develop their children's autonomy (even while guiding their children through more subtle influence).[10] Like immigrant Asian parents, they emphasize what they have learned in their own lives. For them, athletic recruiting is one pathway to get into the most selective colleges. And when public school doesn't seem to meet their kids' needs, many white parents in Woodcrest are willing and able to pull them out and transfer them to a private school.

White and Asian parents alike in Woodcrest—and around the country—also worry that their children are overscheduled, with negative consequences for their emotional health. Even Asian parents downplayed their expectations for their kids because of this concern. When these concerns crescendo, some families begin to ask their schools and fellow parents to dial back schoolwork, while others ask their children to reduce their extracurricular commitments to make time for a rigorous academic course load.

Still, it is important to look beyond what parents say and do in the present, because there is a more complex bundle of decisions that shape what they feel they need to say and do.[11] In other words, direct parent influence may not be the main driver of how parents shape children's behaviors and achievements. This can help us understand why parents all tell their children similar things—across class, geographic, and racial lines, parents tend to express high expectations for their children's education—and yet their children end up behaving differently, with unequal academic outcomes.[12] Bringing children to the Woodcrest environment was enough to set high achievement expectations without stating them explicitly, because the kids were surrounded by high achievers in a well-resourced district. With those expectations already very clear, albeit implicitly, parents could say al the right things about wanting to lower their kids' stress. Parents' degrees were compounded by the degrees of peers' parents and the colleges peers just ahead of them attended. Of course, sometimes that community influence was more than what parents had bargained for—when parents felt the environment emphasized academic excellence too strongly, they sometimes moved their children to private schools or exhorted them to take fewer honors classes. When academic strain grows alongside shifting demographics, it is perhaps unsurprising that some white parents attributed it to ethnic change.

From the moment I arrived at Woodcrest, it was clear that a jumble of tensions was simmering just below the surface. What role should parents play? Is it okay to prepare over the summer for an advanced class in the fall? Who deserves to be in honors classes? How much cajoling is too much? When should a parent stop a striving child from taking on too much? What is a reasonable expectation of practice hours per week for a varsity sports team? What is *too* much?

These questions that parents in Woodcrest spent a considerable amount of time asking themselves emerged from a broad gamut of pressures—from economic anxiety to social striving to worries about children's mental health—and yet these many questions, and the many pressures behind them, more often than not manifested in a single activity: judging the moral worth of *other* parents. These judgments were often based upon moral boundaries related to what it meant to be a good parent. In other words, parents worked hard to defend their own parenting by looking down on *other* parents. And most of the time, those other parents who were the problem were people who looked different from them. This ended up increasing the distance between white and Asian parents, even while some Asian parents rejected white critiques of their parenting, drawing a parallel between Asian families' emphasis on the highest levels of academic excellence with white families' focus on athletic excellence.

When Asian Americans surpass their white neighbors in significant numbers, the whispers of judgment can morph into broader anti-Asian feelings. These fears, though cloaked in liberal identities, are not unlike the fears of working-class whites who blame immigrants for their declining fortunes, a narrative fueled by recent political rhetoric.[13] And they suggest that skill-based immigration policies, as advocated by some conservatives eager to admit only the "right" kind of immigrants, are not a panacea to quell anti-immigrant sentiments, and may even fuel them. On the one hand, previous studies have shown that even Americans who seek more restrictions on who can enter the country often think that immigrants with high levels of education should be allowed in.[14] These immigrants are "good" immigrants and seem to exist in a separate category. On the other hand, many in Woodcrest also found fault with this group of immigrants. Rather than depict immigrants as rapists and drug dealers as Donald Trump did to stoke anti-immigrant sentiments, they portrayed immigrant Asian parents as unreasonably focused on academic pursuits and lacking in attention to children's emotional well-being in the right ways. While these parents did not express views that immigration should be curtailed, I wondered if in the future experiences like theirs just may lead some to that view.

My time in Woodcrest along with my reading of the research on race and education made me realize that to be accepted by white parents and school officials, parents of color often have to fit into a narrow definition of good parents—Black and Latinx parents often are stereotyped by whites as not focused enough on education, while Asian American parents are seen as *too* focused on it. Of course, there is nothing inherently related to race or ethnicity in these issues. But when parents tend to clump with their coethnics in terms of their take on them, individuals attach ethnic labels to those differences, as we have seen throughout this book.

PROTECTING STATUS

One of the most intriguing parts of talking to parents was that, almost across the board, all of their hopes for their kids sounded so reasonable.

When white parents expressed their desires for balance, and for school-work that did not overload their children, I found myself nodding my head in agreement over and over again. Their wishes were so heartfelt, and their hopes were so sensible. And when Asian parents told me that every family should make its own decisions about how much to take on, and that the school should run intramural sports as an option for kids to destress without the intensive commitments of varsity sports, I kept on nodding. Who wouldn't agree with such practical solutions? Over time, I came to realize something more complex: these solutions were absolutely genuine, and also strategic. Parents tended to see the world in ways that privileged their own status. White parents wanted to lessen academics, a domain in which Asian Americans were outperforming their kids; Asian parents disagreed with anything that would reduce the potential to achieve in the academic realm.

I doubt that these were conscious, strategic visions for getting ahead. Rather, for each parent these wishes were unconscious and unexplored—they just seemed like the obvious right way to do things.[15] In other words, the parenting strategies I found in Woodcrest were not necessarily deliberate attempts to improve the standing of all white families or to bolster the status of all Asian families; they just seem like the "natural" way of doing things. And that is why they are so pernicious. The sincerity of parents' good intentions means that these seemingly obvious decisions can morph into stereotypes and biases.[16]

Amidst the many "obvious" decisions that we all make, upper-middle-class whites are particularly adept at getting schools to align with their preferences. In Woodcrest, many white parents diverted energy in the district away from academic achievement in order to preserve children's emotional well-being. And it helped that most school staff, like themselves, were college-educated whites who probably shared much of their cultural repertoires. They tended to set the tone and norms for "good" parenting, leading many town efforts to address students' emotional well-being. This included pushing for reducing homework at the high school level as a mechanism to reduce student stress. The alignment between this perspective and the declining status of white students in Woodcrest's academic hierarchy should not come as a surprise. These white parents did not, for example, argue for fewer hours of sports practice for teams already on the field fifteen hours per week.[17]

The Woodcrest of today is certainly not the first place or time in which this has happened in the world. The people in power have always found ways to justify and maintain their position. We have seen, for example, that white UCLA students downplay the importance of grade point average (GPA) for college admissions when reminded that Asian Americans are overrepresented on University of California campuses under the current system, which uses GPA.[18] In my own research based on interviews with Ivy League and Oxford students, I found that white students in the United States define what a fair system of admissions is very differently from British students, but what students at elite universities in both places share is a belief that admissions should be done the way that their own universities are already doing it. That across-the-board belief in the validity of the system that admitted them has a very simple explanation: believing in the system that rewarded them bolsters their identities as winners of the admissions competition.[19] Institutions do this too. One hundred years ago Ivy League universities run by white Protestant leaders redefined merit in admissions when they wanted to limit the number of Jewish students admitted under the old exam-based system.[20]

White parents in Woodcrest tended to identify as liberal and expressed great appreciation for the racial diversity in their town that came from the busing program and Asian immigration. Over 80 percent of adults in town voted for Joe Biden in the 2020 presidential election. But their appreciation for diversity only went so far. When that growing diversity led to their children seeming less accomplished academically, they pushed back. In other words, when Asian Americans outperformed white teens, white parents worked to shift the very terms of the competition. And they defined their way as the right way to parent. They wanted their children to benefit from moving to a place like Woodcrest, which was supposed to ensure that they came out ahead of everyone else, but when Asian families followed in their footsteps and Asian American kids bested their children, white parents attempted to alter the very system designed to privilege them. Many Asian parents also accepted these narratives and responded by distancing themselves from the supposedly unworthy parenting of many other Asian parents. They agreed, in other words, that Asians are often bad parents, even if they themselves were not.

Still, it is important to keep in mind that Asian Americans also benefited from a broader system of racial exclusion that makes towns like Woodcrest possible in the first place.[21] When ethnic tensions abound it is easy to forget the plethora of privileges enjoyed by Asian American and white families alike in Woodcrest. After all, the town (and many suburbs like it around the country) was designed historically to keep African Americans out, especially poor and working-class African Americans. In other words, when Asian Americans come to Woodcrest, they benefit from the Black exclusion the town was built upon. The concentration of high incomes and levels of education in Woodcrest provide world-class resources and opportunities for all of Woodcrest's students. Professional Asian immigrant families in towns like Woodcrest have the financial and cultural resources to succeed at the competitive processes designed by and for white success. But towns like Woodcrest, needless to say, are inaccessible to most American families. Though Woodcrest's Asian Americans are certainly not white, and while it is important to recognize various kinds of discrimination they face and the ways they continue to be treated as outsiders, the Asian families in Woodcrest are certainly more privileged than most American families.

In towns like Woodcrest, white and Asian families alike benefit from an American system of meritocracy that rewards the children who are already ahead—children whose parents went to college and who have high incomes. This system, in turn, seems designed to punish kids who are working class, Black, or Latinx, not for their lack of ambition or hard work, but for their lower social status. When privileged children work incredibly hard in school, it's easy to forget the ways in which private music lessons, expensive tutors, and a privileged community also enable their achievements. In Woodcrest, this meant that most parents I met, whether Asian or white, seemed unaware of the advantages their children held over children in other school districts. Though most parents chose to live in Woodcrest for its highly regarded school system, they did not fully grasp the influence of that system, instead assuming their children's achievements were a result of individual smarts and hard work. In other words, American meritocracy is built on exclusion—on a rigid class hierarchy, and on a slightly more mutable racial hierarchy, all covered with a shiny veneer of possibility for everyone to get ahead, which masks the hierarchies that make getting ahead so difficult for certain people. So immigrants coming with high levels of education are able to benefit from that system, which can lead them to fail to notice its problems. Ultimately, when Asian and white families in towns like Woodcrest are locked in a struggle to define the terms of fair ways of supporting their children's success, it is easy to forget that children living beyond the town's limits are the ones that really lose out. The problem of privilege in Woodcrest is not white and Asian parents doing everything they can to help their children get ahead; all parents do that. Rather, the problem is a housing and schooling system in the United States that enables them to do so with so many more advantages than others.

We can—and should—marvel over the audacity of people who use their fame and power to curry further fame and power, whether criminal cases like Lori Loughlin faking her children's athletic skills to get them into USC, or the more banal but more pervasive privilege that comes from getting an admissions boost when applying to Harvard as a legacy. But these are merely the most egregious examples of a system that is fundamentally problematic. Ultimately, *most* students attending selective residential colleges are privileged compared to the average teen in the US—let alone compared to those whose families sit in the bottom half of the income distribution.[22] But the disdain we pour on people like Loughlin and her associates actually maintains our belief in our meritocracy—these people, we believe, are the exceptions that prove the rule of meritocracy. If we just root out these bad apples, then the system will be fair. But of course, that is true, and it is not. Asian Americans and whites who go to college are twice as likely as Black, Latinx, and Native American college students to attend selective colleges—colleges with higher graduation rates and more resources and opportunities for their students.[23] Life in an affluent suburb, whether white or Asian, nearly guarantees a spot close to the top.

IMMIGRANT ASSIMILATION

My time in Woodcrest reveals the complexity of the assimilation process, especially for Asian Americans. The old story of immigrant assimilation was that all immigrants would do what they could to dissolve the boundary between themselves and the dominant group—middle-class whites—because of the racial exclusion that shaped so much of American society, everything from citizenship laws to housing to schooling.[24] Simultaneously, the old story was that numerous elements of American life—living in suburbs, academic achievement, professional jobs, and beliefs in multiculturalism—would facilitate that assimilation.[25] But it is clear that in places like Woodcrest, despite being a typical upper-middle-class suburb where we previously would have expected to see straightforward assimilation, Asian immigrants are experiencing something far more complex. Asian Americans have endured ongoing racial stereotypes and still reckon with discrimination. In fact, brutal racialized attacks on Asian Americans are on the rise.[26] Substantial evidence also exists for Asian Americans experiencing bamboo ceilings in the workplace.[27] Yet they have also attained academic and socioeconomic success—even beyond the most privileged race group in the United States, whites.

One surprise to me was just how similar Indian and Chinese parents in Woodcrest were when it came to parenting. When I embarked on this study I assumed that ethnicity would play a more important role, given the myriad differences between India and China, even among the well-educated. Of course there were differences—they attended different religious institutions, and the parents had separate social networks, for example. But what they shared was their origins in countries in which standardized tests play a central role in determining a person's success. That success was what led them to their elite university degrees and the STEM jobs that most of them held. Without these credentials, living in Woodcrest would have been out of reach, as it is to most Americans, given property prices and rents. These findings suggest that our instinct to study immigrants by their countries of origin can lead us to miss similarities between immigrant groups.[28] Immigrant parents' educational experiences in India and China seemed to matter much more in Woodcrest. The lives of parents I met in Woodcrest were dramatically different from those of the Indian parents I met in an earlier study of children of Indian immigrants attending a low-performing high school in Queens, New York, most of whom did not have college degrees.[29]

The parenting strategies of highly skilled Chinese and Indian parents seem to be working: Asian American youth in the United States are outperforming their peers of all other races in a variety of measures of academic achievement, including GPAs, SAT scores, and more.[30] Among Asian Americans and whites growing up middle class, Asian Americans are more likely than whites to end up in the top income quintile and less likely than whites to end up in the bottom income quintile.[31] Young adults born in the US to two Asian parents are more likely to hold a graduate degree than those born to one Asian and one white parent.[32] This is true even when we compare children of the same social class across race lines.[33] Following these national patterns, Asian American youth in Woodcrest outperformed their white peers academically, as we have seen. And across generations, Asian American adults who grew up in Woodcrest have higher incomes, on average, than white adults who grew up in Woodcrest.[34]

So the question remains: will Asian Americans slip into the dominant group—currently defined as "white"—just as later-generation Irish, Italian, and Jewish Americans did in the twentieth century?[35] Evidence in this book suggests that the incorporation process will be more complex, as Asian Americans forge their own pathways to success in the United States. Ironically, as the United States becomes more welcoming of racial diversity, Asian Americans may also feel less compelled to attempt to blend into the dominant white group.[36] At the same time, when Asian Americans catapult ahead of whites in significant numbers they may meet resistance by whites, some of whom may simply move to other suburban communities—a suburban version of white flight that already seems to be happening around the country—or shift the terms of success or redefine what it means to be a good parent.[37] We can especially expect to see this occur in communities with large and growing Asian populations, and where Asian Americans are outperforming whites. Sociologist Richard Alba lists three criteria necessary for the dissolution of the boundary between ethnic groups: (1) a situation of expanding opportunity, so one group's success does not require another's demotion; (2) groups living side-by-side; and (3) a removal of stigma, or a "moral elevation" of the immigrant group.[38] It is clear that in towns like Woodcrest, well-off Asian Americans and whites live side by side, but it remains to be seen whether the moral boundaries drawn between white and Asian parenting and perceptions of Asian American success negatively affecting white youth will decline over time to facilitate that dissolution.

Given that Asian Americans seemed to succeed in Woodcrest by *not* becoming more like their white neighbors, it is reasonable to ask whether the opposite happened. That is, whether their white neighbors shifted toward the cultural repertoires of Asians, as they saw them pulling ahead in academic achievement. Quite simply, they did not. Instead, white parents insisted on the moral worthiness of their own style of parenting. Here we can see the enduring power of whiteness in American society, which takes for granted the superiority of white cultural repertoires, even when Asian Americans catapult ahead on traditional measures of "success." In a study of Cupertino, California—a west coast town similar to Woodcrest—Tomás Jiménez suggests that Asian Americans have flipped the meaning of whiteness, such that Asians are now seen as having higher status than whites because of their academic success.[39] But the tensions I observed suggest that at least in Woodcrest, this conclusion is premature. While Asians in Woodcrest are worthwhile competitors—and often victors—in the race to get ahead, they are still dogged by judgments of bad parenting. Certainly, whites do not strive to take their place by doing the same things—they hold on to their own ways of parenting as the best, most morally defensible style.

Some suggest that assimilation is in fact the wrong question, because it ignores the roles of white privilege and even US imperialism and treats whites as the universal to which minorities must be compared.[40] Certainly, the emphasis of previous research on the extent to which Asian Americans have achieved socioeconomic and educational parity with whites has brought insufficient attention to some of the conflicts I highlight in this book. The ability of whites in Woodcrest to align school policy with their own cultural repertoires is another clear sign of their ongoing power and status in Woodcrest.

In addition, we should pay more attention to race. Would the tensions I saw in Woodcrest have arisen if the growing immigrant groups in town were white (or if there were no immigrants at all)? How would the school district have addressed emotional well-being if the high achievers were not predominantly Asian?[41] We know that Asian immigrants have faced decidedly harsher forms of racial exclusion and overt racism than European immigrants for centuries—from the Chinese Exclusion Acts to Japanese internment during World War II to the growing attacks on Asian Americans when COVID-19 emerged. Even when European immigrants faced racialized exclusion it was fundamentally and undeniably harsher for Asian immigrants.[42] On the other hand, immigrants in Woodcrest benefit from the exclusion of African Americans enabled by housing segregation and test-based systems of selection in the United States. My hope is not only that scholarship will continue to ask questions about group differences and boundaries related to immigration, but also that sociologists elevate and attend to power and racial hierarchy in their analyses of immigration for a fuller picture of the shaping of immigrant life. Together, these ways of analyzing immigration build up a broader, more incisive picture of immigration in the United States.

The findings in this book also show the importance of looking beyond levels of education, incomes, and intermarriage when studying how immigrants incorporate into American society. Taking culture seriously—not just as a lay explanation for supposedly different "values" in groups—means paying attention to, for example, the cultural repertoires that immigrants bring with them and how those shift over time, depending on the neighborhood in which they live, the friends they spend time with, and more.

It remains to be seen how the Asian American teens I interviewed will parent their own children. Will they increasingly adopt the parenting styles and foci of their white peers, or will they maintain the (seemingly successful) strategies for success imparted by their parents? Like myself, many born in the US to highly skilled Asian immigrants who arrived after 1965 have come of age and are creating families of their own. They continue to thrive socioeconomically. They also marry non-Asians at high rates (marrying whites most frequently), perhaps drawing them closer to the perspectives I tended to hear from white parents in Woodcrest.[43] Indeed, US-born Asian American parents I met in Woodcrest seemed to straddle the perspectives of the US-born white parents and immigrant Asian parents I met. More research on Asian American parenting needs to systematically look at the trajectories of later generations. Emerging evidence suggests that later-generation Asian Americans have educational, occupational, and income outcomes that are closer to those of comparable whites than those of immigrant Asians, even if both US-born and immigrant Asians fare better than whites overall.[44] We should also consider whether some whites who grew up in Woodcrest adopt the cultural repertoires of their Asian American peers after seeing their success, or whether instead they follow in their parents' footsteps, finding ways to maintain their sense of moral superiority.

WHAT IS TO BE DONE?

As I was revising this book, Senator Kamala Harris, the daughter of Jamaican and Indian immigrants, was elected vice president of the United States. She embodies both a strong Black identity—she attended a historically Black college and was a member of a Black sorority—alongside strong ties to India—she spent summers as a child there and was raised by her Indian mother. The coexistence of these facets within the vice president has a larger relevance, I believe, and suggests that Asian Americans can (and I would argue, should) maintain strong ethnic identities while also recognizing the historical exclusion of African Americans from the American dream and the ways that well-educated Asian immigrants (not unlike Harris's mother) have benefited from systems of segregation and exclusion that were designed to keep African Americans out. Rather than extol the meritocracy that punishes far more people than it rewards, Asian Americans should recognize more fully the reasons we need, for example, affirmative action, and more generally expansion of opportunities for all Americans to realize the American dream. Asian Americans should also support greater class and racial integration in neighborhoods through, for example, expanding low- and mixed-income housing in their communities, increasing housing density through zoning, and more. I remain hopeful on this front. Asian Americans for decades have participated in progressive politics, both as a panethnic "Asian American" group as well as by their countries of origin, including in movements against colonialism, as allies in the Black power movement, and in protests against the Vietnam War.[45]

Of course, white residents in towns like Woodcrest should also recognize the legacy of racism that built their towns and perpetuated their privilege. It is not enough to praise the diversity that comes from bringing a few Black students to schools through a busing program that ultimately taxes Black students the most—long commutes, school away from their communities, and feelings of social exclusion, especially for girls.[46] Programs like this are simply not enough. Whites in Woodcrest seem to genuinely appreciate the cultural diversity that immigration also brings—interesting foods at the international potlucks in elementary schools and a boost to their liberal credentials.

But we need more than just an appreciation of diversity and the standard liberal rejection of overt racism. Instead, we need more privileged whites to become *antiracist*. An antiracist stance means being willing to give up one's privileges. It means whites not rejecting Asian cultural repertoires outright. This includes not shaming Asian neighbors who send their children to supplementary math classes, nor assuming that Asians are less deserving of spots in honors classes, nor advocating for reductions in academic expectations while ignoring the expectations for sports teams. It means not assuming that their children will and always should be the ones whose priorities the school district emphasizes, whose talents elite colleges should reward. It means forging relationships with Asian neighbors and working hard to understand their perspectives, and their hopes and dreams for their children. For Asian Americans and whites alike, it means supporting policies that increase opportunities for Black, Latinx, and Native American youth even if those programs and policies do not directly benefit our own children or might diminish our property values. It means recognizing the problems with college admissions and standardized tests—systems of meritocracy—that reward a disproportionate number of already well-off students, including our own. And in communities like Woodcrest it means supporting policies that enable—not prevent—working-class families to live and thrive in their community. We need changes that go beyond talking about individual attitudes. They must include equitable and inclusive organizational practices and social policies as well.

The hopes and dreams we all have for our children are more similar than different. We want them to experience happiness, have some level of material well-being, and perhaps experience some kind of professional success and self-fulfillment. But the enduring power of whiteness means that we have unequal opportunities to fulfill those hopes and dreams. As upper-middle-class whites and Asians engage in a race at the very top of the status hierarchy, it is easy to miss the ways that whiteness perpetuates privileges for whites, and also the ways that Asian Americans sometimes benefit from the white supremacy that built America.

Acknowledgments

THE ACKNOWLEDGMENTS ARE ONE OF my favorite parts of a book, both as a reader and as a writer. It is there that we learn with whom the author has been in conversation, who their mentors have been, and where their intellectual debts lie. Sometimes we get a glimpse of who they are as a person. And when writing, it is an opportunity to remember all the shoulders on which our work stands, and the gifts we have been given. Remembering all those gifts brings me great joy. Without them, there would be no book, so I relish this opportunity to acknowledge them with gratitude.

First and foremost, I thank all the residents and school staff and administrators in Woodcrest who, in small and big ways, facilitated this research. So many people shared their stories and observations, opened up their classrooms, invited me to sit with them and their friends at lunch, connected me to others, and guided me. Being a qualitative researcher helps you see the goodness in people—teachers pour their hearts into connecting with and teaching their students. Parents do everything they can to support their children, and sometimes their neighbors' children, too. Coaches put in long hours to guide their teams and enable children to become their best selves. And of course, kids do their best to heed the advice of the adults around them while being true to their inner selves as they stumble through adolescence. While I cannot name any of these people because I want to protect their and their town's privacy, I am forever grateful to them.

Tomás Jiménez has been a helpful sounding board throughout this project, from its inception to feedback on a draft of the manuscript. I am grateful for his time and friendship. Thank you also to the generous students who provided feedback on a draft of this manuscript: Maya Cohen, Nadirah Farah Foley, Liu Jiang, Lisa Utzinger Shen, and Xin Xiang. Helen Marrow read multiple chapters of the book—sometimes twice—and, as always, was generous with her time, ideas, and insights. Bart Bonikowski, Zoya Kumar-Warikoo, Michèle Lamont, and Cinzia Solari also read portions of the book and shared their ideas on how to strengthen it. Shelby Austin-Manning, Michael Koplow, David Lobenstine, and Nora Reavey-Gilbert provided editorial feedback to ensure my arguments and writing were clear and error-free.

Numerous colleagues around the country were helpful in this project, whether through conversations we had, questions they asked at talks, or feedback they provided on work related to this project. Thank you to Stefan Beljean, Amy Binder, Joe Blatt, Mary Brinton, Prudence Carter, Margaret Chin, Peter Demerath, Pawan Dhingra, Amy Hsin, Phil Kasinitz, Michèle Lamont, Pei-Chia Lan, Annette Lareau, Jennifer Lee, Suniya Luthar, OiYan Poon, Stacey Sinclair, Van Tran, Leslie Wang, Mary Waters, Rick Weissbourd, and Janelle Wong. Excellent research assistants also strengthened this project and enabled me to get it done: thank you to Mark Chin, Maya Cohen, Nadirah Farah Foley, and Jessica Rieger. I love the conversations after talks, and audiences for this project did not disappoint—thank you to those who engaged with me at the Eastern Sociological Society annual conference; the University of Potsdam Conference on Cultural Diversity, Migration and Education; and talks at University of Birmingham's Centre for Research on Race and Education, Harvard's Culture and Social Analysis Workshop, and Harvard's Migration and Immigrant Integration Workshop. A Guggenheim Foundation fellowship and grants from Russell Sage Foundation and Tufts University made this research possible.

At Harvard, Dean Jim Ryan was generous with resources and time to help get this project off the ground. At Tufts, I am ever grateful to Paul Joseph, Bárbara Brizuela, and Jim Glaser, who invited me to join their faculty and provided the time and mental space to focus on this project amidst a professional move. Michèle Lamont, Nitika Raj, and Mary

Waters were important sounding boards as I made critical life decisions along the way.

My marvelous editor at University of Chicago Press, Elizabeth Branch Dyson, seemed to understand this project from the start. Conversations with her are always filled with laughter and keen insights into the story I want to tell. Elizabeth read and provided feedback at multiple stages of this project, always making it better as she did so. I feel so lucky to have had this second opportunity to work with her. The reviewers Elizabeth enlisted also provided very helpful insights that strengthened the manuscript. Elizabeth's assistants Mollie McFee and Dylan Montanari made sure everything went off without a hitch. So did Kevin Walsh at Harvard, and John LiBassi at Tufts. Teresa Bergen transcribed recorded interviews with care and precision. Thank you to June Sawyers for creating an index to help readers dig into the book.

Most important throughout this journey have been my family and friends. Every morning I meditate to help clear my mind. As I visualize warm, bright sunlight all around that reaches beyond the stars, I am learning to accept the world as it is, focus on what role I want to play in it, and how to strengthen my relationships and support those around me. Friends and family near and far, too numerous to name, are in my heart even when the pandemic has kept us apart. My parents are my biggest cheerleaders, and the more I am imperfect the more they seem to shower me with unconditional love. My husband Ramesh Kumar has taught me that having a plan is not always the best way to live our lives, and for this and so much more, I am truly grateful. My daughter Zoya has taught me to slow down and savor each moment. My son Kavi has unleashed an adventurous spirit in me (usually at the top of some snowy ski mountain), and my daughter Nuria a creativity that brings me much joy. I trust they are learning at least as much from me as I am from them. Life in our house is often loud and unpredictable, but I wouldn't trade it for anything.

I am so grateful for all of these wonderful people, and for so much more. Writing a book is laborious, but I have finally made it to the best part!

Research Methods

IN ORDER TO ANSWER MY questions about the impact of Asian American immigration in well-off suburban communities, I knew I needed to identify a community to study in-depth. I chose Woodcrest for three reasons. First, I wanted an upper-middle-class community with a large and growing Asian immigrant population. This would allow me to investigate how Asian and white families together made sense of achievement and meritocracy in a changing community. Second, I was interested in a community that until recently was predominantly white, so that I could understand the impact of a changing population. Third, I wanted to study a locale on the east coast, because early studies of Asian Americans in suburban communities were located on the west coast; I also knew that an east coast locale would facilitate more frequent research trips since it would be closer to my home in Massachusetts.[1]

Woodcrest has experienced dramatic ethnic change over the past quarter century. From 1990 to 2019 the Asian American share of the town's population grew five times, to over 30 percent. Nearly half of Asian Americans in Woodcrest are Chinese, over one-third are Indian, and the remainder are predominantly Korean.[2] Less than 5 percent of Woodcrest residents identify as black, Hispanic, or some other race.[3] The median household income in Woodcrest is over $150,000, with Asian American households earning more on average than others.[4] Less than 5 percent of Woodcrest's residents live below the poverty line.[5]

Given the high incomes, it will be no surprise that adults in Woodcrest also have high levels of education. Over 80 percent of them hold a Bachelor's degree; this percentage is slightly higher for Asian residents than for white residents.[6] In my research I found that many of those degrees are from the most elite colleges in the United States, China, and India. Many parents in Woodcrest, but especially Asian parents, work in engineering, science, or technology firms. This includes 60 percent of the Chinese parents interviewed (and 50 percent of the jobs reported by Chinese American students that their parents held), 53 percent of Indian parents interviewed (and 61 percent of jobs reported by Indian American students), and 24 percent of white parents interviewed (and 27 percent of the jobs reported by white students).

Housing makes life in Woodcrest out of reach for most Americans— the median home value is close to $900,000.[7] Over 80 percent of residents in Woodcrest own their homes.[8] Renters spend, on average, over $2,000 per month on rent.[9]

Like most school districts in the metro area, multiple elementary and middle schools in Woodcrest feed into one high school, currently home to over 2,000 students. One-third of students at Woodcrest High School are Asian, reflecting both the younger profile of Asians in Woodcrest as well as white residents' higher propensity to send their children to private schools. Still, over 90 percent of school-age children in Woodcrest attend its public schools. Around 5 percent of students at Woodcrest High, most of whom are part of the busing program from the nearby urban center, are eligible for free or reduced-price school meals.

While this book focuses on parents, the project was different at the outset. I first set out to understand the broader culture of teens in an area of ethnic change, akin to my study of youth cultures among children of immigrants in New York City and London schools.[10] I began by spending time at Woodcrest High School during and after school hours, hanging out with students and observing their experiences in school. During my visits I shadowed students in two different eleventh-grade homeroom classes through their school days. I also conducted four focus-group discussions with six or seven students in each. Each group of students shared a homeroom group that was deliberately mixed by ethnicity and achievement levels. Fifty-three students took part in more in-depth interviews. I met most of those students during my classroom observations. In-depth interviews touched on social life at school; how the

TABLE A.1. Comparative demographics, Woodcrest and U.S.

	WOODCREST	U.S.
RACE (PERCENTAGE OF POPULATION)		
White (non-Hispanic)	60–65	61
Asian	30–35	6
Indian	10–15	1
Chinese	10–15	1
Other Asian	5–10	3
Hispanic or Black	<5	30
AIAN, NHOPI, other, or two or more races	<5	9
IMMIGRATION		
Percentage foreign born	25–30	14
Countries of origin— top 3	China India Korea	Mexico India China
INCOME AND HOUSING		
Median household income	$150,000–$200,000	$63,000
Percentage with bachelor's degree or higher (age 25+)	80–85	32
Median home value	approx. $900,000	$218,000

Race: US Census Bureau 2019c. Immigration: US Census Bureau 2019a. Countries of origin: US Census Bureau 2019a. Income: US Census Bureau 2019f. Educational attainment: US Census Bureau 2019d. Median home value: US Census Bureau 2019b. I give data ranges to protect the identity of the community.

students spend weekdays and weekends; extracurricular activities; how the students define success and achievement; academic achievement; experiences with racial diversity; ethnic identity; and more.[11] Beyond the school day I attended sports games, music concerts, town events, and other activities.

I wanted to make sure that I captured a variety of student experiences, so I used students' level of chemistry in eleventh grade—college prep, remedial, honors, or AP—to make sure I captured a quorum of students in each major ethnic group (Chinese, Indian, white) in each track. When the number of participants fell short, I visited chemistry classes to recruit more participants of the underrepresented tracks by ethnicity; I ended up having to recruit additional Indian and Chinese students in non-AP chemistry. While I conducted forty-nine of the fifty-three student interviews, a research assistant who had been hard at work processing and analyzing transcripts (and who had accompanied me during focus group discussions) stepped in to conduct four interviews at the end of the school year when we needed additional participants and I could not make it to the school.

Interviews took place during a student's free period or after school. All students had at least two free periods a week, thanks to newly instituted all-school study hall periods every week, designed to attenuate stress and provide opportunities for students to catch up on work and make appointments with teachers for extra help. Interviews lasted, on average, forty-four minutes, similar to the length of a class period. At school I also interviewed seven school staff, including school administrators, teachers, and guidance counselors. I also spoke with three ethnic community leaders and a local real estate agent who helped me understanding the shifting housing market in town.

As my research at Woodcrest High School wound down, I started speaking with parents. Most studies of the children of immigrants and intensive parenting take the kids' words at face value; they describe parenting only through the lens of their children (sometimes they are adult children reflecting back on their childhoods).[12] But I knew that if someone interviewed me about my parents' parenting, I would be able to list all the things they did wrong, and I probably would misattribute the reasons for at least some of their actions and expectations. I knew that my parents would describe their parenting in very different ways than I would. These concerns led me to also speak with parents. I wanted to understand the extent to which parents and teens were aligned in their emphases and in their accounts of why students participated in the activities they did and the levels of classes they were in. Altogether I interviewed sixty white, Indian, and Chinese parents. We spoke about a range of topics, including how they ended up living in Woodcrest; their likes and dislikes about their children's schools; how they define success and achievement; their views on stress and competition, especially related to student life at Woodcrest High School; and their perceptions of ethnic change in Woodcrest.[13] While I relied on my time at school and with students to get a broad understanding of the student experience at Woodcrest High School, most of the material in this book relies on the perspectives of parents.

Much to my surprise, I found that parents' and kids' emphases often flipped the usual narratives about parent-child differences, with parents insisting that their children chill out and not overload themselves with schoolwork or extracurricular activities. And I soon realized that parenting was an important site of ethnic tension over what was happening in Woodcrest schools. In other words, I began to understand what I saw in the schools through the lens of parents—their parenting practices and beliefs as well as how they understood the behaviors and actions of other parents. These tensions surfaced most commonly in discussions about their children's achievement and success.

An early set of interviews confirmed that my own experience as a US-born Asian American is not unique. That is, I found that US-born Asian American parents, like myself, tended to share some perspectives and behaviors with US-born whites, and others with immigrant Asian parents. Of course, all of these groups have considerable variation— ethnicity and birthplace do not drive all things parenting. While my primary focus in the book is foreign-born Asian parents, in part because they are the vast majority of Asian parents in Woodcrest (and in the United States), I also include the voices of US-born Asian American parents, to give a sense of how parenting can shift over generations. In the end I interviewed twenty-two Chinese parents (fourteen China-born, one Hong Kong-born, and seven US-born), twenty-one Indian parents (sixteen India-born, four US-born, and one born in Ireland), and seventeen white parents (all US-born). A majority of the parents were mothers, not because I intentionally sought them, but probably because mothers tend to be the primary caretakers of children, so they were the ones who responded most to my requests to speak.[14] Parent interviews ran from thirty minutes to more than two hours, with an average of fifty-five minutes. I met with parents in a variety of locations, including coffee shops, their homes, and, most often, private conference rooms in the Woodcrest public library.

TABLE A.2. Interview participants

| | Ethnicity/Race | | | |
	CHINESE	INDIAN	WHITE	TOTAL
PARENTS				
Immigrant	15	17	0	32
U.S. born	7	4	17	28
	22	**21**	**17**	**60**
STUDENTS				
College prep, remedial, or honors chemistry	8	5	12	25
AP chemistry	11	13	4	28
	19	**18**	**16**	**53**
SCHOOL STAFF AND COMMUNITY LEADERS	4	3	8	15

I connected with parents in a variety of ways. I first contacted parents who gave permission for their children to participate in in-depth interviews at school to solicit their participation, and nine did so. I also tapped my personal networks. Though I don't live in Woodcrest, being a South Asian American professional married to an immigrant South Asian tech entrepreneur meant that my social networks had some connections that were helpful, especially in connecting with Indian parents. Finally, I contacted school and district leaders, leaders in local ethnic organizations, and leaders of other local nonprofits to solicit interviews. Once I interviewed parents, I asked them to connect me with other Woodcrest parents of high school students or recent graduates. I wanted to make sure that I didn't simply interview people in one social network, so I mapped each potential interviewee to make sure that no more than four participants stemmed initially from the same source. Once a source had provided three additional interviewees that participated, I cut off that network and didn't interview any more people

through it. Most parent respondents had children who are either current students at or recent graduates of Woodcrest High School. While
this was the group I targeted, a handful of parents interviewed had
younger children.

Beyond parents of children attending Woodcrest's public schools, I
also wanted to hear from parents who left the public schools. I asked
parents I interviewed, acquaintances, and community leaders if they
knew of parents who either moved away from Woodcrest because of
dissatisfaction with the schools, or whose children moved from public
schools in Woodcrest to private schools. Many connected me to parents
of children attending private schools, but none could point me to a family that moved to another school district in the local area (that is, not
further away because a job took them to an entirely different area of the
country). Ultimately, six of the parents I interviewed had at least one
child attend a private school for at least part of their schooling.

Going into this research I assumed I would have the easiest time recruiting and speaking with Indian parents because of my own Indian
background and a harder time getting white parents to open up given
potential ethnic tensions in town. I was wrong. White parents were the
quickest to agree to speak with me and schedule an interview. I was surprised by their willingness to speak, sometimes in not-so-subtle ways,
about their frustrations with immigrant parents. I soon realized that
they saw me as one of their own. I was born in the United States, have
an American accent, and at the time was a professor of education. White
parents seemed to assume that their take on the world was right and
that as a professional scholar of education I would understand that. I
sensed much less anxiety, and more ease, in their takes on life in Woodcrest.

Chinese parents were the most elusive. Fewer agreed to participate,
and when they did many backed out after an initial response. I offered
interviews with a Mandarin translator, but no one took me up on that
offer. Some Chinese parents asked me to send their interview transcripts after their interviews so that they could clarify anything they
felt did not sound right. This may have been related to comfort with
English, though I suspect it had more to do with concerns about how
their perspectives would be portrayed. As the interviews unfolded, I
wondered if some Chinese parents worried that I would portray them

as at fault for high stress in Woodcrest, as many in the community did. Indian parents showed less concern, perhaps because they shared my ethnicity.

Ultimately, what participants perceive in our mannerisms, race, and accent are always a part of research. Our identities, in turn, shape how we make sense of interviews. I do not promise unfiltered words from my respondents, an impossible task. But I do strive to achieve an empathetic perspective on everyone I encountered. Rather than judge, even when I felt instinctually offended or perplexed, I began by trying to understand. I hope readers will feel I have been successful in this goal.

Student and Parent Interview Questions

STUDENTS

Introduction

- How would you describe Woodcrest to someone who doesn't know this town?

Youth culture

- What are the major social groups at your school?

- What kinds of kids are well-liked at your school? What kinds of kids are not? Please refrain from naming particular students; if you do, those names will be deleted from the transcript.

- What kinds of kids are popular? Unpopular?

- Do you notice any patterns related to ethnicity or race in how kids socialize in or out of school?

- Tell me about your closest friends. Probes:

  - *How and when did you became friends?*

  - *Mutual interests?*

- *How do you spend time together?*

- *How do you communicate?*

- *What is his/her ethnicity?*

- *Do your families ever spend time together? If so, describe that time—activities, meals, etc.*

- What are your favorite music artists, and why? How did you come to listen to that music?

Activities

- Tell me about any extracurricular activities you are involved in. Probes for each activity:

  - *How many hours per week, either as planned practices, lessons, or practicing/homework at home do you spend on that activity?*

  - *Who is in the activity with you—friends, ethnicity, etc.?*

  - *How did you get involved in that activity?*

  - *Did you ever think of ending your participation? What kept you in it?*

  - *Any activities you used to do (since start of ninth grade), but not anymore? How did your participation end?*

  - *Do you know how much, if anything, it costs (if so, please tell me)? What supplies do/did you need to buy or pay for to participate (e.g., uniforms, instruments, transportation, etc.)?*

  - *What is the ethnic make-up of that activity?*

- Do you have a job? (If not: did you ever have a job?) Probes:

  - *How many hours per week?*

  - *How did you get involved?*

  - *What do you like about it?*

  - *What do you dislike about it?*

  - *What you do with the money you earn?*

- Walk me through a typical school day, from the time you wake up until the time you go to bed. Now walk me through a typical Saturday; a typical Sunday.

    - *What time do you go to bed/wake up?*

- What are your plans for the summer?

Success and achievement

- What are your goals in school? Outside of school?

- What are the goals of most kids in this school? What does success mean to them?

- What goals do your parents have for you? How do those connect to your own goals?

    - *How involved are your parents in school? (volunteer activities, talking with your teachers, keeping track of your performance, etc.)*

    - *Do your parents talk with you about school? How frequently? What do they emphasize? How does that compare to other kids' parents in your school?*

- Imagine you are successful in the future. What does that look like ten years from now?

    - *What does not being successful look like ten years from now?*

    - *What will it take for you to be successful?*

    - *What do you worry about?*

- Are you doing anything to prepare for college or other future plans these days?

- Some people say your school is very competitive—what do you think of that? Probes if they agree:

    - *What are the sources of that competition?*

    - *What is good about the competition?*

    - *What is bad about the competition?*

- What kinds of students tend to do well here? What kinds of students tend not to do well?

- What classes are you currently enrolled in?

  - *How did you end up in those classes?*

  - *What grades do you usually get? (ask about specific classes)*

Race and Identity

- What is your ethnic or racial identity? How does your identity shape your experiences in school, if at all?

- Do your parents talk with you about your identity? What do they say?

- Tell me about the different ethnic and racial groups in your school.

  - *For each group: How would you characterize that group?*

- Everyone has had good and bad experiences with people who don't look like them. I know I have. Describe a positive experience you've had with someone of a difference race or ethnicity.

  - *Now describe a negative experience you've had with someone of a different race or ethnicity.*

- Have you ever experienced discrimination? Explain.

- What is your religious identity, if any? Probe if states religious identity:

  - *Do you attend any religious classes like Sunday school?*

  - *Do you go to a church/synagogue/temple? (if yes) How often?*

- Do you speak any other languages?

Family

- Where was your mother born?

- What kind of work, if any, does your mom do outside home? (If used to work: what profession?)

- Do you know if your mom attended college? (Probes: Did she complete college? Any graduate degrees?)

- Where was your father born?

- What kind of work, if any, does your dad do outside home? (If used to work: what profession?)
- Do you know if your dad attended college? (Probes: Did he finish college? Any graduate degrees?)
- How many siblings do you have, and what grades are they in? (If a sibling is finished with high school, probes: What does he/she do now? [If relevant] Where does he/she attend college? What kind of work does he/she do?)
- Do you know whether your family rents or owns your home? How long has your family lived there?

PARENTS

Identity and Background

- How did you end up living in this town?
- Who are your closest friends in town?
- Do you rent or own your home? How long have you lived there?
- How would you describe Woodcrest to someone who doesn't know it?
    - *How has it changed since you moved here (/since you were young)?*
- If you were to do it again, would you move to Woodcrest? Explain.
- Where were you born? (If foreign-born: when did you move to the US?)
- What is your ethnic or racial identity? How does this compare to your children's identities? What do you think of that?
- What kind of work do you do, if any, outside home? (If used to work: what profession?)
- What is the highest level of education you've attended/completed?

Woodcrest High School

- What is your favorite part of Woodcrest High School?
- If you could change one thing about Woodcrest High School, what would it be?

- What do you make of the new homework policy in Woodcrest?

- Have you ever considered changing your child's school, either by moving or shifting to a private or parochial school? How did you resolve that issue?

- What challenges does your child face at school?

- Some people say Woodcrest High School is very competitive—what do you think of that? Probes if yes:

  - *What are the sources of that competition?*

  - *Is it actually competitive?*

  - *Do you like that competition?*

  - *What's good about it?*

  - *What's bad about it?*

- Some people say Woodcrest High School is a school where there are a lot of mental health issues. What do you think of all this talk about mental health?

- What classes is your child currently enrolled in? How did he/she end up in those classes?

- What are your child's grades? Which classes (AP, etc.)?

- What are your child's summer plans?

Success and achievement

- What goals do you have for your child(ren) in school? For the future?

  - *What about other parents in the town—what goals do they have for their children?*

- Imagine that your child is successful in the future—what does that look like ten years from now?

  - *Imagine now that your child is not successful—what does that future look like ten years from now?*

  - *What will it take for your child to be successful?*

  - *What do you worry about?*

- *On a scale of 1–10, how certain are you that your kids will have just as good or better a life than you?*

- How is your parenting style similar to or different from other parents in Woodcrest? Any similarities or differences by ethnicity? How has your style changed over time?

Racial change

- Tell me about the other parents at your child's school. Probes:

  - *In what ways are you similar?*

  - *In what ways are you different?*

  - *Any differences by ethnicity that you notice?*

  - *Who are you closest to?*

- We have all had positive and negative experiences with people of different races. I know I have. Describe a positive experience you've had with someone of a difference race or ethnicity.

  - *Now describe a negative experience you've had with someone of a different race or ethnicity.*

Notes

1. As with all individuals' names, I use a pseudonym to protect Sabrina's identity. Beyond pseudonyms, I sometimes change characteristics of individuals, such as their gender, specific occupation, or specific extracurricular activity to further protect their identities. I sometimes replace a college's name with that of a college that has a similar admit rate, as well.
2. Throughout this book I have edited quotes for clarity only, and mostly for immigrant speakers' verb tenses, missing articles, and other grammatical issues that would not change the meaning of the quote.
3. Economically advantaged and college educated parents tend to push for their children to be in higher academic tracks, and are more likely to advocate for their children at school overall compared to parents with fewer economic resources and less cultural know-how. Lareau 2011; Lareau, Weininger, and Cox 2018; Useem 1992.
4. On intensive parenting, see Hays 1996; Nelson 2010; Sayer et al. 2004.
5. I use the gender-inclusive term "Latinx" to include all people whose ancestry includes anywhere in Latin America. While a majority of Americans who identify as Hispanic or Latino do not self-identify as Latinx, its usage has grown over time. Noe-Bustamante, Mora, and Lopez 2020. For detailed discussion about the term Latinx, see Salinas and Lozano 2021; Torres 2018.
6. Sabrina may have been referring to Thomas Friedman's book *The World Is Flat* (2006), in which Friedman argues that globalization has virtually removed national boundaries, such that talent in places like India and China can now be rewarded on the global stage like never before.
7. Throughout this book I use "Asian" to indicate race, including immigrant Asians and US-born Asians. When describing the foreign-born I write "immigrant Asian," and when describing the US-born and those who came to the US as children, I write "Asian American" (or "Indian American" or "Chinese American").
8. In Warikoo 2020 I refer to the town as "Collegiate."

9. U.S. Census Bureau 2019c.

10. U.S. Census Bureau 2019d.

11. Alba 2009, 2020; Portes, Fernández-Kelly, and Haller 2009; Portes and Zhou 1993.

12. For exceptions see Dhingra 2007; Jiménez 2017; Lung-Amam 2017.

13. On assimilation, see Alba 2020; Alba and Nee 1997; Kasinitz et al. 2008; Portes, Fernández-Kelly, and Haller 2005; Portes and Zhou 1993; Waters and Jiménez 2005. For critiques of assimilation theory for inattention to race, see Jung 2009; Sáenz and Manges Douglas 2015; Treitler 2015.

14. Karabel 2005.

15. Karabel 2005.

16. For example, see Lewis and Diamond 2015; Lucas 1999; Orfield, Kucsera, and Siegel-Hawley 2012; Tyson 2011.

17. Erickson 2016; Geismer 2015; Joffe-Walt 2020.

18. Hays 1996; Sayer et al. 2004.

19. For example, see Abeles 2015; Demerath 2009; Lund and Dearing 2013; Luthar, Barkin, and Crossman 2013; Luthar and Becker 2002; Mueller and Abrutyn 2016.

20. Deresiewicz 2014.

21. Chua 2011; Lythcott-Haims 2015; Schiffrin et al. 2014.

22. Carnevale and Strohl 2013; Lucas 1999; Tyson 2011.

INTRODUCTION

1. Crenshaw et al. 1995.

2. Zuberi 2001.

3. Freedle 2008; Reeves and Halikias 2017; Sackett et al. 2009.

4. Tenenbaum and Ruck 2007; Tyson 2011.

5. Skiba et al. 2011.

6. Starck et al. 2020; Tenenbaum and Ruck 2007.

7. Carnevale and Strohl 2013.

8. Alexander 2010.

9. Choi et al. 2019; Lacy 2007.

10. Kang et al. 2016; Neckerman and Kirschenman 2014; Pager, Bonikowski, and Western 2009.

11. Grogger 2011; Harris 2014.

12. Alba 1985; Ignatiev 1995; Jacobson 1998; Waters 1990.

13. Haney-López 1996.

14. Berrey 2015.

15. On Black hair, see Randle 2015. On workplace discrimination, see Roscigno, Williams, and Byron 2012.

16. Perry 2003.

17. Feliciano and Lanuza 2016; Haller, Portes, and Lynch 2011; Portes and Zhou 1993.

18. Agius Vallejo 2012; Neckerman, Carter, and Lee 1999.

19. Among immigrants this is sometimes described as "selective acculturation," and among African Americans as "cultural straddling" or "code-switching." P. Carter 2005; Dhingra 2007; Portes and Zhou 1993; Warikoo 2011.

20. Feliciano and Lanuza 2016; Fuligni 1997; Kao and Tienda 1995.

21. Carnevale and Strohl 2013; Espenshade and Radford 2009; Hsin and Xie 2014; Kao 1995.

22. Chetty et al. 2019.

23. Chetty et al. 2019. I thank Sebastian Puerta of Opportunity Insights for analyzing the underlying data (available at https://opportunityinsights.org/data/?geographic _level=0&topic=0&paper_id=1652#resource-listing).
24. Batalova, Hanna, and Levesque 2021.
25. U.S. Census Bureau 2019c.
26. Half of Chinese immigrant adults age twenty-five or older have at least a bachelor's degree, compared to only 4 percent of adults in China; this means that Chinese immigrants in the United States are more than twelve times as likely to have a college degree as those who did not immigrate. More than three-in-four adult Indian immigrants have a bachelor's degree or higher, compared to less than 5 percent of adults in India and one-third of US adults overall. In addition, over nine-tenths of Indians in the United States are from a dominant caste, compared to just one-fourth of Hindus in India. Chakravorty, Kapur, and Singh 2017; Kapur 2010; J. Lee and Zhou 2015; U.S. Census Bureau 2019d.
27. Pew Research Center 2017a. This compares to one-third of Americans overall holding a bachelor's degree, and 12 percent holding an advanced degree. U.S. Census Bureau 2019d.
28. Pew Research Center 2017b.
29. U.S. Census Bureau 2019f. Of course, important differences exist between Indian and Chinese immigrants, just as there are differences within each of these immigration streams. To take a few examples, a greater proportion of Chinese immigrants are working class or poor; Indian immigrants tend to identify as more liberal politically and more religious than Chinese; and Confucianism is an important part of Chinese society but not Indian society. Inglehart 1997; Ramakrishnan et al. 2016. However, these differences are far outweighed by the overlaps across much of upper-middle-class Indian and Chinese immigrants in terms of academic achievement. In contrast, Southeast Asian immigrants have much lower levels of educational attainment and household income. For a review of research on Southeast Asian Americans and education, see Ngo and Lee 2007. See also S. J. Lee 2005.
30. Kao 1995; Hsin and Xie 2014.
31. College Board 2019; Reeves and Halikias 2017; U.S. Department of Education 2016, 2018.
32. Dhingra 2020.
33. Carnevale and Strohl 2013.
34. Harvard College Admissions & Financial Aid 2019. Of course, Asian Americans are incredibly diverse, and we should also not forget that 14 percent of the unauthorized population in the United States is Asian, and some Asian groups are among the poorest in the United States. Migration Policy Institute n.d. For example, over one third of Burmese and Bhutanese Americans live in poverty, and another six of the eighteen Asian American national groups in the US have poverty rates above the national poverty rate. U.S. Census 2019g. Nevertheless, on average, Asian Americans are doing well academically and socioeconomically, even if that average masks a lot of internal diversity.
35. Charles 2014; Choi et al. 2019; Logan, Alba, and Leung 1996; Pew Research Center 2012.
36. Frey 2011.
37. Saxenian 1996, 2006. Lareau and Goyette show that the definition of "best" schools is often vague, and determined by hearsay from social networks. Lareau and Goyette 2014. Still, Weininger finds that professional African Americans are more likely than whites to make use of test score data in evaluating communities,

probably due to a lack of dense upper-middle-class social networks for information. Weininger 2014. The same may be true for Asian Americans, though researchers have not yet investigated this question.

38. Alba 1985; Ignatiev 1995; Jacobson 1998; Waters 1990.
39. Alba and Nee 2003; National Academies of Sciences, Engineering, and Medicine 2015.
40. Alba 2020; Alba and Nee 2003; Nee and Holbrow 2013.
41. Tuan 1998.
42. Fox 2012; Haney-López 1996; Sáenz and Manges Douglas 2015. On Asian Americans as excluded from US citizenship, see also Cheryan and Monin 2005; R. G. Lee 1999; Lowe 1996; Takaki 1998.
43. Fong 1994; Horton and Calderon 1995; Saito 1998.
44. Ramakrishnan et al. 2017.
45. Anti-Defamation League 2020; Human Rights Watch 2020; Levin 2016.
46. Kasinitz et al. 2008; Qin, Way, and Rana 2008; Rivas-Drake, Hughes, and Way 2008; Warikoo 2011.
47. Chin 2020; Huang 2020; Tran, Lee, and Huang 2019; Woo 2000. Lu, Nisbett, and Morris 2020 suggest that this ceiling applies to East Asians, but not South Asians.
48. Alba and Yrizar Barbosa 2016; C. Kim and Sakamoto 2010; C. Kim and Zhao 2014. Others come to the conclusion that there is no wage differential once taking into account Asian Americans' preference for living in high cost-of-living regions of the country. S. X. Wang, Takei, and Sakamoto 2017.
49. J. Lee and Zhou 2015; Louie 2004; Sue and Okazaki 1990; Xie and Goyette 2003.
50. The uniqueness of Asian American discrimination stems at least in part from distinct racial stereotypes. The pervasive stereotype of Asian Americans is that they are on the one hand highly competent, but on the other lacking warmth and sociability. Fiske et al. 1999; Lin et al. 2005. This stereotype can lead to "stereotype promise" in school (in which educators assume Asian American students are high achievers), which can also bolster Asian Americans' academic success. J. Lee and Zhou 2015. See also S. J. Lee 1996; Louie 2004; Ochoa 2013. However, stereotype promise can have negative repercussions as well, when struggling students have their educational needs overlooked by adults who assume they are competent at all tasks. J. Lee and Zhou 2015; S. J. Lee 1996; Louie 2004; Ochoa 2013. In addition, even positive stereotypes can make individuals feel excluded from society. Cheryan and Monin 2005; Siy and Cheryan 2013. Indeed, Asian Americans are often seen as less American than Americans of other races. Cheryan and Monin 2005. Given the complexity of Asian American experiences with stereotypes and discrimination and the differences between their experiences and those of other racial minorities, Claire Kim suggests a better way to understand anti-Asian discrimination is to consider "racial triangulation" in which on the one hand "model minority" stereotypes use Asian Americans to disparage Black Americans, and on the other hand Asian Americans are stereotyped as "foreign" and thus excluded from American society more than Black Americans. C. J. Kim 1999.
51. See also Dhingra 2020.
52. Carson 2003; Zuberi and Bonilla-Silva 2008.
53. Jiménez 2017. See also Kye 2018; Lung-Amam 2017.
54. Jiménez 2017.
55. L. L.-C. Wang 1988.
56. Samson 2013.

57. New York State Education Department 2019a, 2019b; NAACP Legal Defense and Educational Fund 2012.
58. See Dwyer 2018 for a similar point.
59. Geismer 2015.
60. For example, see Kaushal, Magnuson, and Waldfogel 2011; Snellman et al. 2015; Weis, Cipollone, and Jenkins 2014. On college admissions, see Stevens 2007.
61. Covay and Carbonaro 2010; Weininger, Lareau, and Conley 2015.
62. On students getting teacher attention, see Calarco 2018; Lareau 2011. On parents advocating for their children, see Lareau, Weininger, and Cox 2018; Posey-Maddox 2013.
63. Lareau 2011.
64. Hays 1996; Sayer, Bianchi, and Robinson 2004. See also Nelson 2010.
65. Hamilton 2016; Lareau 2011; Nelson 2010; Rivera 2015; Stevens 2007.
66. Hagerman 2018; Lewis and Diamond 2015; Lewis-McCoy 2014.
67. Dow 2019; Hannah-Jones 2016; Lacy 2007.
68. Altschul, Oyserman, and Bybee 2006; D. Carter 2008; Sellers, Chavous, and Cooke 1998.
69. Park 2020; Zhou and Kim 2008.
70. Agius Vallejo 2012; Louie 2012; Smith 2008.
71. Agius Vallejo 2012; Dhingra 2020; Imoagene 2017; Louie 2004.
72. Chao 1994; Farver et al. 2007; Sahithya, Manohari, and Vijaya 2019; Sapru 2006; Steinberg, Dornbusch, and Brown 1992.
73. Zhou and Wang 2019.
74. Trines 2018; Wu 2017; Walder, Li, and Treiman 2000. In fact, Chinese college entrance examinations have made study in the United States at the undergraduate level an attractive alternative for many Chinese students whose families can afford to pay for education abroad. Gu et al. 2019; Tu, forthcoming.
75. Bray and Lykins 2012; Ørberg 2018; Sancho 2016; Subramanian 2019; Zhou and Kim 2008. Of course, the families of many Chinese and Indian students cannot afford to provide quality shadow education to their children, or they provide it only to their children who they feel have a chance of excelling. Hansen 2015. Chinese and Indian immigrants in Woodcrest mostly arrived in the United States from families that could provide those resources.
76. See also Feliciano 2006; Feliciano and Lanuza 2017; Luthra, Soehl, and Waldinger 2018.
77. Trines 2018; Walder, Li, and Treiman 2000; Wu 2017.
78. On elite colleges as the pathway to jobs in finance, law, and consulting, see Rivera 2015.
79. Brint and Yoshikawa 2017. Still, cultural elites in the United States are more likely to hold degrees from elite colleges. Brint et al. 2020.
80. J. Lee and Zhou 2015. This includes academic extracurriculars as a pathway to college success, a strategy Dhingra describes as an "Asian American style of concerted cultivation." Dhingra 2020, 15.
81. J. Lee and Zhou 2015, 6. See also Louie 2004.
82. Fishman 2020; Goyette and Xie 1999; Kao and Tienda 1998; Luthra, Soehl, and Waldinger 2018; Tao and Hong 2014.
83. Selective migration is not the only factor in Asian American–white differences in achievement. In particular, it cannot explain achievement differences between Asian American and white youth in lower-income families, which are in fact

greater than differences between high-income white and Asian American youth. Fishman 2020; Liu and Xie 2016. Consistent and higher educational aspirations, greater understandings of pathways to success, greater academic effort, and beliefs about the connection between effort and achievement also matter. Farver et al. 2007; Fishman 2020; Fuligni 1997; Goyette and Xie 1999; Hsin and Xie 2014; Kao 1995; Kao and Tienda 1998; Liu and Xie 2016. These differences are related to messages they receive from their parents about the importance of hard work over innate ability, as well as mothers' beliefs about their own role in child-development. Chao 1994; Stevenson et al. 1990. Other research has shown that high parental expectations in education among immigrants can be found among non-Asian immigrants as well, at least in part because immigrants as a group have higher levels of education on average compared to people from their countries of origin. Feliciano 2006; Feliciano and Lanuza 2016; Xie and Goyette 2003.

84. Roza 2010.
85. Hextrum 2018.
86. Bunch 2020; Ripley 2013.
87. Kaushal, Magnuson, and Waldfogel 2011; Snellman et al. 2015; Thompson 2019.
88. Fairclough 2008.
89. Won and Han 2010.
90. I use the term "emotional well-being" to include a broad set of concerns about children's inner worlds, including happiness, lack of stress, and feelings of fulfillment as well as lack of clinical aspects of mental health—depression, anxiety, or suicidal ideation.
91. Giddens 1991; Madsen 2014; Rieff 1966.
92. Demerath 2009; Lareau 2000, 2011; Mueller and Abrutyn 2016; Nelson 2010; Weis, Cipollone, and Jenkins 2014.
93. Levine 2006; Pope, Brown, and Miles 2015.
94. Lythcott-Haims 2015.
95. Challenge Success n.d.
96. Abeles 2015; Hinshaw and Kranz 2009; Levine 2006; Luthar, Barkin, and Crossman 2013; Lythcott-Haims 2015; Marano 2008; Rosin 2015; Twenge, Campbell, and Freeman 2012.
97. Twenge et al. 2019. Psychologist Suniya Luthar finds that rates of maladjustment among upper-middle-class teens are higher than rates among more disadvantaged teens. Luthar, Barkin, and Crossman 2013; Luthar and Becker 2002.
98. Demerath 2009; Lund and Dearing 2013; Mueller and Abrutyn 2016.
99. Bachman et al. 2011; U.S. Department of Health and Human Services Office of Minority Health n.d.
100. J. Lee and Zhou 2015; Louie 2004; Tao and Hong 2014; Warikoo et al. 2020.
101. For example, see V. Wang and Hernandez 2020.
102. Lan 2018, 30.
103. Atterberry 2020; Kuan 2015; Lan 2018; Sahithya, Manohari, and Vijaya 2019; Way et al. 2013.
104. Hansen 2015; Kuan 2015; Naftali 2014; Raval et al. 2013; Sancho 2016; Saraswathi and Pai 1997; Tuli and Chaudhary 2010.
105. Atterberry 2020; Lan 2018.
106. Kuan 2015; Lan 2018; Xu 2017.
107. Dhingra 2020; Pugh 2015; Sherman 2017b; Thomas, Keogh, and Hay 2015. In interactions with teachers, for example, parents frequently signal knowledge of their

children's flaws and bring up attempts to address them in order to support their identities as "good" parents. Pillet-Shore 2015.

108. On coddling, see Lukianoff and Haidt 2018. On hard work, see Dhingra 2020; Sherman 2017a. On expectations, see Aizenman 2018.

109. For example, see Jiménez 2017; C. Katz 2017; Lung-Amam 2017. This has also been found in Britain, Canada, and Australia. Archer and Francis 2007; Butler, Ho, and Vincent 2017; Davidson 2011; Watkins, Ho, and Butler 2017; Watkins and Noble 2013.

110. Swidler 1986, 273.

111. For example, see Kasinitz et al. 2008; Portes and Rumbaut 2001; Rumbaut 2008. Notable exceptions are Agius Vallejo 2012; Jiménez 2017; Li 2009; Lung-Amam 2017; Matsumoto 2018. For a similar critique, see Singer 2008. On suburbanization, see Berube et al. 2010.

112. Singer 2008.

113. There are thirty-four American cities with median household income above the top household income quintile in the United States in 2010 (that is, above $100,000) and whose Asian American share of the population remained stable or increased from 2000 to 2010 and was at least 20 percent by 2010 (author's analysis). U.S. Census Bureau 2000, 2010a, 2010b. I chose the 20 percent cutoff because research on neighborhood change and "tipping points" finds that when the percentage of racial minorities reaches a certain tipping point—between 5 percent and 20 percent, depending on the context—whites start to move out of the neighborhood. Card, Mas, and Rothstein 2008.

114. Kye 2018.

115. Geismer 2015.

116. U.S. Census Bureau 1970.

117. I do not provide references for these historical events in order to protect the identity of the community.

118. Woodcrest district profile, state department of education 2019.

119. See Jung 2009 for a similar point. Jung writes, "'outsiders' becoming a part of the mainstream may require them to participate in keeping out others, foremost Blacks" (384).

120. U.S. Census Bureau 2019e, 2019f.

121. Woodcrest district profile, state department of education 2018. Most Black and Latinx students are part of the busing program. I focus on white and Asian American students at Woodcrest high in this study because they are the largest groups at the school, and are most relevant to the questions on parenting and Asian American achievement I wanted to address in this project. For studies of student experiences in a busing program to suburban schools, see Eaton 2001; Holland 2012; Ispa-Landa 2013.

122. State department of education 2017.

123. College Board 2017; Woodcrest district profile, state department of education 2017; U.S. Department of Education 2018.

124. U.S. News and World Report n.d.b.

125. Woodcrest school data 2017.

126. Woodcrest school data 2017.

127. Woodcrest district profile, state department of education 2015.

128. Woodcrest school data 2020.

129. Woodcrest school data 2020.

130. Data from local newspaper article 2020.
131. Go 2020.
132. Cooper 2014; C. Katz 2008; Nelson 2010.

CHAPTER 1

1. Similarly, in a study of parents who enroll their children in supplementary education, Dhingra 2020 finds that white parents who do so sometimes view immigrant Asian parents as embodying the American spirit of hard work, in contrast to "lazy" white parents.
2. Dow 2019; Lacy 2007; Lareau 2011.
3. U.S. Census Bureau 2010b.
4. Lan 2018. See also Atterberry 2020.
5. On upper-middle-class parents choosing school districts, see Hagerman 2018; Lareau and Goyette 2014.
6. Still, research on middle-class suburbs shows that when Asians become an increasing share of the community some whites move to other, less diverse towns. Jiménez 2017; Kye 2018. In Woodcrest, as we'll see in chapter 4, white families seemed to stay in town but transfer their children to private schools.
7. Woodcrest High School Youth Risk and Behavior Survey, 2017.
8. Woodcrest district profile, state department of education 2019.
9. The town's poverty rate is more than four times Woodcrest's, and Woodcrest's median household income is more than 2.5 times that of Jaya's old town.
10. U.S. News & World Report n.d.a.
11. Carnevale and Strohl 2013.
12. Carnevale and Strohl 2013.
13. Woodcrest High School Youth Risk and Behavior Survey, 2017.
14. Dworkin, Larson, and Hansen 2003.
15. Covay and Carbonaro 2010; Eccles and Templeton 2002; Feldman and Matjasko 2005; Lareau 2011.
16. These patterns of excellence resonate with Pawan Dhingra's study of Asian and white families' participation in academic extracurriculars, which shows white and Asian families alike having similar explanations for why they encourage (or sometimes require) their children's participation, rooted in desires for instilling values of hard work and competitive spirit. Dhingra 2020.
17. This analysis is based on graduates of Woodcrest High School and the Barron's College Rankings, using Woodcrest school data 2020.
18. Opportunity Insights n.d.
19. OECD 2015; Robinson and Harris 2014.
20. Harris 2011; Warikoo 2011.
21. Swidler 1986.
22. Hoxby and Turner 2015.

CHAPTER 2

1. Swidler 1986, 273. See also Hannerz 1969.
2. Trines 2018; Walder, Li, and Treiman 2000; Wu 2017.

3. Other research has shown that Asian Americans often experience "bamboo ceilings" in the labor market, being passed over for promotion because of racial stereotypes. Chin 2020; Huang 2020; Tran, Lee, and Huang 2019.

4. Brint and Yoshikawa 2017.

5. Hansen 2015; Harding 2007; Lan 2018.

6. See also Dhingra 2020; Sherman 2017b.

7. Interestingly, unlike Chinese students, Indian students have not done well on international tests meant to compare students around the world. In fact, on the 2009 Programme for International Student Assessment (PISA), India ranked seventy-third out of seventy-four countries, leading the country to withdraw from the assessment in 2015. Walker 2011. On that most recent assessment China ranked fourth, behind Singapore, Japan, and Estonia; the United States ranked twenty-fifth. OECD 2018. Still, there is dramatic inequality in Indian schools in terms of how children from upper- versus lower-class families perform, surpassed only by inequality in South African schools. Das and Zajonc 2010. The vast majority of Indian immigrants in Woodcrest come from schools at the top of the achievement distribution in India, which prepared them for success in higher education in India and, for many, in the United States, even while Indian children attending lower-status schools fare much worse. Indian schools serving upper-class families, indeed, are likely to hold high standards in mathematics compared to schools in the United States. They also benefit from shadow education. Bray and Lykins 2012. Das and Zajonc describe the inequality in Indian education as "Indian shining and Bharat drowning." Das and Zajonc 2010.

8. Dhingra found this desire to have children experience hard work among white parents who sent their children to supplementary education as well. Those parents often expressed admiration for immigrant parents who, as they perceived it, instilled more appreciation for the value of hard work than many American parents. Dhingra 2020. See also Sherman 2017b.

9. Like Ruby, Taiwanese middle-class parents in Pei-Chia Lan's study of parenting in Taiwan and the United States also frequently described transnational influences on their parenting. In other words, they took into account strategies for success in two different national contexts. Lan 2018.

10. Half of white parents spoke of the importance of "balance" in their children's lives during in-depth interviews, compared to one-third of immigrant parents. One-fourth of white parents used the word more than once, compared to less than one-fifth of immigrant parents doing so.

11. Woodcrest High School Youth Risk and Behavior Survey, 2017; Woodcrest school data 2017.

12. Woodcrest district profile, state department of education 2019.

13. Woodcrest High School Youth Risk and Behavior Survey, 2017.

14. Dale and Krueger 2002, 2011.

15. See also Dhingra 2020; Ho 2017.

16. While some suggest that fear of racial discrimination in the labor market drives Asian Americans' focus on achievement, especially in STEM fields (for example, see J. Lee and Zhou 2015; Louie 2004; Sue and Okazaki 1990; Xie and Goyette 2003), no parent expressed this concern to me. Some did express fear of discrimination in college admissions—the lawsuit against Harvard claiming racial discrimination against Asian Americans in admissions was ongoing during the time of this research. Still, this fear could make Asian Americans focus *less* on STEM

fields, to counter stereotypes about Asian Americans. Beljean 2019. Indeed, colleges seem to give a boost to applicants that defy stereotypes. Kaufman and Gabler 2004.

17. Woodcrest school data 2020.

18. On Asian Americans and assimilation, see Alba and Nee 2003; Nee and Holbrow 2013.

CHAPTER 3

1. Roza 2010.

2. Won and Han 2010.

3. Bowen and Levin 2003.

4. Arcidiacono, Kinsler, and Ransom 2019.

5. Anderson and Svrluga 2019. Still, college admissions alone cannot fully explain the American emphasis on sports compared to other national contexts. In Canada, a country with more equity and less stratification between universities, parents also emphasize the importance of extracurricular activities, citing the importance of supporting their children's interests and their physical health. Canadian parents describe benefits to extracurricular activities similar to the benefits cited by US parents: life skills, socialization, exercise, and confidence. Aurini, Missaghian, and Milian 2020.

6. Lareau 2011.

7. Social psychologists have shown variation in how individuals make sense of passion—that is, whether a person's passions are innate or developed. They find that when individuals understand passions as "fixed," on the one hand they pour all their energy into a passion and forgo others, but on the other hand they are more likely to disengage when they encounter difficulties. Chen, Ellsworth, and Schwarz 2015; O'Keefe, Dweck, and Walton 2018. On upper-middle-class families and schools cultivating students' "passions," see Davidson 2011.

8. Lareau 2011.

9. Inglehart 1997; Markus and Kitayama 1991; Sahithya, Manohari, and Vijaya 2019; Sapru 2006; Tao and Hong 2014; Tuli 2012; Tuli and Chaudhary 2010.

10. Chao 1994; Farver et al. 2007; Fuligni 1998; Steinberg, Dornbusch, and Brown 1992.

11. Fuligni 1998; Iyengar and Lepper 1999. Ideas about autonomy are shifting in Asia. A recent study of upper-middle-class urban Indian parents finds that they increasingly cultivate a sense of individual motivation, because of the value they place in seeing their children as autonomous. Sancho 2016. They do so in part because they recognize autonomy and individuality as important for success in global markets—this is also true of upper-middle-class parents in other parts of Asia. Lan 2018; Sancho 2016. That is, when professionals are increasingly linked to multinational firms, and jobs in those firms are especially coveted, Western ideals of autonomy and individuality get prioritized. Lan 2018. See also Hansen 2015 for a similar finding in rural China, but related to the role of the state in simultaneously cultivating autonomy yet adherence to state authority.

12. See Weininger and Lareau 2009 for a discussion of how upper-middle-class parents simultaneously express the importance of children's autonomy and exert subtle but impactful influence on the activities in which their children engage.

13. Khan and Jerolmack 2013; Lizardo 2017; Weininger and Lareau 2009.

14. Dhingra 2020 finds that many Indian immigrants believe that their children are

genetically physically weak, making academic extracurriculars a better domain in which to cultivate their competitive talent than sports.

15. Woodcrest High School Youth Risk and Behavior Survey, 2017; Woodcrest school data, 2017.

16. Woodcrest High School Youth Risk and Behavior Survey, 2017.

17. Meier, Hartmann, and Larson 2018; Okamoto, Herda, and Hartzog 2013. Carter found race differences in which particular sports students played in integrated schools in the US South and in South Africa as well. P. Carter 2012.

18. Twenty-eight percent of Asian students reported that they had tried out but didn't make the cut for something at school, in contrast to 17 percent of white students. Woodcrest High School Youth Risk and Behavior Survey, 2017.

19. Arcidiacono, Kinsler, and Ransom 2019.

20. Arcidiacono, Kinsler, and Ransom 2019. The percentage is similar for Latinx and Asian students, but Black students admitted to Harvard are twice as likely as Asian students (but half as likely as white students) to be recruited athletes.

21. Arcidiacono, Kinsler, and Ransom 2019; Bowen and Levin 2003; Hextrum 2018.

22. Author calculation based on Woodcrest school data 2020.

23. For a similar finding, see Dhingra 2020.

CHAPTER 4

1. Woodcrest High School Youth Risk and Behavior Survey, 2017.

2. For example, see Luthar, Barkin, and Crossman 2013; Mueller and Abrutyn 2016; Nelson 2010.

3. Demerath 2009; Lareau 2000, 2011; Mueller and Abrutyn 2016; Nelson 2010.

4. Stearns 2003.

5. Weis, Cipollone, and Jenkins 2014.

6. Abeles 2015; Hinshaw and Kranz, 2009; Levine 2006; Luthar, Barkin, and Crossman 2013; Lythcott-Haims 2015; Rosin 2015; Twenge, Campbell, and Freeman 2012.

7. Ruth Frankenberg 1993 shows how white is often seen as the universal, nonmarked race. See also Brekhus 1998.

8. Chua 2011.

9. J. Lee and Zhou 2015, 184. See also Louie 2004.

10. Fishman 2020; Goyette and Xie 1999; Kao and Tienda 1998; Luthra, Soehl, and Waldinger 2018; Tao and Hong 2014; Warikoo et al. 2020.

11. Bachman et al. 2011; U.S. Department of Health and Human Services Office of Minority Health, n.d.

12. McKim 2019.

13. Substance Abuse and Mental Health Services Administration 2015. 46 percent of whites with mental illness have utilized some form of mental health service in the past year, compared to 18 percent of Asian Americans with mental illness.

14. Lan 2018. See also Kuan 2015; Naftali 2014; Way et al. 2013.

15. Zelizer 1985.

16. Warner 2010. See Kusserow 2004 for a similar finding at the preschool level.

17. Warner 2010, 704.

18. It is important to keep in mind that the definition of "happiness" can also vary, including how people conceptualize happiness and how they seek to achieve it, as we'll see. See Shoshana 2019.

19. This was five immigrant parents (three Chinese, two Indian) and one US-born Chinese American parent.
20. This was four of the fifteen immigrant Chinese parents and three of the seventeen immigrant Indian parents interviewed.
21. Bourdieu 1986; Coleman 1988.
22. While some Asian parents in Woodcrest, including Priya, cited wealth differences between Asian and white families in Woodcrest to explain this difference, I could not confirm the influence of wealth for white versus Asian families.
23. On meritocracy benefiting whites, see Bourdieu 1996; Karabel 2005; Zuberi and Bonilla-Silva 2008.
24. Tocqueville 1994. See also Bellah 1985.
25. Lareau, Weininger, and Cox 2018; Lewis and Diamond 2015; Lewis-McCoy 2014; Posey-Maddox 2013.
26. Lareau, Weininger, and Cox 2018.
27. Lareau, Weininger, and Cox 2018.
28. Report on race/ethnicity in school staff for Woodcrest's state department of education 2017.
29. Lewis-McCoy 2014.
30. Similarly, Park finds that immigrant Asian parents do not see engagement with school administrators or teachers as a viable option for addressing their concerns about their children's schooling, in part because of fears of feeding into stereotypes about Asian parenting. Park 2020.
31. Torres 2019.
32. Stevens also explains that most large public school guidance counselors shepherd much larger numbers of students through the college application process than private school guidance counselors. Stevens 2007.
33. Woodcrest district profile, state department of education 2017; U.S. Census Bureau 2019c.
34. Woodcrest district profile, state department of education, multiple years.
35. U.S. Census Bureau 2014, 2019c.
36. National Center for Education Statistics 2020. Three of the Asian parents I met did enroll their children in private schools for some of their schooling. One was a US-born parent (Grace, above). Another sent her child to the same US boarding school that she herself attended for high school. Lastly, one was an Indian immigrant mother whose children attended a private school in India when the family moved there for four years (in the US, her children always attended public schools).
37. Scholars of culture describe cultural brokers as "intermediaries" who define tastes in society—for example, television producers or magazine editors. Bourdieu 1984; DiMaggio 1977. Scholars of immigration describe cultural brokers as individuals who play a bridging role between immigrants and nonimmigrants. For example, Jennifer Lee 2002 describes Korean small business owners' strategic hiring of black managers in stores in which the majority of clientele are black. Vikki Katz 2014 describes children of immigrants who act as cultural brokers between their parents and health care professionals.
38. On shaping conceptions of morality, see Hitlin and Vaisey 2013, 58–60.
39. Students were asked, "During the past 12 months, did you ever feel so sad or hopeless almost every day (for two weeks or more in a row) that you stopped doing some usual activities?" Woodcrest High School Youth Risk and Behavior Survey, 2017.
40. Woodcrest High School Youth Risk and Behavior Survey, 2017.
41. Redfield et al. 2018.

42. Of course, suicide ideation is not the only measure of mental health. However, it was the only data for which comparable data exists for both students at Woodcrest High School and teens in the United States overall.

43. Other research shows that parent-child relationships play a more significant role in shaping children's emotional well-being than children's perceptions of their parents' expectations. Warikoo et al. 2020.

44. Stanley Cohen describes moral panics as shared concerns about a "condition, episode, person or group of persons" that are seen as a threat, and are exaggerated either compared to their own significance or in relation to other social phenomena. Cohen 1972, 9. Moral panics are constructed by the media and by community leaders. In the case of moral panic about teen mental health in Woodcrest, it seemed sometimes that all parents, and at other times specifically immigrant Asian parents, were blamed for supposed elevated levels of teen anxiety, depression, and even suicide ideation. Moral panics involve hostility toward the group at fault; hence, as we'll see, the boundary making parents engaged around their own parenting and the problematic parenting of others. See also Goode and Ben-Yehuda 1994.

45. For a discussion of differences between what people say and what they do, see Khan and Jerolmack 2013; Lamont and Swidler 2014; Lizardo 2017.

46. I suggest that these perspectives may be related to group interest rather than simply individual interest because a number of parents expressed views in line with their group interest even if they did not seem to further their individual children's interests. For example, Jennifer was a white mother whose two children were attending an Ivy League university when I met her. Despite her children's strong academic achievement, Jennifer was active in promoting interventions to address emotional health among Woodcrest teens by reducing academic work. On the other hand, Fan, an immigrant Chinese mother, expressed concern about a data disaggregation bill that some Chinese Americans feared would make college admission even harder for their children. Yet she also told me that her son was not doing well in school and despite her desire for him to attend "Harvard, MIT, or something. . . . He wants to become a policeman and maybe join the army."

47. For similar findings of whites rejecting Asians' focus on academics to maintain their sense of status, see Archer and Francis 2007; Jiménez 2017; C. Katz 2017; Lung-Amam 2017.

48. Beljean 2019. Other research has shown that elite colleges do indeed prefer applicants who do not fit stereotypes—for example, male applicants who participate in their school's yearbook club. Kaufman and Gabler 2004.

CHAPTER 5

1. Lamont and colleagues define moral boundaries as "moral distinctions that people draw between more and less worthy individuals." Lamont et al. 1996, 32. Lamont also shows how individuals draw distinctions between themselves and other groups based on, among other things, moral worth; how they define moral worth, however, varies by race and national origin, as Lamont shows. Lamont 1992, 2000.

2. I use the concept of symbolic boundaries—"conceptual distinctions made by social actors to categorize objects, people, practices, and even time and space." Lamont and Molnar 2002, 168.

3. Bernhard 2013.

4. Among recent arrivals from India to the United States, there are more South Indians than North Indians, and South Indian immigrants in the United States on average have higher levels of education than Punjabis, who are from Northern India. Chakravorty, Kapur, and Singh 2017.
5. J. Lee and Zhou 2015; Louie 2004.
6. Hoxby and Turner 2015; Jack 2019.
7. See Harding 2007 for a discussion of cultural heterogeneity in poor neighborhoods.
8. In a study of parents whose children participate in academic competitions and supplementary academic classes, Dhingra 2020 finds that some express moral disdain for white parenting as teaching children to be lazy and not instilling value for hard work. Dhingra finds this among white parents whose children participate in "hyper education" as well. I did not find this in Woodcrest, perhaps because participation in academic competitions was uncommon, even among Asian Americans, so parents whose children participate in academic competitions may have a particularly strong view on the importance of academic extracurriculars as necessary for moral development. White parents in Dhingra's study who had children enrolled in academic extracurriculars also sometimes expressed this critique of *other* white parents; but again, they are outliers, even among parents in towns like Woodcrest, which may explain this difference among whites.
9. On gender, see Kanter 1977; Westervelt 2018. On class, see Johnson 2006.
10. Cooper 2014; Pugh 2015.
11. Holmstrom, Karp, and Gray 2011; see also Zaloom 2019.
12. Roda 2017.
13. Sherman 2017b.
14. Pillet-Shore 2015; Thomas, Keogh, and Hay 2015.
15. For example, see Farver et al. 2007; Inglehart 1997; Lan 2018; Sahithya, Manohari, and Vijaya 2019.
16. Zelizer 1985.
17. Stearns 2003.
18. Farver et al. 2007; Lan 2018; Raval et al. 2013.
19. See also Davidson 2011; Jiménez 2017; Lung-Amam 2017.
20. Whites have distanced themselves from Chinese parenting in Australia, Britain, and Canada as well, for similar reasons. Archer and Francis 2007; Watkins, Ho, and Butler 2017.
21. See Edgell, Gerteis, and Hartmann 2006 for a discussion of the use of moral boundaries to strengthen in-group identity.
22. For example, see Goldstein 2019; Narizhnaya and Algar 2020; Spencer 2015.
23. Shapiro 2020.

CONCLUSION

1. Pew Research Center 2020.
2. Mijs 2021; Owens 2020. Parents are likely unaware that social policies already protect wealthy Americans' class status—tax policies and weak provisions for social mobility for the poor and working classes mean it is harder than ever for disadvantaged Americans to reach the upper class. In fact, intergenerational mobility is lower in the United States than in most Western, developed countries. Corak 2013.
3. Cooper 2014.

4. Cooper 2014.
5. Duru-Bellat and Tenret 2012; Mijs 2021.
6. Lareau 2011; Lareau and Goyette 2014.
7. Lareau, Weininger, and Cox 2018; Posey-Maddox 2013.
8. On the role of discrimination, see Chua 2011; J. Lee and Zhou 2015; Sue and Okazaki 1990; Xie and Goyette 2003.
9. See also Dhingra 2020.
10. See also Weininger and Lareau 2009.
11. For a similar argument, see Hagerman 2018.
12. OECD 2015; Robinson and Harris 2014. Further, academic tracking at Woodcrest High School meant that students experienced different levels of peer pressures to achieve, even within the same school. Other research has shown how academic tracking can lead to the racialization of achievement in integrated schools—for example, when upper tracks are dominated by white students but lower tracks are dominated by Black students, Black students in high tracks can be seen as "acting white." Tyson, Darity, and Castellino 2005.
13. Bohman 2011.
14. Connor and Ruiz 2019; Hainmueller and Hopkins 2015.
15. Other studies have also shown how advantaged parents engage in practices that unwittingly place their children at an advantage in school. For example, see Kusserow 2004; Lareau 2011; Lewis and Diamond 2015; Lewis-McCoy 2014; Warikoo 2020.
16. Pierre Bourdieu calls the assumed "better" ways of doing things and taste preferences of elites as the "cultural arbitrary." Bourdieu and Passeron 1977. According to Bourdieu, those in power believe their cultures are the "right" or "better" way of doing things and designate them as such, despite the actually arbitrary nature of those cultures. In this way, those in power are able to maintain their status position via their cultural capital. Bourdieu calls the imposition of the cultural arbitrary on lower-status groups "symbolic violence." In Woodcrest, Asian and white parents employ different cultural repertoires, and those of white parents resonate most with school officials, in line with their status position in American society, as Bourdieu would predict. However, as I highlight throughout this book, Asian Americans may be charting new pathways to the top in American society, despite different cultural repertoires from those of school officials and the established elites.
17. Future studies should also examine whether parents' "constructed criteria" for school quality vary according to the domains in which their in-group excels. Uhlmann and Cohen 2005. It may be, for example, that white American parents call for a reduction in academic emphasis only in contexts where white students are outperformed overall academically by Asian American (or other) peers. Furthermore, it may be that Asian American parents emphasize academic achievement only in communities in which their children outperform their white peers academically.
18. Samson 2013.
19. Warikoo 2016.
20. Karabel 2005.
21. See also Jung 2009.
22. Arcidiacono, Kinsler, and Ransom 2019; Carnevale and Strohl 2013; Kahlenberg 2010.
23. Carnevale and Strohl 2013.
24. Haney-López 1996; Massey and Denton 1993.

25. Alba and Nee 2003; Portes, Fernández-Kelly, and Haller 2009.
26. Dhingra 2021.
27. Chin 2020; Huang 2020; Tran, Lee, and Huang 2019. This blocked mobility at the top of the status hierarchy may not be fully captured by aggregate data on social mobility, given that studies showing Asian American social mobility group all college graduates together rather than look at differences between them. Indeed, controlling for occupation, education, field of study, geographic location, and type of college attended, white men earn more than Asian American men, and Asian women also face labor market disadvantages compared to white women. Alba and Yrizar Barbosa 2016; C. Kim and Sakamoto 2010; C. Kim and Zhao 2014. Still, Wang and colleagues suggest that this difference may be due to Asian Americans' preferences for living in high-cost-of-living regions, rather than due to discrimination. S. X. Wang, Takei, and Sakamoto 2017.
28. In other words, national origin is not always the most salient variable for understanding immigrant incorporation, despite the repeated use of national origin as a primary unit of analysis for studying immigrant assimilation. For a similar argument, see Brubaker 2004; Luthra, Soehl, and Waldinger 2018; Wimmer 2013.
29. Warikoo 2011.
30. Hsin and Xie 2014; Kao 1995; U.S. Department of Education 2018.
31. Badger et al. 2018.
32. Alba 2020.
33. Badger et al. 2018.
34. Opportunity Insights n.d. This is also true when looking at total household income, and when comparing only Asian American and white adults who grew up in high-income households in Woodcrest.
35. Alba 1985; Ignatiev 1995; Jacobson 1998; Waters 1990.
36. Alba 2020; Alba and Nee 1997.
37. On moving to places with fewer Asians, see Kye 2018.
38. Alba 2020. In Woodcrest, questions of moral worth were used to maintain the boundary between Asian and white, not shift it.
39. Jiménez 2017.
40. See, for example, Go 2020; Jung 2009; Romero 2008; Sáenz and Manges Douglas 2015; Treitler 2015.
41. Studies of predominantly white upper-middle-class towns have found, for example, that white children experience high levels of academic competition and sometimes suffer from mental health issues due to academic pressure. Parents in those communities cannot lay blame on a supposed negative influence from Asian immigrants, in contrast to white Woodcrest parents. For examples, see Lund and Dearing 2013; Mueller and Abrutyn 2006; Weis, Cipollone, and Jenkins 2014.
42. Sáenz and Manges Douglas 2015.
43. As of 2017, Asian Americans were the most likely of any racial group to intermarry; 29 percent of Asian American newlyweds were intermarried (36 percent of newlywed Asian American women and 21 percent of newlywed Asian American men). The likelihood of intermarriage is even higher for US-born Asian Americans: 46 percent of U.S.-born Asian American newlyweds have a spouse of a different race or ethnicity, while 24 percent of foreign-born Asian American newlyweds do. Livingston and Brown 2017.
44. Alba and Yrizar Barbosa 2016; Chetty et al. 2019; Sakamoto, Goyette, and Kim 2009.
45. Daryl 2009; Okamoto 2003; Sohi 2014; Wei 1993.
46. Ispa-Landa 2013.

APPENDIX A

1. For studies of Asian Americans in west coast suburbs, see Fong 1994; Horton and Calderon 1995; Jiménez 2017; Lung-Amam 2017; Saito 1998.
2. U.S. Census Bureau 2019c.
3. U.S. Census Bureau 2019c.
4. U.S. Census Bureau 2019f.
5. U.S. Census Bureau 2019e.
6. U.S. Census Bureau 2019d.
7. U.S. Census Bureau 2019b.
8. U.S. Census Bureau 2019b.
9. U.S. Census Bureau 2019b.
10. Warikoo 2011.
11. See appendix B for interview questions.
12. For example, see Hamilton 2016; J. Lee and Zhou 2015; Louie 2004; Luthar, Barkin, and Crossman 2013; Luthar and Becker 2002.
13. See appendix B for interview questions.
14. Cooper 2014; Hays 1996; Sayer, Bianchi, and Robinson 2004.

References

Abeles, Vicki. 2015. *Beyond measure: rescuing an overscheduled, overtested, underesti-mated generation*. New York: Simon & Schuster.

Agius Vallejo, Jody. 2012. *Barrios to burbs: the making of the Mexican American middle class*. Stanford: Stanford University Press.

Aizenman, Nurith. 2018. "Your turn: when parents push too hard ... or not enough." NPR: Goats and Soda: Stories of Life in a Changing World. Accessed June 30, 2020. https://www.npr.org/sections/goatsandsoda/2018/07/12/627674865/your-turn -when-parents-push-too-hard-or-not-enough.

Alba, Richard D. 1985. *Italian Americans: into the twilight of ethnicity*. Englewood Cliffs, NJ: Prentice-Hall.

———. 2009. *Blurring the color line: the new chance for a more integrated America*. Cambridge, MA: Harvard University Press.

———. 2020. *The great demographic illusion: majority, minority, and the expanding American mainstream*. Princeton: Princeton University Press.

Alba, Richard, and Victor Nee. 1997. "Rethinking assimilation theory for a new era of immigration." *International Migration Review* 31 (4): 826–874. https://doi.org/10 .2307/2547416.

———. 2003. *Remaking the American mainstream: assimilation and contemporary immigration*. Cambridge, MA: Harvard University Press.

Alba, Richard, and Guillermo Yrizar Barbosa. 2016. "Room at the top? Minority mobility and the transition to demographic diversity in the USA." *Ethnic and Racial Studies* 39 (6): 917–938. https://doi.org/10.1080/01419870.2015.1081966.

Alexander, Michelle. 2010. *The new Jim Crow: mass incarceration in the age of colorblindness*. New York: New Press.

Altschul, Inna, Daphna Oyserman, and Deborah Bybee. 2006. "Racial-ethnic identity in mid-adolescence: content and change as predictors of academic achievement." *Child Development* 77: 1155–1169. https://doi.org/10.1111/j.1467-8624.2006 .00926.x.

Anderson, Nick, and Susan Svrluga. 2019. "Varsity athletes, admissions and enroll-

ment at top colleges." *Washington Post.* Accessed March 4, 2021. https://www
.washingtonpost.com/education/2019/06/12/varsity-athletes-admissions
-enrollment-top-colleges/.

Anti-Defamation League. 2020. "Reports of anti-Asian assaults, harassment and hate
crimes rise as coronavirus spreads." *American Defamation League.* Accessed June 18,
2020. https://www.adl.org/blog/reports-of-anti-asian-assaults-harassment-and
-hate-crimes-rise-as-coronavirus-spreads.

Archer, Louise, and Becky Francis. 2007. *Understanding minority ethnic achievement:
race, gender, class and "success."* London: Routledge.

Arcidiacono, Peter, Josh Kinsler, and Tyler Ransom. 2019. "Legacy and athlete preferences at Harvard." *National Bureau of Economic Research Working Paper Series* No.
26316.

Atterberry, Adrienne Lee. 2020. "Cultivating India's new transnational elite: parenting, schooling, and belonging in the age of global IT." Doctoral diss. draft, Syracuse
University.

Aurini, Janice, Rod Missaghian, and Roger Pizarro Milian. 2020. "Educational status
hierarchies, after-school activities, and parenting logics: lessons from Canada."
Sociology of Education 93 (2): 173–189. https://doi.org/10.1177/0038040720908173.

Bachman, Jerald G., Patrick M. O'Malley, Peter Freedman-Doan, Kali H. Trzesniewski,
and M. Brent Donnellan. 2011. "Adolescent self-esteem: differences by race/eth-
nicity, gender, and age." *Self and Identity* 10 (4): 445–473. https://doi.org/10.1080
/15298861003794538.

Badger, Emily, Claire Cain Miller, Adam Pearce, and Kevin Qealy. 2018. "Income mobility charts for girls, Asian-Americans and other groups. Or make your own." *New
York Times.* Accessed August 24, 2020. https://www.nytimes.com/interactive/2018
/03/27/upshot/make-your-own-mobility-animation.html.

Batalova, Jeanne, Mary Hanna, and Christopher Levesque. 2021. "Frequently requested statistics on immigrants and immigration in the United States." Migration
Policy Institute. Accessed March 3, 2021. https://www.migrationpolicy.org/article
/frequently-requested-statistics-immigrants-and-immigration-united-states
-2020#demographic-educational-linguistic.

Beljean, Stefan. 2019. "The pressures of status reproduction: upper-middle-class
youth and the transition to higher education in Germany and the United States."
Ph.D. diss., Harvard University, Department of Sociology.

Bellah, Robert N. 1985. *Habits of the heart: individualism and commitment in American
life.* Berkeley: University of California Press.

Bernhard, Meg. 2013. "The making of a Harvard feeder school." *Crimson,* December
13. Accessed October 16, 2020. https://www.thecrimson.com/article/2013/12/13
/making-harvard-feeder-schools/.

Berrey, Ellen. 2015. *The enigma of diversity: the language of race and the limits of racial
justice.* Chicago: University of Chicago Press.

Berube, Alan, William H. Frey, Alec Friedhoff, Emily Garr, Emilia Istrate, Elizabeth
Kneebone, Robert Puentes, Audrey Singer, Adie Tomer, Howard Wial, and Jill H.
Wilson. 2010. *State of metropolitan America: on the front lines of demographic trans-
formation.* The Brookings Institution Metropolitan Policy Program.

Bohman, Andrea. 2011. "Articulated antipathies: political influence on anti-immigrant
attitudes." *International Journal of Comparative Sociology* 52 (6): 457–477. https://
doi.org/10.1177/0020715211428182.

Bourdieu, Pierre. 1984. *Distinction: a social critique of the judgement of taste.* Cambridge,
MA: Harvard University Press.

————. 1986. "The forms of capital." In *Handbook of Theory and Research for the Sociology of Education*, edited by John G. Richardson. New York: Greenwood Press.

————. 1996. *The state nobility: elite schools in the field of power.* Stanford: Stanford University Press.

Bourdieu, Pierre, and Jean-Claude Passeron. 1977. *Reproduction in education, society and culture.* Translated by Richard Nice. London: SAGE.

Bowen, William G., and Sarah A. Levin. 2003. *Reclaiming the game: college sports and educational values.* Princeton: Princeton University Press.

Bray, Mark, and Chad Lykins. 2012. *Shadow education: private supplementary tutoring and its implications for policy makers in Asia.* Asian Development Bank, Mandaluyong City, Philippines. https://www.adb.org/sites/default/files/publication/29777/shadow-education.pdf.

Brekhus, Wayne. 1998. "A sociology of the unmarked: redirecting our focus." *Sociological Theory* 16 (1): 34–51. https://doi.org/10.1111/0735-2751.00041.

Brint, Steven, and Sarah R. K. Yoshikawa. 2017. "The educational backgrounds of American business and government leaders: inter-industry variation in recruitment from elite colleges and graduate programs." *Social Forces* 96 (2): 561–590. https://doi.org/10.1093/sf/sox059.

Brint, Steven, Komi T. German, Kayleigh Anderson-Natale, Zeinab F. Shuker, and Suki Wang. 2020. "Where ivy matters: the educational backgrounds of U.S. cultural elites." *Sociology of Education* 93 (2): 153–172. https://doi.org/10.1177/0038040719898505.

Brubaker, Rogers. 2004. *Ethnicity without groups.* Cambridge, MA: Harvard University Press.

Bunch, Will. 2020. "State of play." *Brown Alumni Magazine*, October 26. Accessed March 8, 2021. https://www.brownalumnimagazine.com/articles/2020-10-26/state-of-play.

Butler, Rose, Christina Ho, and Eve Vincent. 2017. "'Tutored within an inch of their life': morality and 'old' and 'new' middle class identities in Australian schools." *Journal of Ethnic and Migration Studies* 43 (14): 2408–2422. https://doi.org/10.1080/1369183X.2017.1315867.

Calarco, Jessica McCrory. 2018. *Negotiating opportunities: how the middle class secures advantages in school.* New York: Oxford University Press.

Card, David, Alexandre Mas, and Jesse Rothstein. 2008. "Tipping and the dynamics of segregation." *Quarterly Journal of Economics* 123 (1): 177–218. http://www.jstor.org/stable/25098897.

Carnevale, Anthony P., and Jeff Strohl. 2013. "Separate and unequal: how higher education reform reinforces the intergenerational reproduction of white racial privilege." Georgetown Public Policy Institute. Accessed April 2, 2015. https://cew.georgetown.edu/wp-content/uploads/2014/11/SeparateUnequal.FR_.pdf.

Carson, John. 2003. "The culture of intelligence." In *The Cambridge history of science*, edited by Theodore M. Porter and Dorothy Ross. Cambridge: Cambridge University Press.

Carter, Dorinda. 2008. "Achievement as resistance: the development of a critical race achievement ideology among Black achievers." *Harvard Educational Review* 78 (3): 466–497. https://doi.org/doi:10.17763/haer.78.3.83138829847hw844.

Carter, Prudence. 2005. *Keepin' it real: school success beyond black and white.* New York: Oxford University Press.

Carter, Prudence L. 2012. *Stubborn roots: race, culture, and inequality in U.S. and South African schools.* New York: Oxford University Press.

Chakravorty, Sanjoy, Devesh Kapur, and Nirvikar Singh. 2017. *The other one percent: Indians in America*. New York: Oxford University Press.

Challenge Success, n.d. "About Challenge Success." Accessed July 15, 2021. https://challengesuccess.org/who-we-are/#.

Chao, Ruth K. 1994. "Beyond parental control and authoritarian parenting style: understanding Chinese parenting through the cultural notion of training." *Child Development* 65 (4): 1111–1119. https://doi.org/10.2307/1131308.

Charles, Camille Zubrinsky. 2014. "Neighborhood racial-composition preferences: evidence from a multiethnic metropolis." *Social Problems* 47 (3): 379–407. https://doi.org/10.2307/3097236.

Chen, Patricia, Phoebe C. Ellsworth, and Norbert Schwarz. 2015. "Finding a fit or developing it: implicit theories about achieving passion for work." *Personality and Social Psychology Bulletin* 41 (10): 1411–1424. https://doi.org/10.1177/0146167215596988.

Cheryan, Sapna, and Benoît Monin. 2005. "Where are you *really* from? Asian Americans and identity denial." *Journal of Personality and Social Psychology* 89 (5): 717–730. https://doi.org/10.1037/0022-3514.89.5.717.

Chetty, Raj, Nathaniel Hendren, Maggie R. Jones, and Sonya R. Porter. 2019. "Race and economic opportunity in the United States: an intergenerational perspective." *Quarterly Journal of Economics* 135 (2): 711–783. https://doi.org/10.1093/qje/qjz042.

Chin, Margaret May. 2020. *Stuck: why Asian Americans don't reach the top of the corporate ladder*. New York: New York University Press.

Choi, Ann, Keith Herbert, Olivia Winslow, and Arthur Browne. 2019. "Long Island divided." *Newsday*, November 17. Accessed March 4, 2021. https://projects.newsday.com/long-island/real-estate-agents-investigation/.

Chua, Amy. 2011. *Battle hymn of the tiger mother*. New York: Penguin Press.

Cohen, Stanley. 1972. *Folk devils and moral panics: the creation of the Mods and Rockers*. London: MacGibbon and Kee.

Coleman, James S. 1988. "Social capital in the creation of human capital." *American Journal of Sociology* 94: S95–S120. https://doi.org/10.1086/228943.

College Board. 2017. *Class of 2017 SAT results*. Accessed August 9, 2021. https://reports.collegeboard.org/archive/sat-suite-program-results/2017/class-2017-results.

College Board. 2019. *SAT results: class of 2019*. Accessed June 16, 2020. https://reports.collegeboard.org/sat-suite-program-results/class-2019-results.

Connor, Phillip, and Neil G. Ruiz. 2019. "Majority of U.S. public supports high-skilled immigration." Pew Research Center, January. Accessed March 3, 2021. https://www.pewresearch.org/global/wp-content/uploads/sites/2/2019/01/Pew-Research-Center_Majority-of-U.S.-Public-Supports-High-Skilled-Immigration_2019-01-22_Report.pdf.

Cooper, Marianne. 2014. *Cut adrift: families in insecure times*. Berkeley: University of California Press.

Corak, Miles. 2013. "Income inequality, equality of opportunity, and intergenerational mobility." *Journal of Economic Perspectives* 27 (3): 79–102. https://doi.org/doi:10.1257/jep.27.3.79.

Covay, Elizabeth, and William Carbonaro. 2010. "After the bell: participation in extracurricular activities, classroom behavior, and academic achievement." *Sociology of Education* 83 (1): 20–45. https://doi.org/10.1177/0038040709356565.

Crenshaw, Kimberlé, Neil Gotanda, Gary Peller, and Kendall Thomas, eds. 1995. *Critical race theory: the key writings that formed the movement*. New York: New Press.

Dale, Stacy Berg, and Alan B. Krueger. 2002. "Estimating the payoff to attending a more selective college: an application of selection on observables and unobserv-ables." *Quarterly Journal of Economics* 117 (4): 1491–1527. https://doi.org/10.1162/003355302320935089.

———. 2011. "Estimating the return to college selectivity over the career using administrative earnings data." NBER Working Paper 17159. Accessed April 3, 2015. http://www.nber.org/papers/w17159.pdf.

Daryl, J. Maeda. 2009. *Chains of Babylon: the rise of Asian America*. New ed. Minneapolis: University of Minnesota Press.

Das, Jishnu, and Tristan Zajonc. 2010. "India shining and Bharat drowning: Compar-ing two Indian states to the worldwide distribution in mathematics achievement." *Journal of Development Economics* 92 (2): 175–187. https://doi.org/10.1016/j.jdeveco.2009.03.004.

Davidson, Elsa. 2011. *The burdens of aspiration: schools, youth, and success in the divided social worlds of Silicon Valley*. New York: New York University Press.

Demerath, Peter. 2009. *Producing success: the culture of personal advancement in an American high school*. Chicago: University of Chicago Press.

Deresiewicz, William. 2014. *Excellent sheep: the miseducation of the American elite and the way to a meaningful life*. New York: Free Press.

Dhingra, Pawan. 2007. *Managing multicultural lives: Asian American professionals and the challenge of multiple identities*. Stanford: Stanford University Press.

———. 2020. *Hyper education: why good schools, good grades, and good behavior are not enough*. New York: New York University Press.

———. 2021. "Racism is behind anti-Asian American violence, even when it's not a hate crime." *The Conversation*, March 19. Accessed March 26, 2021. https://theconversation.com/racism-is-behind-anti-asian-american-violence-even-when-its-not-a-hate-crime-157487.

DiMaggio, Paul. 1977. "Market structure, the creative process, and popular culture: to-ward an organizational reinterpretation of mass-culture theory." *Journal of Popular Culture* 11 (2): 436–452. https://doi.org/10.1111/j.0022-3840.1977.00436.x.

Dow, Dawn Marie. 2019. *Mothering while black: boundaries and burdens of middle-class parenthood*. Oakland: University of California Press.

Duru-Bellat, Marie, and Elise Tenret. 2012. "Who's for meritocracy? Individual and contextual variations in the faith." *Comparative Education Review* 56 (2): 223–247. http://www.jstor.org/stable/10.1086/661290.

Dworkin, Jodi B., Reed Larson, and David Hansen. 2003. "Adolescents' accounts of growth experiences in youth activities." *Journal of Youth and Adolescence* 32 (1): 17–26. https://doi.org/10.1023/A:1021076222321.

Dwyer, Jim. 2018. "Decades ago, New York dug a moat around its specialized schools." *New York Times*, June 8. Accessed March 8, 2021. https://www.nytimes.com/2018/06/08/nyregion/about-shsat-specialized-high-schools-test.html?

Eaton, Susan E. 2001. *The other Boston busing story: what's won and lost across the boundary line*. New Haven: Yale University Press.

Eccles, Jacquelynne S., and Janice Templeton. 2002. "Chapter 4: extracurricular and other after-school activities for youth." In *Review of Research in Education* 26: 113–180.

Edgell, Penny, Joseph Gerteis, and Douglas Hartmann. 2006. "Atheists as 'other': moral boundaries and cultural membership in American society." *American Socio-logical Review* 71 (2): 211–234. https://doi.org/10.1177/000312240607100203.

Erickson, Ansley T. 2016. *Making the unequal metropolis: school desegregation and its limits*. Chicago: University of Chicago Press.

Espenshade, Thomas J., and Alexandria Walton Radford. 2009. *No longer separate, not yet equal: race and class in elite college admission and campus life.* Princeton: Princeton University Press.

Fairclough, Gordon. 2008. "In China, jocks don't rule school; but the smart kids, they're cool." *Wall Street Journal*, August 19. Accessed July 29, 2021. https://www.wsj.com/articles/SB121909869003651101.

Farver, JoAnn M., Yiyuan Xu, Bakhtawar R. Bhadha, Sonia Narang, and Eli Lieber. 2007. "Ethnic identity, acculturation, parenting beliefs, and adolescent adjustment: a comparison of Asian Indian and European American families." *Merrill-Palmer Quarterly* 53 (2): 184–215. www.jstor.org/stable/23096105.

Feldman, Amy F., and Jennifer L. Matjasko. 2005. "The role of school-based extracurricular activities in adolescent development: a comprehensive review and future directions." *Review of Educational Research* 75 (2): 159–210. https://doi.org/10.3102/00346543075002159.

Feliciano, Cynthia. 2006. *Unequal origins: immigrant selection and the education of the second generation.* New York: LFB Scholarly Pub.

Feliciano, Cynthia, and Yader R. Lanuza. 2016. "The immigrant advantage in adolescent educational expectations." *International Migration Review* 50 (3): 758–792. https://doi.org/10.1111/imre.12183.

———. 2017. "An immigrant paradox? Contextual attainment and intergenerational educational mobility." *American Sociological Review* 82 (1): 211–241. https://doi.org/10.1177/0003122416684777.

Fishman, Samuel H. 2020. "Educational mobility among the children of Asian American immigrants." *American Journal of Sociology* 126 (2): 260–317. https://doi.org/10.1086/711231.

Fiske, Susan T., Juan Xu, Amy C. Cuddy, and Peter Glick. 1999. "(Dis)respecting versus (dis)liking: status and interdependence predict ambivalent stereotypes of competence and warmth." *Journal of Social Issues* 55 (3): 473–489. https://doi.org/doi:10.1111/0022-4537.00128.

Fong, Timothy P. 1994. *The first suburban Chinatown: the remaking of Monterey Park, California.* Philadelphia: Temple University Press.

Fox, Cybelle. 2012. *Three worlds of relief: race, immigration, and the American welfare state from the Progressive Era to the New Deal.* Princeton: Princeton University Press.

Frankenberg, Ruth. 1993. *White women, race matters: the social construction of whiteness.* Minneapolis: University of Minnesota Press.

Freedle, Roy. 2008. "Correcting the SAT's ethnic and social-class bias: a method for reestimating SAT scores." *Harvard Educational Review* 73 (1): 1–43. https://doi.org/10.17763/haer.73.1.8465k88616hn4757.

Frey, William H. 2011. *Melting pot cities and suburbs: racial and ethnic change in metro America in the 2000s.* Washington, DC: Brookings Institution. Accessed July 29, 2021. https://www.brookings.edu/wp-content/uploads/2016/06/0504_census_ethnicity_frey.pdf.

Friedman, Thomas L. 2006. *The world is flat: a brief history of the twenty-first century.* 1st updated and expanded ed. New York: Farrar, Straus and Giroux.

Fuligni, Andrew J. 1997. "The academic achievement of adolescents from immigrant families: the roles of family background, attitudes, and behavior." *Child Development* 68 (2): 351–363. https://doi.org/10.2307/1131854.

———. 1998. "Authority, autonomy, and parent–adolescent conflict and cohesion: a study of adolescents from Mexican, Chinese, Filipino, and European backgrounds."

Developmental Psychology 34 (4): 782–792. https://doi.org/10.1037/0012-1649.34 .4.782.

Geismer, Lily. 2015. *Don't blame us: suburban liberals and the transformation of the Democratic Party.* Princeton: Princeton University Press.

Giddens, Anthony. 1991. *Modernity and self-identity: self and society in the late modern age.* Stanford: Stanford University Press.

Go, Julian. 2020. "Race, empire, and epistemic exclusion: or the structures of sociological thought." *Sociological Theory* 38 (2): 79–100. https://doi.org/10.1177 /0735275120926213.

Goldstein, Dana. 2019. "Where civility is a motto, a school integration fight turns bitter." *New York Times*, November 12. Accessed October 20, 2020. https://www .nytimes.com/2019/11/12/us/howard-county-school-redistricting.html.

Goode, Erich, and Nachman Ben-Yehuda. 1994. "Moral panics: culture, politics, and social construction." *Annual Review of Sociology* 20 (1): 149–171. https://doi.org/10 .1146/annurev.so.20.080194.001053.

Goyette, Kimberly, and Yu Xie. 1999. "Educational expectations of Asian American youths: determinants and ethnic differences." *Sociology of Education* 72 (1): 22–36. https://doi.org/10.2307/2673184.

Grogger, Jeffrey. 2011. "Speech patterns and racial wage inequality." *Journal of Human Resources* 46 (1): 1–25. https://doi.org/10.3368/jhr.46.1.1.

Gu, Mini, Rachel Michael, Claire Zheng, and Stefan Trines. 2019. "Education in China." Education System Profiles. World Education News and Reviews. Accessed June 16, 2020. https://wenr.wes.org/2019/12/education-in-china-3.

Hagerman, Margaret A. 2018. *White kids: growing up with privilege in a racially divided America.* New York: New York University Press.

Hainmueller, Jens, and Daniel J. Hopkins. 2015. "The hidden American immigration consensus: a conjoint analysis of attitudes toward immigrants." *American Journal of Political Science* 59 (3): 529–548. https://doi.org/https://doi.org/10.1111/ajps.12138.

Haller, William, Alejandro Portes, and Scott M. Lynch. 2011. "Dreams fulfilled, dreams shattered: determinants of segmented assimilation in the second generation." *Social Forces* 89 (3): 733–762. https://doi.org/10.1353/sof.2011.0003.

Hamilton, Laura T. 2016. *Parenting to a degree: how family matters for college women's success.* Chicago: University of Chicago Press.

Haney-López, Ian. 1996. *White by law: the legal construction of race.* New York: New York University Press.

Hannah-Jones, Nikole. 2016. "Choosing a school for my daughter in a segregated city." *New York Times*, June 9. Accessed January 7, 2021. https://www.nytimes.com/2016 /06/12/magazine/choosing-a-school-for-my-daughter-in-a-segregated-city .html.

Hannerz, Ulf. 1969. *Soulside: inquiries into ghetto culture and community.* New York: Columbia University Press.

Hansen, Mette Halskov. 2015. *Educating the Chinese individual: life in a rural boarding school.* Seattle: University of Washington Press.

Harding, David J. 2007. "Cultural context, sexual behavior, and romantic relationships in disadvantaged neighborhoods." *American Sociological Review* 72 (3): 341–364. https://doi.org/10.2307/25472467.

Harris, Angel. 2011. *Kids don't want to fail: oppositional culture and Black students' academic achievement.* Cambridge, MA: Harvard University Press.

Harris, Fredrick C. 2014. "The rise of respectability politics." *Dissent*, Winter. Ac-

cessed March 4, 2021. https://www.dissentmagazine.org/article/the-rise-of
-respectability-politics.

Harvard College Admissions & Financial Aid. 2019. "Admissions statistics: a brief
profile of the admitted class of 2023." Harvard College. Accessed December 5, 2019.
https://college.harvard.edu/admissions/admissions-statistics.

Hays, Sharon. 1996. *The cultural contradictions of motherhood*. New Haven: Yale University Press.

Hextrum, Kirsten. 2018. "The hidden curriculum of college athletic recruitment."
Harvard Educational Review 88 (3): 355–377. https://doi.org/10.17763/1943-5045
-88.3.355.

Hinshaw, Stephen P., and Rachel Kranz. 2009. *The triple bind: saving our teenage girls
from today's pressures*. New York: Ballantine Books.

Hitlin, Steven, and Stephen Vaisey. 2013. "The new sociology of morality." *Annual
Review of Sociology* 39 (1): 51–68. https://doi.org/doi:10.1146/annurev-soc-071312
-145628.

Ho, Christina. 2017. "The new meritocracy or over-schooled robots? Public attitudes
on Asian–Australian education cultures." *Journal of Ethnic and Migration Studies* 43
(14): 2346–2362. https://doi.org/10.1080/1369183X.2017.1315855.

Holland, Megan M. 2012. "Only here for the day: the social integration of minority
students at a majority white high school." *Sociology of Education* 85 (2): 101–120.
https://doi.org/10.1177/0038040712440789.

Holmstrom, Lynda Lytle, David A. Karp, and Paul S. Gray. 2011. "Why parents pay
for college: the good parent, perceptions of advantage, and the intergenerational
transfer of opportunity." *Symbolic Interaction* 34 (2): 265–289. https://doi.org/10
.1525/si.2011.34.2.265.

Horton, John, and Jose Calderon. 1995. *The politics of diversity: immigration, resistance,
and change in Monterey Park, California*. Philadelphia: Temple University Press.

Hoxby, Caroline, and Sarah Turner. 2015. "What high-achieving low-income students
know about college." *American Economic Review* 105 (5): 514–517.

Hsin, Amy, and Yu Xie. 2014. "Explaining Asian Americans' academic advantage over
whites." *Proceedings of the National Academy of Sciences* 111 (23): 8416–8421.

Huang, Tiffany J. 2020. "Negotiating the workplace: second-generation Asian American professionals' early experiences." *Journal of Ethnic and Migration Studies* 47 (11):
1–20. https://doi.org/10.1080/1369183X.2020.1778455.

Human Rights Watch. 2020. "Covid-19 fueling anti-Asian racism and xenophobia
worldwide." May 12. Accessed July 29, 2021. https://www.hrw.org/news/2020/05
/12/covid-19-fueling-anti-asian-racism-and-xenophobia-worldwide.

Ignatiev, Noel. 1995. *How the Irish became white*. New York: Routledge.

Imoagene, Onoso. 2017. *Beyond expectations: second-generation Nigerians in the United
States and Britain*. Oakland: University of California Press.

Inglehart, Ronald. 1997. *Modernization and postmodernization: cultural, economic, and
political change in 43 societies*. Princeton: Princeton University Press.

Ispa-Landa, Simone. 2013. "Gender, race, and justifications for group exclusion: urban
Black students bussed to affluent suburban schools." *Sociology of Education* 86 (3):
218–233. https://doi.org/10.1177/0038040712472912.

Iyengar, Sheena S., and Mark R. Lepper. 1999. "Rethinking the value of choice: a
cultural perspective on intrinsic motivation." *Journal of Personality and Social Psychology* 76 (3): 349–366. http://dx.doi.org/10.1037/0022-3514.76.3.349.

Jack, Anthony Abraham. 2019. *The privileged poor: how elite colleges are failing disadvantaged Students*. Cambridge, MA: Harvard University Press.

Jacobson, Matthew Frye. 1998. *Whiteness of a different color: European immigrants and the alchemy of race*. Cambridge, MA: Harvard University Press.

Jiménez, Tomás R. 2017. *The other side of assimilation: how immigrants are changing American life*. Oakland: University of California Press.

Joffe-Walt, Chana. 2020. "Nice white parents." *New York Times*, July 23. Accessed July 29, 2021. https://www.nytimes.com/2020/07/23/podcasts/nice-white-parents-serial.html.

Johnson, Heather Beth. 2006. *The American dream and the power of wealth: choosing schools and inheriting inequality in the land of opportunity*. New York: Routledge.

Jung, Moon-Kie. 2009. "The racial unconscious of assimilation theory." *Du Bois Review* 6 (2): 375–395. https://doi.org/10.1017/S1742058X09990245.

Kahlenberg, Richard D. 2010. *Affirmative action for the rich: legacy preferences in college admissions*. New York: Century Foundation Press.

Kang, Sonia K., Katherine A. DeCelles, András Tilcsik, and Sora Jun. 2016. "Whitened résumés: race and self-presentation in the labor market." *Administrative Science Quarterly* 61 (3): 469–502. https://doi.org/10.1177/0001839216639577.

Kanter, Rosabeth M. 1977. *Men and women of the corporation*. New York: Basic Books.

Kao, Grace. 1995. "Asian Americans as model minorities? A look at their academic performance." *American Journal of Education* 103 (2): 121–159. www.jstor.org/stable/1085574.

Kao, Grace, and Marta Tienda. 1995. "Optimism and achievement: the educational performance of immigrant youth." *Social Science Quarterly* 76 (1): 1–19. http://www.jstor.org/stable/44072586.

———. 1998. "Educational aspirations of minority youth." *American Journal of Education* 106 (3): 349–384. www.jstor.org/stable/1085583.

Kapur, Devesh. 2010. *Diaspora, development, and democracy: the domestic impact of international migration from India*. Princeton: Princeton University Press.

Karabel, Jerome. 2005. *The chosen: the hidden history of admission and exclusion at Harvard, Yale, and Princeton*. Boston: Houghton Mifflin.

Kasinitz, Philip, John H. Mollenkopf, Mary C. Waters, and Jennifer Holdaway. 2008. *Inheriting the city: the children of immigrants come of age*. Cambridge, MA: Harvard University Press.

Katz, Cindi. 2008. "Childhood as spectacle: relays of anxiety and the reconfiguration of the child." *Cultural Geographies* 15 (1): 5–17. https://doi.org/10.1177/1474474007085773.

———. 2017. "The angel of geography: Superman, tiger mother, aspiration management, and the child as waste." *Progress in Human Geography* 42 (5): 723–740. https://doi.org/10.1177/0309132517708844.

Katz, Vikki. 2014. "Children as brokers of their immigrant families' health-care connections." *Social Problems* 61 (2): 194–215. https://doi.org/10.1525/sp.2014.12026.

Kaufman, Jason, and Jay Gabler. 2004. "Cultural capital and the extracurricular activities of girls and boys in the college attainment process." *Poetics* 32 (2): 145–168. https://doi.org/10.1016/j.poetic.2004.02.001.

Kaushal, Neeraj, Katherine Magnuson, and Jane Waldfogel. 2011. "How is family income related to investments in children's learning?" In *Whither opportunity? Rising inequality, schools, and children's life chances*, edited by Greg J. Duncan and Richard J. Murnane. New York: Russell Sage Foundation.

Khan, Shamus, and Colin Jerolmack. 2013. "Saying meritocracy and doing privilege." *Sociological Quarterly* 54 (1): 9–19. https://doi.org/10.1111/tsq.12008.

Kim, ChangHwan, and Arthur Sakamoto. 2010. "Have Asian American men achieved labor market parity with white men?" *American Sociological Review* 75 (6): 934–957. https://doi.org/10.1177/0003122410388501.

Kim, ChangHwan, and Yang Zhao. 2014. "Are Asian American women advantaged? Labor market performance of college educated female workers." *Social Forces* 93 (2): 623–652. https://doi.org/10.1093/sf/sou076.

Kim, Claire Jean. 1999. "The racial triangulation of Asian Americans." *Politics & Society* 27 (1): 105–138. https://doi.org/10.1177/0032329299027001005.

Kuan, Teresa. 2015. *Love's uncertainty: the politics and ethics of child rearing in contemporary China.* Oakland: University of California Press.

Kusserow, Adrie. 2004. *American individualisms: child rearing and social class in three neighborhoods.* New York: Palgrave Macmillan.

Kye, Samuel H. 2018. "The persistence of white flight in middle-class suburbia." *Social Science Research* 72: 38–52. https://doi.org/10.1016/j.ssresearch.2018.02.005.

Lacy, Karyn R. 2007. *Blue-chip Black: race, class, and status in the new Black middle class.* Berkeley: University of California Press.

Lamont, Michèle. 1992. *Money, morals, and manners: the culture of the French and American upper-middle class.* Chicago: University of Chicago Press.

———. 2000. *The dignity of working men: morality and the boundaries of race, class, and immigration.* New York: Russell Sage Foundation; Cambridge, MA: Harvard University Press.

Lamont, Michèle, and Virag Molnar. 2002. "The study of boundaries in the social sciences." *Annual Review of Sociology* 28: 167–95.

Lamont, Michèle, John Schmalzbauer, Maureen Waller, and Daniel Weber. 1996. "Cultural and moral boundaries in the United States: structural position, geographic location, and lifestyle explanations." *Poetics* 24 (1): 31–56. https://doi.org/10.1016/0304-422X(96)00005-8.

Lamont, Michèle, and Ann Swidler. 2014. "Methodological pluralism and the possibilities and limits of interviewing." *Qualitative Sociology* 37 (2): 153–171. https://doi.org/10.1007/s11133-014-9274-z.

Lan, Pei-Chia. 2018. *Raising global families: parenting, immigration, and class in Taiwan and the US.* Stanford: Stanford University Press.

Lareau, Annette. 2000. *Home advantage: social class and parental intervention in elementary education.* 2nd ed. Lanham, MD: Rowman & Littlefield.

———. 2011. *Unequal childhoods: class, race, and family life.* 2nd ed., updated. Berkeley: University of California Press.

Lareau, Annette, and Kimberly A. Goyette. 2014. *Choosing homes, choosing schools.* New York: Russell Sage Foundation.

Lareau, Annette, Elliot B. Weininger, and Amanda Cox. 2018. "Parental challenges to organizational authority in an elite school district: the role of cultural, social, and symbolic capital." *TC Record* 120 (1): 1–46. https://www.tcrecord.org/content.asp?contentid=21978.

Lee, Jennifer. 2002. *Civility in the city: Blacks, Jews, and Koreans in urban America.* Cambridge, MA: Harvard University Press.

Lee, Jennifer, and Min Zhou. 2015. *The Asian American achievement paradox.* New York: Russell Sage Foundation.

Lee, Robert G. 1999. *Orientals: Asian Americans in popular culture.* Philadelphia: Temple University Press.

Lee, Stacey J. 1996. *Unraveling the "model minority" stereotype: listening to Asian American youth.* New York: Teachers College Press.

———. 2005. *Up against whiteness: race, school, and immigrant youth.* New York: Teachers College Press.

Levin, Brian. 2016. *Special status report: hate crime in the United States.* Center for the Study of Hate & Extremism, California State University San Bernardino. Accessed July 29, 2021. https://www.csusb.edu/sites/default/files/SPECIAL%20STATUS%20REPORT%20Final%20Draft.pdf.

Levine, Madeline. 2006. *The price of privilege: how parental pressure and material advantage are creating a generation of disconnected and unhappy kids.* New York: HarperCollins.

Lewis, Amanda E., and John Diamond. 2015. *Despite the best intentions: how racial inequality thrives in good schools.* New York: Oxford University Press.

Lewis-McCoy, R. L'Heureux. 2014. *Inequality in the promised land: race, resources, and suburban schooling.* Stanford: Stanford University Press.

Li, Wei. 2009. *Ethnoburb: the new ethnic community in urban America.* Honolulu: University of Hawai'i Press.

Lin, Monica H., Virginia S. Y. Kwan, Anna Cheung, and Susan T. Fiske. 2005. "Stereotype content model explains prejudice for an envied outgroup: scale of anti–Asian American stereotypes." *Personality and Social Psychology Bulletin* 31 (1): 34–47. https://doi.org/10.1177/0146167204271320.

Liu, Airan, and Yu Xie. 2016. "Why do Asian Americans academically outperform whites? The cultural explanation revisited." *Social Science Research* 58: 210–226. https://doi.org/http://dx.doi.org/10.1016/j.ssresearch.2016.03.004.

Livingston, Gretchen, and Anna Brown. 2017. *Intermarriage in the U.S. 50 years after Loving v. Virginia.* Pew Research Center, May 18. Accessed July 29, 2021. https://www.pewsocialtrends.org/2017/05/18/intermarriage-in-the-u-s-50-years-after-loving-v-virginia/.

Lizardo, Omar. 2017. "Improving cultural analysis: considering personal culture in its declarative and nondeclarative modes." *American Sociological Review* 82 (1): 88–115. https://doi.org/10.1177/0003122416675175.

Logan, John R., Richard D. Alba, and Shu-Yin Leung. 1996. "Minority access to white suburbs: a multiregional comparison." *Social Forces* 74 (3): 851–881. https://doi.org/10.1093/sf/74.3.851.

Louie, Vivian S. 2004. *Compelled to excel: immigration, education, and opportunity among Chinese Americans.* Stanford: Stanford University Press.

———. 2012. *Keeping the immigrant bargain: the costs and rewards of success in America.* New York: Russell Sage Foundation.

Lowe, Lisa. 1996. *Immigrant acts: on Asian American cultural politics.* Durham: Duke University Press.

Lu, Jackson G., Richard E. Nisbett, and Michael W. Morris. 2020. "Why East Asians but not South Asians are underrepresented in leadership positions in the United States." *Proceedings of the National Academy of Sciences* 117 (9): 4590–4600. https://doi.org/10.1073/pnas.1918896117.

Lucas, Samuel Roundfield. 1999. *Tracking inequality: stratification and mobility in American high schools.* New York: Teachers College Press.

Lukianoff, Greg, and Jonathan Haidt. 2018. *The coddling of the American mind: how good intentions and bad ideas are setting up a generation for failure.* New York: Penguin.

Lund, Terese J., and Eric Dearing. 2013. "Is growing up affluent risky for adolescents or is the problem growing up in an affluent neighborhood?" *Journal of Research on Adolescence* 23 (2): 274–282. https://doi.org/10.1111/j.1532-7795.2012.00829.x.

Lung-Amam, Willow S. 2017. *Trespassers? Asian Americans and the battle for suburbia.* Oakland: University of California Press.

Luthar, Suniya S., Samuel H. Barkin, and Elizabeth J. Crossman. 2013. "'I can, therefore I must': fragility in the upper-middle classes." *Development and Psychopathology* 25: 1529–1549. https://doi.org/doi:10.1017/S0954579413000758.

Luthar, Suniya S., and Bronwyn E. Becker. 2002. "Privileged but pressured? A study of affluent youth." *Child Development* 73 (5): 1593–1610. https://doi.org/10.1111/1467-8624.00492.

Luthra, Renee, Thomas Soehl, and Roger Waldinger. 2018. *Origins and destinations: the making of the second generation.* New York: Russell Sage Foundation.

Lythcott-Haims, Julie. 2015. *How to raise an adult: break free of the overparenting trap and prepare your kid for success.* New York: Henry Holt.

Madsen, Ole Jacob. 2014. *The therapeutic turn: how psychology altered Western culture.* Hove, East Sussex: Routledge.

Marano, Hara Estroff. 2008. *A nation of wimps: the high cost of invasive parenting.* New York: Broadway Books.

Markus, Hazel R., and Shinobu Kitayama. 1991. "Culture and the self: implications for cognition, emotion, and motivation." *Psychological Review* 98 (2): 224–253. https://doi.org/10.1037/0033-295X.98.2.224.

Massey, Douglas S., and Nancy A. Denton. 1993. *American apartheid: segregation and the making of the underclass.* Cambridge, MA: Harvard University Press.

Matsumoto, Noriko. 2018. *Beyond the city and the bridge: East Asian immigration in a New Jersey suburb.* New Brunswick: Rutgers University Press.

McKim, Jennifer. 2019. "Harvard student's suicide prompts concern about mental health care on college campuses." *Boston Globe*, September 16. Accessed July 13, 2020. https://www.bostonglobe.com/metro/2019/09/16/harvard-student-suicide-prompts-concern-about-mental-health-care-college-campuses/kKJsMeSrriLeBeD2BZtu4L/story.html?p1=HP_Feed_ContentQuery.

Meier, Ann, Benjamin Swartz Hartmann, and Ryan Larson. 2018. "A quarter century of participation in school-based extracurricular activities: inequalities by race, class, gender and age?" *Journal of Youth and Adolescence* 47 (6): 1299–1316. https://doi.org/10.1007/s10964-018-0838-1.

Migration Policy Institute. n.d. "Profile of the unauthorized population: United States." Accessed August 6, 2021. https://www.migrationpolicy.org/data/unauthorized-immigrant-population/state/US.

Mijs, Jonathan J. B. 2021. "The paradox of inequality: income inequality and belief in meritocracy go hand in hand." *Socio-economic Review* 19 (1): 7-35. https://doi.org/10.1093/ser/mwy051.

Mueller, Anna S., and Seth Abrutyn. 2016. "Adolescents under pressure: a new Durkheimian framework for understanding adolescent suicide in a cohesive community." *American Sociological Review* 81 (5): 877–899. https://doi.org/10.1177/0003122416663464.

NAACP Legal Defense and Educational Fund. 2012. "New York City specialized high school complaint." Accessed March 8, 2021. https://www.naacpldf.org/case-issue/new-york-city-specialized-high-school-complaint/.

Naftali, Orna. 2014. *Children, rights and modernity in China: raising self-governing citizens.* Basingstoke, Hampshire: Palgrave Macmillan.

Narizhnaya, Khristina, and Selim Algar. 2020. "Tensions boil over at rally to keep competitive admissions in NYC schools." *New York Post*, October 23. Accessed October 29, 2020. https://nypost.com/2020/10/23/tensions-boil

-over-at-nyc-school-admissions-rally/?fbclid=IwAR2we8HkEvYSKK
-ShPtD1bFsvtteTedoYVi1mcGnHYHsh9mYUs_4uNlzCLQ.

National Academies of Sciences, Engineering, and Medicine. 2015. *The Integration of Immigrants into American Society*. Washington, DC: National Academies Press.

National Center for Education Statistics. 2020. "Private school enrollment." Accessed March 25, 2021. https://nces.ed.gov/programs/coe/indicator_cgc.asp#:~:text= In%20fall%202017%2C%20about%205.7,of%20Two%20or%20more %20races.

Neckerman, Kathryn M., Prudence Carter, and Jennifer Lee. 1999. "Segmented assimilation and minority cultures of mobility." *Ethnic and Racial Studies* 22 (6): 945–965. https://doi.org/10.1080/014198799329198.

Neckerman, Kathryn M., and Joleen Kirschenman. 2014. "Hiring strategies, racial bias, and inner-city workers." *Social Problems* 38 (4): 433–447. https://doi.org/10 .2307/800563.

Nee, Victor, and Hilary Holbrow. 2013. "Why Asian Americans are becoming mainstream." *Daedalus* 142 (3): 65–75. https://doi.org/10.1162/DAED_a_00219.

Nelson, Margaret K. 2010. *Parenting out of control: anxious parents in uncertain times*. New York: New York University Press.

New York State Education Department. 2019a. "NYC Public Schools enrollment (2018– 19)." Accessed March 8, 2021. https://data.nysed.gov/enrollment.php?year=2019& instid=7889678368.

———. 2019b. "Stuyvesant High School enrollment (2018–19)." Accessed March 8, 2021. https://data.nysed.gov/enrollment.php?year=2019&instid=800000046741.

Ngo, Bic and Stacey J. Lee. 2007. "Complicating the image of model minority success: a review of Southeast Asian American education." *Review of Educational Research* 77 (4): 415-453. https://doi.org/10.3102/0034654307309918.

Noe-Bustamante, Luis, Lauren Mora, and Mark H. Lopez. 2020. "About one-in-four U.S. Hispanics have heard of Latinx, but just 3% use it." Accessed August 27, 2021. https://www.pewresearch.org/hispanic/2020/08/11/about-one-in-four-u-s -hispanics-have-heard-of-latinx-but-just-3-use-it/.

O'Keefe, Paul A., Carol S. Dweck, and Gregory M. Walton. 2018. "Implicit theories of interest: finding your passion or developing it?" *Psychological Science* 29 (10): 1653–1664. https://doi.org/10.1177/0956797618780643.

Ochoa, Gilda L. 2013. *Academic profiling: Latinos, Asian Americans, and the achievement gap*. Minneapolis: University of Minnesota Press.

OECD. 2015. *What do parents look for in their child's school?* Paris: OECD Publishing. https://doi.org/10.1787/5js1qfw4n6wj-en.

———. 2018. *PISA 2015 results in focus*. Paris: OECD Publishing. https://doi.org/10.1787 /aa9237e6-en.

Okamoto, Dina G. 2003. "Toward a theory of panethnicity: explaining Asian American collective action." *American Sociological Review* 68 (6): 811–842. https://doi.org/10 .2307/1519747.

Okamoto, Dina G., Daniel Herda, and Cassie Hartzog. 2013. "Beyond good grades: school composition and immigrant youth participation in extracurricular activities." *Social Science Research* 42 (1): 155–168. https://doi.org/10.1016/j.ssresearch .2012.08.005.

Opportunity Insights. n.d. "The opportunity atlas." Accessed August 12, 2020. https:// www.opportunityatlas.org/.

Ørberg, Jakob Williams. 2018. "Uncomfortable encounters between elite and 'shadow education' in India: Indian Institutes of Technology and the Joint Entrance Exam-

ination coaching industry." *Higher Education* 76 (1): 129–144. https://doi.org/10
.1007/s10734-017-0202-5.

Orfield, Gary, Erica D. Frankenberg, and Chungmei Lee. 2003. "The resurgence of
school segregation." *Educational Leadership* 60 (4): 16. https://www.ascd.org/el
/articles/the-resurgence-of-school-segregation.

Orfield, Gary, John Kucsera, and Genevieve Siegel-Hawley. 2012. "*E pluribus* . . . sepa-
ration: deepening double segregation for more students." Civil Rights Project, University of California Los Angeles. Accessed June 25, 2013. http://civilrightsproject
.ucla.edu/research/k-12-education/integration-and-diversity/mlk-national/e
-pluribus . . . separation-deepening-double-segregation-for-more-students
/orfield_epluribus_revised_omplete_2012.pdf.

Owens, Ann. 2020. "Unequal opportunity: school and neighborhood segregation in the
USA." *Race and Social Problems* 12 (1): 29–41. https://doi.org/10.1007/s12552-019
-09274-z.

Pager, Devah, Bart Bonikowski, and Bruce Western. 2009. "Discrimination in a low-
wage labor market: a field experiment." *American Sociological Review* 74 (5): 777-
799. https://doi.org/10.1177/000312240907400505.

Park, Eujin. 2020. "Asian Americans in the suburbs: race, class, and Korean immigrant
parental engagement." *Equity & Excellence in Education* 53 (1–2): 30–49. https://
doi.org/10.1080/10665684.2020.1758974.

Perry, Theresa. 2003. "Freedom for literacy and literacy for freedom: the African-
American philosophy of education." In *Young, gifted, and Black: promoting high
achievement among African-American students*, edited by Theresa Perry, Claude
Steele, and Asa Hilliard III. Boston: Beacon.

Pew Research Center. 2012. "The rise of Asian Americans." Accessed July 30, 2021.
https://www.pewresearch.org/social-trends/2012/06/19/the-rise-of-asian
-americans/.

———. 2017a. "Chinese in the U.S. fact sheet." Accessed August 7, 2020. https://www
.pewsocialtrends.org/fact-sheet/asian-americans-chinese-in-the-u-s/.

———. 2017b. "Indians in the U.S. fact Sheet." Accessed August 7, 2020. https://www
.pewsocialtrends.org/fact-sheet/asian-americans-indians-in-the-u-s/.

———. 2020. "Most Americans say there is too much economic inequality in the U.S.
but fewer than half call it a top priority." Accessed August 24, 2020. https://www
.pewsocialtrends.org/2020/01/09/trends-in-income-and-wealth-inequality/#fn
-27657-9.

Pillet-Shore, Danielle. 2015. "Being a 'good parent, in parent-teacher conferences."
Journal of Communication 65 (2): 373–395. https://doi.org/10.1111/jcom.12146.

Pope, Denise Clark, Maureen Brown, and Sarah B. Miles. 2015. *Overloaded and underprepared: strategies for stronger schools and healthy, successful kids*. San Francisco:
Jossey-Bass.

Portes, Alejandro, Patricia Fernández-Kelly, and William Haller. 2005. "Segmented
assimilation on the ground: the new second generation in early adulthood." *Ethnic
& Racial Studies* 28 (6): 1000–1040. https://doi.org/10.1080/01419870500224117.

———. 2009. "The adaptation of the immigrant second generation in America: a
theoretical overview and recent evidence." *Journal of Ethnic & Migration Studies* 35
(7): 1077–1104. https://doi.org/10.1080/1369183090300127.

Portes, Alejandro, and Rubén G. Rumbaut. 2001. *Legacies: the story of the immigrant
second generation*. Berkeley: University of California Press; New York: Russell Sage
Foundation.

Portes, Alejandro, and Min Zhou. 1993. "The new second generation: segmented assimilation and its variants." *Annals of the American Academy* 530: 74–96. https://doi.org/10.1177/0002716293530001006.

Posey-Maddox, Linn. 2013. "Professionalizing the PTO: race, class, and shifting norms of parental engagement in a city public school." *American Journal of Education* 119 (2): 235–260. https://doi.org/10.1086/668754.

Pugh, Allison J. 2015. *The tumbleweed society: working and caring in an age of insecurity.* New York: Oxford University Press.

Qin, Desiree Baolian, Niobe Way, and Meenal Rana. 2008. "The 'model minority' and their discontent: examining peer discrimination and harassment of Chinese American immigrant youth." *New Directions for Child & Adolescent Development* 2008 (121): 27–42. https://doi.org/10.1002/cd.221.

Ramakrishnan, S. Karthick, Jennifer Lee, Taeku Lee, and Janelle Wong. 2016. "National Asian American Survey." Accessed February 22. http://naasurvey.com/.

Ramakrishnan, Karthick, Janelle Wong, Jennifer Lee, and Taeku Lee. 2017. *2016 Post-Election National Asian American Survey.* Accessed July 30, 2021. http://naasurvey.com/wp-content/uploads/2017/05/NAAS16-post-election-report.pdf.

Randle, Brenda A. 2015. "'I am not my hair': African American women and their struggles with embracing natural hair." *Race, Gender & Class* 22 (1–2): 114–121. https://www.jstor.org/stable/26505328.

Raval, Vaishali V., Pratiksha H. Raval, Jennifer M. Salvina, Stephanie L. Wilson, and Sharon Writer. 2013. "Mothers' socialization of children's emotion in India and the USA: a cross- and within-culture comparison." *Social Development* 22 (3): 467–484. https://doi.org/10.1111/j.1467-9507.2012.00666.x.

Redfield, Robert R., Anne Schuchat, Leslie Dauphin, Joanne Cono, Chesley L. Richards, and Michael F. Iademarco. 2018. "Youth risk behavior surveillance: United States, 2017." *Morbidity and Mortality Weekly Report Surveillance Summaries* 67 (8): 1–114. http://dx.doi.org/10.15585/mmwr.ss6708a1.

Reeves, Richard V., and Dimitrios Halikias. 2017. "Race gaps in SAT scores highlight inequality and hinder upward mobility." Brookings Institution, February 1. Accessed July 30, 2021. https://www.brookings.edu/research/race-gaps-in-sat-scores-highlight-inequality-and-hinder-upward-mobility/.

Rieff, Philip. 1966. *The triumph of the therapeutic: uses of faith after Freud.* New York: Harper & Row.

Ripley, Amanda. 2013. "The case against high-school sports." *The Atlantic*, October. Accessed March 8, 2021. https://www.theatlantic.com/magazine/archive/2013/10/the-case-against-high-school-sports/309447/.

Rivas-Drake, Deborah, Diane Hughes, and Niobe Way. 2008. "A closer look at peer discrimination, ethnic identity, and psychological well-being among urban Chinese American sixth graders." *Journal of Youth & Adolescence* 37 (1): 12–21. https://doi.org/10.1007/s10964-007-9227-x.

Rivera, Lauren A. 2015. *Pedigree: how elite students get elite jobs.* Princeton: Princeton University Press.

Robinson, Keith, and Angel L. Harris. 2014. *The broken compass: parental involvement with children's education.* Cambridge, MA: Harvard University Press.

Roda, A. 2017. "Parenting in the age of high-stakes testing: gifted and talented admissions and the meaning of parenthood." *Teachers College Record* 119(8): 1–53. https://www.tcrecord.org/content.asp?contentid=21930.

Romero, Mary. 2008. "Crossing the immigration and race border: A critical race theory approach to immigration studies." *Contemporary Justice Review* 11 (1): 23–37. https://doi.org/10.1080/10282580701850371.

Roscigno, Vincent J., Lisa M. Williams, and Reginald A. Byron. 2012. "Workplace racial discrimination and middle class vulnerability." *American Behavioral Scientist* 56 (5): 696–710. https://doi.org/10.1177/0002764211433805.

Rosin, Hanna. 2015. "The Silicon Valley suicides." *The Atlantic*, December. Accessed January 6, 2016. http://www.theatlantic.com/magazine/archive/2015/12/the -silicon-valley-suicides/413140/.

Roza, Marguerite. 2010. *Educational economics: where do school funds go?* Washington, DC: Urban Institute Press.

Rumbaut, Rubén G. 2008. "The coming of the second generation: immigration and ethnic mobility in southern California." *Annals of the American Academy of Political and Social Science* 620: 196–236. www.jstor.org/stable/40375817.

Sackett, Paul R., Nathan R. Kuncel, Justin J. Arneson, Sara R. Cooper, and Shonna D. Waters. 2009. "Socioeconomic status and the relationship between the SAT and freshman GPA: an analysis of data from 41 colleges and universities." College Board Research Report No. 2009-1. Accessed March 4, 2021. https://files.eric.ed.gov /fulltext/ED562860.pdf.

Sáenz, Rogelio, and Karen Manges Douglas. 2015. "A call for the racialization of immigration studies: on the transition of ethnic immigrants to racialized immigrants." *Sociology of Race and Ethnicity* 1 (1): 166–180. https://doi.org/10.1177 /2332649214559287.

Sahithya, B. R., S. M. Manohari, and Raman Vijaya. 2019. "Parenting styles and its [sic] impact on children: a cross cultural review with a focus on India." *Mental Health, Religion & Culture* 22 (4): 357–383. https://doi.org/10.1080/13674676.2019.1594178.

Saito, Leland T. 1998. *Race and politics: Asian Americans, Latinos, and whites in a Los Angeles suburb.* Urbana: University of Illinois Press.

Sakamoto, Arthur, Kimberly A. Goyette, and ChangHwan Kim. 2009. "Socioeconomic attainments of Asian Americans." *Annual Review of Sociology* 35 (1): 255–276. https://doi.org/10.1146/annurev-soc-070308-115958.

Salinas, Cristobal, and Adele Lozano. 2021. "The history and evolution of the term Latinx." In *Handbook of Latinos and Education: Theory, Research, and Practice*, edited by Enrique G. Murillo Jr. et al. New York: Routledge.

Samson, Frank L. 2013. "Multiple group threat and malleable white attitudes towards academic merit." *Du Bois Review* 10 (1): 233–260. https://doi.org/doi:10.1017 /S1742058X1300012X.

Sancho, David. 2016. *Youth, class and education in urban India: the year that can break or make you.* New York: Routledge.

Sapru, Saloni. 2006. "Parenting and adolescent identity: a study of Indian families in New Delhi and Geneva." *Journal of Adolescent Research* 21 (5): 484–513. https://doi .org/10.1177/0743558406291766.

Saraswathi, T. S., and Shefali Pai. 1997. "Socialization in the Indian context." In *Asian perspectives on psychology*, edited by Henry S. R. Rao and Durganand Sinha. Thousand Oaks, CA: SAGE, Inc.

Saxenian, AnnaLee. 1996. *Regional advantage: culture and competition in Silicon Valley and Route 128.* Cambridge, MA: Harvard University Press.

———. 2006. *The new argonauts: regional advantage in a global economy.* Cambridge, MA: Harvard University Press.

Sayer, Liana, C., Suzanne M. Bianchi, and John P. Robinson. 2004. "Are parents investing less in children? Trends in mothers' and fathers' time with children." *American Journal of Sociology* 110 (1): 1–43. https://doi.org/10.1086/386270.

Schiffrin, Holly H., Miriam Liss, Haley Miles-McLean, Katherine A. Geary, Mindy J.

Erchull, and Taryn Tashner. 2014. "Helping or hovering? the effects of helicopter parenting on college students' well-being." *Journal of Child and Family Studies* 23 (3): 548–557. https://doi.org/10.1007/s10826-013-9716-3.

Sellers, Robert M., Tabbye M. Chavous, and Deanna Y. Cooke. 1998. "Racial ideology and racial centrality as predictors of African American college students' academic performance." *Journal of Black Psychology* 24 (1): 8–27. https://doi.org/10.1177 /00957984980241002.

Shapiro, Eliza. 2020. "'Fire Carranza!': why Asian-Americans are targeting schools chief." *New York Times*, March 3. Accessed December 2, 2021. http://www.nytimes .com/2020/03/03/nyregion/carranza-asian-americans-schools.html.

Sherman, Rachel. 2017a. "Conflicted cultivation: parenting, privilege, and moral worth in wealthy New York families." *American Journal of Cultural Sociology* 5 (1): 1–33. https://doi.org/10.1057/s41290-016-0012-8.

———. 2017b. *Uneasy street: the anxieties of affluence*. Princeton: Princeton University Press.

Shoshana, Avihu. 2019. "Youth, class, and happiness." *Children and Youth Services Review* 99: 64–73. https://doi.org/10.1016/j.childyouth.2019.01.034.

Singer, Audrey. 2008. "Twenty-first-century gateways: an introduction." In *Twenty-First-Century Gateways: Immigrant Incorporation in Suburban America*, edited by Audrey Singer, Susan W. Hardwick and Caroline Brettell. Washington, DC: Brookings Institution Press.

Siy, John Oliver, and Sapna Cheryan. 2013. "When compliments fail to flatter: American individualism and responses to positive stereotypes." *Journal of Personality and Social Psychology* 104 (1): 87–102. https://doi.org/10.1037/a0030183.

Skiba, Russell J., Robert H. Horner, Choong-Geun Chung, M. Karega Rausch, Seth L. May, and Tary Tobin. 2011. "Race is not neutral: a national investigation of African American and Latino disproportionality in school discipline." *School Psychology Review* 40 (1): 85–107. https://doi.org/10.1080/02796015.2011.12087730.

Smith, Robert Courtney. 2008. "Horatio Alger lives in Brooklyn: extra family support, intrafamily dynamics, and socially neutral operating identities in exceptional mobility among children of Mexican immigrants." *Annals of the American Academy of Political and Social Science* 620 (1): 270–290. https://doi.org/10.1177 /0002716208322988.

Snellman, Kaisa, Jennifer M. Silva, Carl B. Frederick, and Robert D. Putnam. 2015. "The engagement gap: social mobility and extracurricular participation among American youth." *Annals of the American Academy of Political and Social Science* 657 (1): 194–207. https://doi.org/10.1177/0002716214548398.

Sohi, Seema. 2014. *Echoes of mutiny: race, surveillance, and Indian anticolonialism in North America*. Oxford: Oxford University Press.

Spencer, Kyle. 2015. "New Jersey school district eases pressure on students, baring an ethnic divide." *New York Times*, December 25. Accessed January 6, 2016. http:// www.nytimes.com/2015/12/26/nyregion/reforms-to-ease-students-stress-divide -a-new-jersey-school-district.html.

Starck, Jordan G., Travis Riddle, Stacey Sinclair, and Natasha Warikoo. 2020. "Teachers are people too: examining the racial bias of teachers compared to other American adults." *Educational Researcher* 49 (4): 273–284. https://doi.org/10.3102 /0013189x20912758.

Stearns, Peter N. 2003. *Anxious parents: a history of modern childrearing in America*. New York: New York University Press.

Steinberg, Laurence, Sanford M. Dornbusch, and B. Bradford Brown. 1992. "Ethnic differences in adolescent achievement: an ecological perspective." *American Psychologist* 47 (6): 723–729. https://doi.org/10.1037/0003-066X.47.6.723.

Stevens, Mitchell L. 2007. *Creating a class: college admissions and the education of elites.* Cambridge, MA: Harvard University Press.

Stevenson, Harold W., Shin-Ying Lee, Chuansheng Chen, James W. Stigler, Chen-Chin Hsu, Seiro Kitamura, and Giyoo Hatano. 1990. "Contexts of achievement: a study of American, Chinese, and Japanese children." *Monographs of the Society for Research in Child Development* 55 (1/2): i–119. https://doi.org/10.2307/1166090.

Subramanian, Ajantha. 2019. *The caste of merit: engineering education in India.* Cambridge, MA: Harvard University Press.

Substance Abuse and Mental Health Services Administration. 2015. "Racial/ethnic differences in mental health service use among adults." HHS Publication No. SMA-15-4906. Rockville, MD: Substance Abuse and Mental Health Services Administration. Accessed April 23, 2019. https://www.samhsa.gov/data/sites/default/files/MHServicesUseAmongAdults/MHServicesUseAmongAdults.pdf.

Sue, Stanley, and Sumie Okazaki. 1990. "Asian-American educational achievements: a phenomenon in search of an explanation." *American Psychologist* 45: 913–20. https://doi.org/10.1037/1948-1985.S.1.45.

Swidler, Ann. 1986. "Culture in action: symbols and strategies." *American Sociological Review* 51 (2): 273–286. https://doi.org/10.2307/2095521.

Takaki, Ronald T. 1998. *Strangers from a different shore: a history of Asian Americans.* 1st ed. Boston: Little, Brown.

Tao, Vivienne Y. K., and Ying-yi Hong. 2014. "When academic achievement is an obligation: perspectives from social-oriented achievement motivation." *Journal of Cross-Cultural Psychology* 45 (1): 110–136. https://doi.org/10.1177/0022022113490072.

Tenenbaum, Harriet R., and Martin D. Ruck. 2007. "Are teachers' expectations different for racial minority than for European American students? A meta-analysis." *Journal of Educational Psychology* 99 (2): 253–273. https://doi.org/10.1037/0022-0663.99.2.253.

Thomas, Sue, Jayne Keogh, and Steve Hay. 2015. "Discourses of the good parent in attributing school success." *Discourse* 36 (3): 452–463. https://doi.org/10.1080/01596306.2014.901489.

Thompson, Derek. 2019. "Meritocracy is killing high-school sports." *The Atlantic*, August 30. Accessed March 4, 2021. https://www.theatlantic.com/ideas/archive/2019/08/meritocracy-killing-high-school-sports/597121/.

Tocqueville, Alexis de. 1994. *Democracy in America.* New York: Knopf.

Torres, Amanda. 2019. "Research insights: why parents choose independent schools." National Association of Independent Schools. Accessed March 11, 2021. https://www.nais.org/magazine/independent-school/winter-2019/research-insights-why-parents-choose-independent-schools/.

Torres, Lourdes. 2018. "Latinx?" *Latino Studies* 16: 283–285. https://doi.org/10.1057/s41276-018-0142-y.

Tran, Van C., Jennifer Lee, and Tiffany J. Huang. 2019. "Revisiting the Asian second-generation advantage." *Ethnic and Racial Studies* 42 (13): 2248-2269. https://doi.org/10.1080/01419870.2019.1579920.

Treitler, Vilna Bashi. 2015. "Social agency and white supremacy in immigration studies." *Sociology of Race and Ethnicity* 1 (1): 153–165. https://doi.org/10.1177/2332649214560796.

Trines, Stefan. 2018. "Education in India." Education System Profiles. World Education

News and Review. Accessed June 16, 2020. https://wenr.wes.org/2018/09/education-in-india.

Tu, Siqi. Forthcoming. "In search of the 'best' option: American private secondary education for upper-middle-class Chinese teenagers." *Current Sociology.*

Tuan, Mia. 1998. *Forever foreigners or honorary whites? The Asian ethnic experience today.* New Brunswick: Rutgers University Press.

Tuli, Mila. 2012. "Beliefs on Parenting and Childhood in India." *Journal of Comparative Family Studies* 43 (1): 81–91. https://doi.org/10.3138/jcfs.43.1.81.

Tuli, Mila, and Nandita Chaudhary. 2010. "Elective interdependence: understanding individual agency and interpersonal relationships in Indian families." *Culture & Psychology* 16 (4): 477–496. https://doi.org/10.1177/1354067x10380157.

Twenge, Jean M., W. Keith Campbell, and Elise C. Freeman. 2012. "Generational differences in young adults' life goals, concern for others, and civic orientation, 1966–2009." *Journal of Personality and Social Psychology* 102 (5): 1045–1062. https://doi.org/10.1037/a0027408.

Twenge, Jean M., A. Bell Cooper, Thomas E. Joiner, Mary E. Duffy, and Sarah G. Binau. 2019. "Age, period, and cohort trends in mood disorder indicators and suicide-related outcomes in a nationally representative dataset, 2005–2017." *Journal of Abnormal Psychology* 128 (3): 185–199. https://doi.org/10.1037/abn0000410.

Tyson, Karolyn. 2011. *Integration interrupted: tracking, Black students, and acting White after Brown.* New York: Oxford University Press.

Tyson, Karolyn, William Darity Jr., and Domini Castellino. 2005. "It's not 'a Black thing': understanding the burden of acting white and other dilemmas of high achievement." *American Sociological Review* 70 (4): 582–605. https://doi.org/10.1177/000312240507000403.

Uhlmann, Eric Luis, and Geoffrey L. Cohen. 2005. "Constructed criteria: redefining merit to justify discrimination." *Psychological Science* 16 (6): 474–480. https://doi.org/10.1111/j.0956-7976.2005.01559.x.

U.S. Census Bureau. 1970. Decennial Census of Population and Housing. Accessed May 15, 2021. www.socialexplorer.com/explore-tables.

———. 2000. Decennial Census of Population and Housing. Accessed May 21, 2015. http://www.s4.brown.edu/us2010/Data/Download1.htm.

———. 2010a. Current Population Survey, Annual Social and Economic Supplements. Table H-1. Accessed July 28, 2021. https://www2.census.gov/programs-surveys/cps/tables/time-series/historical-income-households/h01ar.xlsx.

———. 2010b. Decennial Census of Population and Housing. Accessed May 21, 2015. http://www.s4.brown.edu/us2010/Data/Download1.htm.

———. 2014. American Community Survey 5-Year Estimates, Table DP05. Accessed July 28, 2021. https://data.census.gov.

———. 2019a. American Community Survey 5-Year Estimates, Table B05002. Accessed July 28, 2021. https://data.census.gov.

———. 2019b. American Community Survey 5-Year Estimates, Table DP04. Accessed July 28, 2021. https://data.census.gov.

———. 2019c. American Community Survey 5-Year Estimates, Table DP05. Accessed July 28, 2021. https://data.census.gov.

———. 2019d. American Community Survey 5-Year Estimates, Table S1501. Accessed July 28, 2021. https://data.census.gov.

———. 2019e. American Community Survey 5-Year Estimates, Table S1701. Accessed July 28, 2021. https://data.census.gov.

————. 2019f. American Community Survey 5-Year Estimates, Table S1903. Accessed July 28, 2021. https://data.census.gov.

————. 2019g. American Community Survey 1-Year Estimates, Table S0201. Accessed July 7, 2021. https://data.census.gov.

U.S. Department of Education, National Center for Education Statistics. 2016. "Table 226.10. SAT mean scores of college-bound seniors, by race/ethnicity: selected years, 1986–87 through 2015–16." In *Digest of Education Statistics*. Accessed July 30, 2021. https://nces.ed.gov/programs/digest/d16/tables/dt16_226.10.asp.

————. 2018. "Table 226.10. Number, percentage distribution, and SAT mean scores of high school seniors taking the SAT, by sex, race/ethnicity, first language learned, and highest level of parental education: 2017 and 2018." In *Digest of Education Statistics*. Accessed July 30, 2021. https://nces.ed.gov/programs/digest/d18/tables/dt18_226.10.asp?current=yes.

U.S. Department of Health and Human Services Office of Minority Health. n.d. "Mental health and Asian Americans." Minority Population Profiles. Accessed May 22, 2015. http://minorityhealth.hhs.gov/omh/browse.aspx?lvl=4&lvlID=54.

U.S. News & World Report. n.d.a. "*U.S. News* best colleges." Accessed June 16, 2020. https://www.usnews.com/best-colleges.

————. n.d.b. "*U.S. News* high school rankings." Accessed August 7, 2020. http://www.usnews.com/education/best-high-schools.

Useem, Elizabeth L. 1992. "Middle schools and math groups: parents' involvement in children's placement." *Sociology of Education* 65 (4): 263–279. https://doi.org/10.2307/2112770.

Walder, Andrew G., Bobai Li, and Donald Treiman. 2000. "Politics and life chances in a state socialist regime: dual career paths into the urban Chinese elite, 1949 to 1996." *American Sociological Review* 65 (2): 191-209. https://doi.org/10.2307/2657437.

Walker, Maurice. 2011. *PISA 2009 Plus Results: performance of 15-year-olds in reading, mathematics and science for 10 additional participants*. Melbourne: ACER Press. https://research.acer.edu.au/cgi/viewcontent.cgi?referer=&httpsredir=1&article=1000&context=pisa.

Wang, L. Ling-Chi. 1988. "Meritocracy and diversity in higher education: discrimination against Asian Americans in the post-*Bakke* era." *Urban Review* 20 (3): 189-209. https://doi.org/10.1007/BF01112009.

Wang, Sharron Xuanren, Isao Takei, and Arthur Sakamoto. 2017. "Do Asian Americans face labor market discrimination? Accounting for the cost of living among native-born men and women." *Socius* 3: 1-14. https://doi.org/10.1177/2378023117741724.

Wang, Vivian, and Javier C. Hernandez. 2020. "China long avoided discussing mental health. The pandemic changed that." *New York Times*, December 21. Accessed January 8, 2021. https://www.nytimes.com/2020/12/21/world/asia/china-covid-mental-health.html.

Warikoo, Natasha. 2011. *Balancing acts: youth culture in the global city*. Berkeley: University of California Press.

————. 2016. *The diversity bargain: and other dilemmas of race, admissions, and meritocracy at elite universities*. Chicago: University of Chicago Press.

————. 2020. "Addressing emotional health while protecting status: Asian American and white parents in suburban America." *American Journal of Sociology* 126 (3): 545-576.

Warikoo, Natasha, Mark Chin, Nicole Zillmer, and Suniya Luthar. 2020. "The influence of parent expectations and parent-child relationships on mental health in Asian

American and white American families." *Sociological Forum* 35 (2): 275–296. https://doi.org/10.1111/socf.12583.

Warner, Catharine H. 2010. "Emotional safeguarding: exploring the nature of middle-class parents' school involvement." *Sociological Forum* 25 (4): 703–724. https://doi.org/10.1111/j.1573-7861.2010.01208.x.

Waters, Mary C. 1990. *Ethnic options: choosing identities in America*. Berkeley: University of California Press.

Waters, Mary C., and Tomás R. Jiménez. 2005. "Assessing immigrant assimilation: new empirical and theoretical challenges." *Annual Review of Sociology* 31: 105–125. https://doi.org/10.1146/annurev.soc.29.010202.100026.

Watkins, Megan, Christina Ho, and Rose Butler. 2017. "Asian migration and education cultures in the Anglo-sphere." *Journal of Ethnic and Migration Studies* 43 (14): 2283–2299. https://doi.org/10.1080/1369183X.2017.1315849.

Watkins, Megan, and Greg Noble. 2013. *Disposed to learn: schooling, ethnicity and the scholarly habitus*. London: Bloomsbury Academic.

Way, Niobe, Sumie Okazaki, Jing Zhao, Joanna J. Kim, Xinyin Chen, Hirokazu Yoshikawa, Yueming Jia, and Huihua Deng. 2013. "Social and emotional parenting: mothering in a changing Chinese society." *Asian American Journal of Psychology* 4 (1): 61–70. https://doi.org/10.1037/a0031204.

Wei, William. 1993. *The Asian American movement*. Philadelphia: Temple University Press.

Weininger, Elliot B. 2014. "School choice in an urban setting." In *Choosing Homes, Choosing Schools*, edited by Annette Lareau and Kimberly Goyette. New York: Russell Sage Foundation.

Weininger, Elliot B., and Annette Lareau. 2009. "Paradoxical pathways: an ethnographic extension of Kohn's findings on class and childrearing." *Journal of Marriage and Family* 71 (3): 680–695. https://doi.org/10.1111/j.1741-3737.2009.00626.x.

Weininger, Elliot B., Annette Lareau, and Dalton Conley. 2015. "What money doesn't buy: class resources and children's participation in organized extracurricular activities." *Social Forces* 94 (2): 479–503. https://doi.org/10.1093/sf/sov071.

Weis, Lois, Kristin Cipollone, and Heather Jenkins. 2014. *Class warfare: class, race, and college admissions in top-tier secondary schools*. Chicago: University of Chicago Press.

Westervelt, Amy. 2018. *Forget "having it all": how America messed up motherhood—and how to fix it*. New York: Seal Press.

Wimmer, Andreas. 2013. *Ethnic boundary making: institutions, power, networks*. New York: Oxford University Press.

Won, Seoung Joun, and Seunghee Han. 2010. "Out-of-school activities and achievement among middle school students in the U.S. and South Korea." *Journal of Advanced Academics* 21 (4): 628–661. https://doi.org/10.1177/1932202x1002100404.

Woo, Deborah. 2000. *Glass ceilings and Asian Americans: the new face of workplace barriers*. Walnut Creek, CA: AltaMira Press.

Wu, Xiaogang. 2017. "Higher education, elite formation and social stratification in contemporary China: preliminary findings from the Beijing College Students Panel Survey." *Chinese Journal of Sociology* 3 (1): 3–31. https://doi.org/10.1177/2057150X16688144.

Xie, Yu, and Kimberly Goyette. 2003. "Social mobility and the educational choices of Asian Americans." *Social Science Research* 32 (3): 467–498. https://doi.org/10.1016/S0049-089X(03)00018-8.

Xu, Jing. 2017. *The good child: moral development in a Chinese preschool.* Stanford: Stanford University Press.

Zaloom, Caitlin. 2019. *Indebted: how families make college work at any cost.* Princeton: Princeton University Press.

Zelizer, Viviana A. 1985. *Pricing the priceless child: the changing social value of children.* New York: Basic Books.

Zhou, Min, and Susan Kim. 2008. "Community forces, social capital, and educational achievement: the case of supplementary education in the Chinese and Korean immigrant communities." *Harvard Educational Review* 76 (1): 1–29. https://doi.org/10.17763/haer.76.1.u08t548554882477.

Zhou, Min, and Jun Wang. 2019. "Challenges and strategies for promoting children's education: a comparative analysis of Chinese immigrant parenting in the United States and Singapore." *Genealogy* 3 (2). https://www.mdpi.com/2313-5778/3/2/20.

Zuberi, Tukufu. 2001. *Thicker than blood: how racial statistics lie.* Minneapolis: University of Minnesota Press.

Zuberi, Tukufu, and Eduardo Bonilla-Silva. 2008. *White logic, white methods: racism and methodology.* Lanham: Rowman & Littlefield.

Index

academic tracking, xvi, 32, 39, 62–63, 67, 91, 98–99, 134, 172, 185n3; racialization of achievement, 199n12

advanced classes, 1, 20, 32–33, 36–37, 55–57, 59–63, 66–67, 70–74, 81–83, 89, 95, 97–99, 105, 109–11, 115, 124, 130–31, 149

affirmative action, 8, 148, 163

African Americans, 3, 5, 10, 16, 18–19, 187n37, 188n50; American dream, exclusion from, 163; philosophy of education, 2; "respectability politics," 2; stereotypes of, 6; systemic exclusion of, 7–9, 157, 161–63

Alba, Richard, 160

American dream, xii, 94, 109, 163

Amherst College, 75

Asia, xii, 16, 45, 47, 52, 77, 81–82, 92, 97, 107, 120, 135, 151; Asian professionals, 23; and autonomy, 194n11; cultural repertoires, 49, 164; education system, 10–11; emotional health, concerns over, 13; selective migration from, 10–11; sports industry in, as struggling, 12; standardized tests, 48–49

Asian Americans: academic and socioeconomic success of, xiv, 3–6, 159; assimilation of, xiv, 5–6, 8, 158; attacks on, 6, 159, 161; bamboo ceilings, 6, 159; Black exclusion, benefitting from, 3, 157, 161–62; boundary between Asian Americans and whites, as blurring, xiii, 6, 20, 147; college admissions, fear of discrimination, 193–94n16; cultural brokers, 117–20; discrimination against, 6, 159, 161, 188n50, 193n16; as diverse, 187n34; and diversity, xv; ethnic identities, maintaining of, 163; as highly educated, 11; as highly skilled workers, 4; intermarriage of, 162, 200n43; and meritocracy, xv, 4, 7; neo-assimilation theory, 6; as outsiders, 157; population, growth of, 3–4; privileges enjoyed by, 157; racial exclusion, benefitting from, 156–57; racial stereotyping, 159; racial triangulation and model minority, 188n50; SAT scores, 4; selective migration, 11, 189n83; selective universities, overrepresentation in, 5; social mobility, 200n27; as socioeconomically successful, 6, 160; STEM fields, 6, 193n16; "stereotype promise," 188n50; suburbs, move to, 5; in top income quintile, 159; white peers, as threat to status of, xvi; white supremacy, benefitting from, 164.